Abuse and Religion

Abuse and Religion

When Praying Isn't Enough

Edited by

Anne L. Horton
Brigham Young University

Judith A. Williamson
Department of Family Services

Lexington Books
D.C. Heath and Company/Lexington, Massachusetts/Toronto

Library of Congress Cataloging-in-Publication Data

Abuse and religion.

    Bibliography: p.
    Includes index.
      1. Family violence—United States—Religious
aspects.   2. Abused wives—Counseling of—United States.
3. Abused children—Counseling of—United States.
4. Abused parents—Counseling of—United States.
I. Horton, Anne L. II. Williamson, Judith A.
HQ809.3.U5A28 1988   362.8′2   86–46298
ISBN 0–669–15337–0 (alk. paper)

Published simultaneously in Canada
Printed in the United States of America
International Standard Book Number: 0–669—15337–0
Library of Congress Catalog Card Number: 86–46298

The paper used in this publication meets the minimum requirements of American National Standard for Information Sciences—Permanence of Paper for Printed Library Materials, ANSI Z39.48–1984. ∞™

88 89 90 91 92 8 7 6 5 4 3 2 1

For Frances Lamkin,
my mother,
who taught me that
"Nice people don't hit each other!"

Contents

Treatment

Special Considerations

Section II: Guidelines from Religious Leaders

Roles

Special Considerations

Section III: Guidelines from Research on Victims and Perpetrators

Victim Studies

Perpetrator Studies

Special Considerations

Preface and Acknowledgments

E ach year more abuse victims, perpetrators, and family members seek help from clergy and religious leaders than all other helping profes- sionals combined. In addition, a considerable number of religious cli- ents will seek assistance from secular agencies in their community. Yet many (perhaps most) will go away dissatisfied, uninformed, and unprotected—not because these counselors give bad advice, but because it is often limited. To- day few professional training programs of any kind adequately train their students to work with abusive families.

The clergy are often even more restricted because their focus is theologi- cal, and they frequently feel frustrated and inadequate when approached by victims or abusers whom they have not been trained to help. For this reason religious victims and their families may tend to feel misunderstood and misdi- rected by those helpers, and a poor partnership with these trusted leaders may result. Initial research has also indicated that religious values may be in conflict with certain treatment options. Many agency counselors and thera- pists feel handicapped in working with religious victims whose value differ- ences may affect treatment. Thus, these families currently encounter two poor alternatives. The dual nature of their concerns, religion and abuse, often seems to limit treatment to that which is sensitive to only one need while excluding the other.

This book has been prepared to address the special needs of these victims and those who advise them. It has been prepared from a practical, "how to" perspective, emphasizing the basic information, referral sources, and alterna- tives that victims, religious leaders, and concerned family counselors need to know about in order to work effectively and sensitively with domestic vio- lence. Four helpful and important perspectives are presented here: those of (1) the abuse experts, (2) the religious leaders, (3) the victims, and (4) the perpetrators.

An old Russian proverb says, "Pray to the Lord and row toward the shore." This sound combination of faith and works has served countless vic- tims throughout the ages and is still the key to stopping violence in the home.

Today domestic abuse is not only immoral, but illegal as well. By allowing known abuse to continue without attempting responsible intervention, one becomes a partner with the abuser and, as such, assumes a certain responsibility for the tragic consequences that may result.

The civil rights and women's movements have exposed the exploited condition of abuse victims; as a result, shelters, restraining orders, legal aid, funding sources, and various community services have united to work toward ending this widespread problem. However, the focus of many of these advocacy groups has been separation and blame rather than unity and family treatment. The abuser has been seen as pathological and criminal, and the victim offered sympathy and support. While this crisis approach filled a short-term safety need, it soon became apparent that the approach was inadequate for long-term treatment and certainly did not address the needs of the total family.

A better understanding of abusive families clearly demanded a change-oriented approach. The major discrepancy and failing of the feminist position was and is that it assumes that victims who value their marital relationships do not value their personal well-being. Many of the current treatment facilities and programs address only the abuse and the necessity of ending the relationship, not marital commitment or family priorities.

In the past, secular helping services often assumed a victim was "not serious" about ending the abuse if she was not ready to leave her abusive partner. Meanwhile, many religious advisors urged victims to save their relationships but did not address the fear, pain, and life-threatening aspects of the violence. It is not surprising that these victims became frustrated in their attempts to seek help. On the one hand, personal safety was offered at the cost of a highly prized relationship, and on the other hand, the marital union took precedence over physical well-being, perhaps even life itself. Clearly, if either approach provided all the answers, this complex problem would be resolved by now.

The best efforts of the social sciences can now be marshalled to address both safety and relationship needs in harmony with religious belief systems. The problem of domestic violence demands a repertoire of social and institutional resources such that a new partnership must be formed between the clergy and the community. No one agent has the ability to do it all. Proper treatment demands time, energy, expertise, and facilities. The church needs to explore community resources, and the secular community needs to develop new respect for religious values that may influence treatment.

This book presents a unifying perspective. Religious leaders today are expected not only to be experts on moral and philosophical questions, but also to provide temporal leadership in the areas of health, social problems, family solidarity, morality, and human conduct. What a complex task in a technological and dynamic society! Therefore, this publication aims to educate such leaders about the treatment and prevention of domestic violence. These protective considerations and guidelines are aimed at the physical, emotional, and spiritual well-being of all victims and their families, and we hope they are presented in such a way that all religious leaders and secular counselors will understand the common treatment needs. These needs, not denominational or sectarian differences, form the basis of this manual.

We, the editors, are indebted to many who have influenced us and joined us in the pursuit of this project. Certainly, the contributors, research assistants, many local and national agencies and organizations, and our families have been exceedingly generous with their time, expertise, and concern. We are grateful also to the many clergy, clinicians, and concerned family members who have sought this information and are intent on providing the best care, education, and treatment for all those affected by domestic violence. We wish to thank the Women's Research Institute, Family Living Center, and the College of Family, Home, and Social Sciences at Brigham Young University for their grant and funding support of this project. In addition, special acknowledgments must be extended to the B.Y.U. School of Social Work, Professor Barry Johnson, Martha Webster, Stephanie Wall, Wendy Helms, Brandie Siegfried, Valerie Evans, Amy Cowan, and Malia Howland for their considerable personal contributions. Our aim is to end violence and fear in the home and at the same time uphold a strong spiritual environment. It is with great love for these victims and their religious caregivers and secular advisors—and to their common partnership—that this book is dedicated.

Editor's Note

This book consists largely of chapters written by concerned and sensitive authors. These authors represent many disciplines, institutions, cultural backgrounds, and religious denominations or sects. Throughout the text there has been a considerable effort made to avoid sexist language. Quite obviously this imposes a considerable hardship because no common pronoun which is suitable to both sexes has thus far been found. Therefore, victims will commonly be referred to in the feminine gender, and perpetrators or abusers will be treated in the masculine gender. The authors have done this in an effort to maintain uniformity, but it is not meant to indicate a lack of sensitivity to male victims or homosexual and lesbian relationships. All contributors have had full license to express their own views, and we hope this diversity of style, content, and philosophy will enrich and educate the reader from many perspectives.

1
Abuse in the American Family: The Role of Religion

Mildred Daley Pagelow
Pamela Johnson

For almost three decades, Americans have been coming to the realization, reluctantly and gradually, that some family members are subject to abuse by others in their families. In the 1960s, the issue of child abuse and neglect surfaced; then in the 1970s wife abuse became a topic, followed by the sexual abuse of children, and then abuse of the elderly. In all cases, these are abuses of power: crimes committed by more powerful family members against those with little power to protect or defend themselves. One reason many Americans have been unwilling to probe into the family or intervene is that the family is considered a sacred institution by most members of society. Only when it became undeniably clear that victims of abuse in the family required outside intervention to protect their lives and welfare were leaders and policy makers pushed into action.

Religion is another important institution of American society. It is so closely affiliated with the family that there is a symbiotic relationship between the two institutions. Anything that threatens harm to one can be construed as potentially harmful to the other. Despite this closeness, and despite the growing evidence that there are serious problems in the family that have far-reaching consequences for society as a whole, very little attention has been given to the role of religion—until now, that is. This book brings together viewpoints on abuse in the family, from experts on the family looking at religion and from experts in the field of religion looking at the family. Each discipline has much to learn from the other.

The first section of the book provides insight into the parameters and definitions of specific types of abuse: spouse abuse, child physical abuse, incest, marital rape, and elder abuse. This first chapter presents an overall view of the role religion plays in intrafamily abuse, both as an institution and in relation to the clergy, the faithful, and to a lesser extent, victims and abusers in religious families.

It Happens—But Not Here

Denial, silence, and traditional ideology: these are three terms that have great relevance to understanding abuse in the American family. They are particularly important in a study of the role of religion in intrafamily abuse.

Denial

Denial of abuse in the family is widespread; people prefer to cling to the image of the family as an institution representing the best of human interaction: nurturance, love, support, protection, and comfort among family members. It is painful to admit that the home is a dangerous place and that people have a greater chance of being assaulted and battered, sexually abused, raped, or killed in the home by other family members than by strangers on the streets. This is perhaps especially painful for deeply religious people to admit to themselves or others.

When one of the authors began her study of wife abuse, she discussed the issue with a friend who was both a minister and doctoral candidate in sociology. He was intrigued by the topic, but although he had done extensive pastoral counseling, he was confident that wife abuse did not occur in his congregation because no one had ever come to him with this problem. This is a common misperception. One of the few books on wife abuse found in religious bookstores was written by a Lutheran minister who asserts that "Many people respond to the issue of battering with disbelief or denial in order to protect a certain stubborn pride in their church and community. Many clergy, for example, refuse to believe that abuse exists within their congregations" (Bussert, 1986, p. 2). In presenting the problematic relationship between abuse and religion it is necessary not only to explore but to expose and explode the myth that domestic violence or sexual abuse does not occur in religious families.

It has been estimated that at least a million Christian women are victims of spouse abuse in this country (Ingram, 1985), but this is undoubtedly a gross underestimation. Estimates range widely, depending on definitions used and the way studies were conducted, from two million to over twenty million physically abused wives (Frieze, 1980; Pagelow, 1981a, 1981b, 1984; Russell, 1982; Straus, Gelles, and Steinmetz, 1980). A conservative conclusion is that wives are battered at least once in 25–30 percent of all marriages (Pagelow, 1984, pp. 45–46). In other words, about one out of every three or four wives are beaten by their husbands. One need only look at the houses down the street or at the congregation during services to realize the immensity of the problem and accept the fact that, although hidden, wife abuse exists in our communities.

Research has shown that family violence occurs at all socioeconomic levels and crosses all age, racial and ethnic, and religious boundaries. One study, using a nationally representative sample of intact families, found that parents hit children in 60 percent of all American homes and that siblings hit each other at the same rate (Straus et al., 1980). A National Incidence Study conducted by the National Center on Child Abuse and Neglect (1982) estimated that more than one million children are maltreated each year in the United States. Finkelhor's study (1979) led him to estimate that as many as 30 percent of all females and 10 percent of all males are sexually victimized before they reach the age of eighteen. Russell's study (1982) of wife rape, based on a representative sample, concluded that more than one out of seven, or 14 percent, of all wives are raped by their husbands. Estimates on family abuse of the elderly are not based on large-scale, reliable studies, but there is sufficient evidence to know that it is a widespread problem that will continue to grow as the aged population expands (Pagelow, 1988).

All the studies cited above focused almost entirely on *physical* forms of abuse, but few would deny that *psychological abuse* is far more prevalent. It also accompanies most types of physical abuse, and its effects can be far more long-lasting and damaging to victims (Pagelow, 1984, pp. 53–59).

There should be no doubt that abuse in the family is very common and crosses all boundaries. Victims and abusers belong to a widespread range of religious faiths, and therefore religious leaders and their congregations cannot state unequivocally that wife abuse and other forms of family violence do not occur among them. Denial only perpetuates the problem and impedes solutions.

Silence

There are those who have moved past their initial denial of the pervasiveness of family violence, but who maintain their silence and fail to take an active stance to help victims and abusers. These people include many members of the clergy and their congregations as well as victims. But family violence does occur within religious homes, and our silent treatment makes recovery for those involved especially difficult. Bringing the issue of abuse into the open, ending the silence, and discussing solutions triggers complex feelings of fear and defensiveness among clergy and congregation. Writing about wife abuse in a chapter titled "A Theology of Silence," Bussert explains silence this way:

> [One] reason it is difficult to open the door and hear the women's cries is that it simply hurts to acknowledge suffering—especially meaningless suffering—so close to home. To step beyond the locked door and fully see and hear the reality of abuse down the street, next door, or within one's own church community is to face the fact that if it could happen to "her" (them), it could happen to "me" (us). It is safer to keep the door locked shut, to perpetuate the silence and pretend not to see (1986, p. 3).

The silence must be broken by the clergy, whose position of leadership and responsibility gives unparalleled opportunities to educate the faithful and render assistance to victims and abusers. How the clergy responds to the social problem of family violence is in large part determined by theological beliefs, but it is also often based on individuals' knowledge, or lack of it, about the causes and consequences of intrafamily abuse. For those who simply do not understand and do not know how to intervene effectively, this book will help to light the way, but many have ignored or even condoned abuse of the powerless by other family members in the past, and unfortunately, will continue to do so in the future. One author writes:

> The clergy preaches a male-oriented theology and structure of the marriage relationship. The clergy has not been in the vanguard of help for the battered wife. Instead, its attitudes about woman's place, duty, and nature have added to the problem. Even now, with few exceptions, the silence from the churches on this issue is profound (Davidson, 1978, p. 207).

Davidson (1978, p. 131) wrote from a background of personal experience:

> I would prefer to forget the terrors of my childhood—my life is now far removed from them. But the terrorist was my violent father, a Christian minister. His first target was my mother. And as I grew and tried to be the peacemaker, he turned on me.
> . . . some wifebeating husbands can be helped with therapy when their motivations to change are strong. But this wifebeater, my father, would have never gone for counseling. After all, as a clergyman, he *gave* counseling. He had no intention of reforming.

In the Pagelow (1984) study of wife abuse, several wives were battered by husbands who were ministers, and one in-depth interview was conducted with a young wife with two small children whose violent husband was a student at a theological seminary. She returned to her husband, despite life-threatening abuse, partly because of her personal commitment to her marriage and religion which taught her that she was to "submit"[1] to her husband and partly because he "needed" her. Her husband's career, she felt, hinged on her being there to understand and support him, much like Davidson's long-suffering mother, who told her daughter that if the truth had been known, "it would mean the end of his ministry" (1978, p. 148).

In one sample of 350 battered women, 28 percent said they had sought help from the clergy (Pagelow, 1981b, pp. 277–300). The primary responses these women received were (1) a reminder of their duty and the advice to forgive and forget, (2) a reference elsewhere to avoid church involvement, and (3) useless advice, sometimes based on religious doctrine rather than their own needs. Some were reminded of their vows of "for better or for worse" and admonished to pray more and live more worthy lives. One, scolded by her minister for "betraying" her husband by revealing what had occurred in the privacy of their home, was beaten harder by her husband when the pastors told him of her visit.

Bowker (1982) has written one of the few journal articles on battered women and the clergy (see Chapter 25). Other studies show that battered women turn to the clergy for help: 16 percent of a Kentucky random sample said they talked to their ministers after the incidents (Schulman, 1979), and 39 percent of Freize's Pittsburgh sample of 137 women consulted the clergy (1980). That was twice as many women as those who consulted family doctors, and almost as many who turned to therapists or social service agencies.

One Presbyterian minister who wrote a book on pastoral care of battered women states that there is hope for the future because many churches and their leaders have become involved in helping violent families (Clarke, 1986). Clarke says that most denominations now have literature about wife abuse. Many support shelters for battered women and their children, and "as pastors become aware and educated, they will be more helpful to the battered women in their churches" (1986, p. 24). Change is occurring, albeit slowly.

Traditional Ideology

Obviously, denial of the reality of abuse in the family is lessening, and the wall of silence surrounding the issue is being shattered by many voices; but there is still one factor that greatly impedes progress toward assisting the helpless victims of family violence: traditional ideology.[2] Briefly summarized, traditional ideology is a term for a broad range of internalized beliefs favoring acceptance of the rightness of the patriarchal-hierarchal order of the social structure (Pagelow, 1981a, p. 16). "Patriarchy provides a social structure of ownership of women by men which makes it possible for men to do whatever they want with their woman" (Clarke, 1986, p. 24). Dobash and Dobash, in their "case against the patriarchy," describe connections between patriarchy, abuse of family members, and religious beliefs this way:

> The seeds of wife-beating lie in the subordination of females and in their subjection to male authority and control. This relationship between women and men has been institutionalized in the structure of the patriarchal family and is supported by the economic and political institutions and by a belief system, including a religious one, that makes such relationships seem natural, morally just, and sacred (1979, pp. 33–34).

An issue that must be addressed is how the structure of most (if not all) major religions has contributed to, supported, and legitimized intrafamily abuse. Religion has through the ages constituted a powerful force supporting the hierarchal relationship of humans to each other and to their God (Pagelow, 1981b). This subject has recently been made sensitive by fears of theological anarchy, feminism, and heresy. The subordinate position of the female and the dominant position of the male are major factors in this problem.

> The model of authority for patriarchy is hierarchical. In this pattern, authority comes from the top down. The man is the head of the family, and the wife is the obedient support person . . . . If our culture approves of the hierarchical model, which puts power in the hands of the husband, that power also gives him sanction to punish those who resist his attempts to control them (the wife and children). The inequality in a hierarchical family may initiate a chain reaction running throughout the family (Clarke, 1986, pp. 26–27).

In discussing the "Religious Right," Bussert (1986, pp. 60–61) tells of a woman who went to a shelter for battered women to escape abuse by her husband. Her pastor called the shelter director to say that if the woman was not home by the next morning, "she would be excommunicated from the church because it was her duty to keep the family together and submit to her husband in all things" despite the fact that the children were also abused. Some with great influence in religious communities even suggest that a woman should elevate her husband over God. Bussert (1986, pp. 60–61) quotes a book used in premarital counseling by many clergy throughout the United States:

> Suppose a woman feels God is leading her definitely opposite from what her husband has commanded? Whom should she obey? The Scriptures say a woman must ignore her feelings about the will of God and do what her husband says. She is to obey her husband as if he were God himself. She can be as certain of God's will when her husband speaks as if God had spoken audibly from heaven.

Bussert calls this an idolatrous mentality bent on maintaining the patriarchal-hierarchal structure of the family. She admits that it is an unfortunate legacy of "our theological heritage in the church," but if "submission continues to be the 'theory,' then battering will inevitably continue to be the 'practice'" (1986, p. 61).

One writer says, "All religions preach subordination of women not just to God, but to men, as an article of faith . . . . Moreover, Judeo/Christian theological writings are explicitly misogynous" (Gardner, 1977). The heritage of theological misogyny is well documented in the literature (Bullough, 1974; Hays, 1964). A French monk writing in 1095 is quoted in O'Faolain and Martines: "If her bowels and flesh were cut open, you would see what filth is covered by her white skin. If a fine crimson cloth covered a foul dung, would anyone be foolish enough to love the dung because of it?" (1973, p. xiii). Saint Augustine showed a similar contempt of women, as quoted in Bussert (1986, pp. 7–8): "A good Christian is found in one and the same woman to love the creature of God whom he desires to be transformed and renewed, but to hate in her the corruptible and mortal conjugal connection, sexual intercourse and *all that pertains to her as a wife*" (emphasis added). Another Catholic cleric quoted in Bussert (1986, p. 10) said this to women: "You are the first deserter of the Divine Law. . . . You destroyed so easily God's image, man."

Early laws of marriage came from Rome, where "The man was the absolute patriarch who owned and controlled all properties and people within the family" (Dobash and Dobash, 1978, p. 428). As Roman laws began to modify subordination, a new religious group called Christians gained converts and power, and demanded the continuance and maintenance of the control and authority to the patriarchy. The first Christian Roman emperor, Constantine I the Great (later canonized as a saint) was the first emperor to order the execution of his own wife (Davis, 1971). His empire was obtained by a proxy marriage to an infant, Fausta, but when his young wife was no longer of use to him, he had her scalded to death in a cauldron of water brought to a slow boil over a wood fire because he "suspected her of adultery" (Davis, 1971, p. 236).

The church and the state joined forces to support husbands' dominance and wives' submission, and the writing of Martin Luther, John Knox, and John Calvin, leaders of Christian splinter groups, strongly reinforced that heritage (Davidson, 1977; Dobash and Dobash, 1979). The founder of the Lutheran church, who admitted "boxing" his wife's ear when she got "saucy," compared women to a nail driven into the wall and said, "The rule remains with the husband and the wife is compelled to obey him by God's command" (Luther, cited in Bussert, 1986, p. 11). Bussert also quotes Calvin's response to an abused wife that, except when she might be killed, she must "bear with patience the cross which God has seen fit to place upon her; and meanwhile not to deviate from the duty which she has before God to please her husband, but to be faithful whatever happens" (1986, p. 12). These teachings remain powerful in the present, because as Daly (1973, p. 4) asserts, "theology and ethics which are overtly and explicitly oppressive to women are by no means confined to the past," whether they are manifested in ritual law of Judaism (Richardson, 1974), the theology of Christianity (Daly, 1973), or the Eastern religions such as Islam.

Traditional ideology and the hierarchical structure of the patriarchal family contribute also to the physical, psychological, and sexual maltreatment of children (Dobash and Dobash, 1978, 1979; Pagelow, 1984). Like wives, children were property of their fathers, and although ideas about children have ranged from evil to holy at various times during the centuries, the bulk of the evidence shows what deMause (1975) declares to be child-rearing that is "bloody, dirty, and mean." Parents' justification for maltreatment of children was often based on religious beliefs and practices, as Radbill (1974, p. 3) explains:

> "Spare the rod and spoil the child" was a dictum backed by the Bible and expressed in 1633 in the *Bibliotheca Scholastica*. There was a time in most Christian countries when children were whipped on Innocents Day to make them remember the massacre of the innocents by Herod. Beatings to drive out the devil were a form of psychiatric treatment especially applicable to children.

People fear the unusual. Thus, "In China, India, and throughout the Orient deformed children were usually destroyed at birth; and in sixteenth-century Europe, Martin Luther ordered mentally defective children drowned because he was convinced they were instruments of the devil" (Radbill, 1974, p. 7). In an earlier article, Radbill (1968) wrote that "The beating of very young children, for a time, raised many objections which led to some mitigation. But then as the Calvinistic views that children were imps of darkness became popular, they were again whipped." Another writer adds,

> The purposeful beating of the young has for centuries found legitimacy in beliefs of its necessity for achieving disciplinary, educational or religious obedience. . . . In the seventeenth century, a period dominated by religious values and institutions, severe punishments were considered essential to the "sacred" trust of children (Pfohl, 1977, pp. 310–11).

Acts that are considered by many to be child abuse today were commonly done by parents in earlier years without arousing public outrage or legal censure. The acts have not changed, but the norms and common definitions of right and wrong have. A generation ago it was common for parents to beat their children with straps and belts, and even today the vast majority of Americans, about 90 percent (Stark and McEvoy, 1970), believe that it is not only a parent's right but a duty to spank their children as a form of discipline. Almost all parents accused of child abuse protest that they were only disciplining their victims for the "child's own good." Many parents still view their children as their property, and unfortunately, the old idea of having a "moral obligation" to beat children to ensure obedience persists in some religiously rigid, patriarchal homes. To these people, "goodness" is achieved through fear—fear of authority, whether God or another authority figure in power: husband, parent, or caretaker.

It Does Happen Here—
and What Can Be Done about It

In light of overwhelming evidence, abuse in the family is a serious and widespread social problem that must be addressed by the institution of religion, by its leadership, and by its membership. It cannot be denied that abuse occurs in religious families as well as in nonreligious families. The next step is to break the silence surrounding the issue, and this book takes a giant leap in that direction. Three other excellent sources provide guidelines on how religions and religious communities can effectively gather information, educate, and intervene: Bowker (1982), Bussert (1986), and Clarke (1986). Despite the unwillingness of most Americans to invade the privacy of the family, it is an institution under seige, and members of all Judeo-Christian religious communities should be in the forefront of the movement to prevent abuse and help abused family members.

Leadership in breaking the silence surrounding abuse in the family must be assumed by clerics, who are in positions of trust and guidance unparalleled by other professionals. Sermons can inform entire congregations that their spiritual leaders know that many families are troubled by abuse, including violence, which will not be tolerated or condoned. Words must be followed by action, and the clergy must educate itself on what services are available in the community and what their communities lack. Shelter networks or safe homes have been established in some congregations, while others have become involved in community programs and shelters (Travis, 1981). Some pastors openly admit to having no training or education in counseling victims or abusers and welcome professional secular help.

The silence of religious leaders on intrafamily abuse has perpetuated a shroud of secrecy, shame, and guilt surrounding victims. Afraid to talk with their ministers for fear of being misunderstood, rejected, or blamed for their victimization, victims remain confined in their misery. Sometimes wives are driven from both their churches and their husbands when they find more condemnation than comfort in a setting supposedly representing love and compassion. Silence within the religious community has served to keep the lid on the simmering pain that not only immobilizes victims but encourages the behavior of perpetrators.

Finally, the firmly entrenched hierarchical structure of the patriarchal family must be recognized as a destructive force of traditional ideology. A ranking order of greater to lesser beings that must be enforced by power is a cause of continual conflict in that violence is often an abuse of power. The patriarchy is a man-made invention that has been kept alive through the centuries by force and tradition, transmitted through cultural institutions. By their symbiotic relationship, the institutions of religion and the family have perpetuated and venerated vastly unequal relationships between spouses and parents and children. The time for change is long past due.

Change is not easy, and institutions change very slowly. The institution of religion is no exception, but change must occur in the basic patriarchal structure. The past few years have witnessed enormous challenge, change, and muting of traditional values. Although some welcome reform, many others stubbornly cling to traditional ideology. As medical doctors resisted the use of anesthesia and refused to wash their hands as they went from one birthing mother to the next (meanwhile wondering why so many healthy women died from "childbirth fever"), so do many clerics resist change. The Inquisition, four centuries of "witch" burnings in Europe and "witch" hunts in the Puritan colonies, declarations that scientists such as Galileo were heretics, and support for slavery in the United States are other examples of religion's resistance to enlightenment and change.

Conclusion

But institutions, even religion and the family, must change over time, however grudgingly. And while some will always mourn the passing of the "good old days," there will always be those who remember the past less fondly and who welcome the future and its challenges. The authors share a dream with many others that a new model family will be a vast improvement over the one that has been held out as an ideal for so long. It will be one in which loving adults share their lives as equals and children obey their parents, not because of fear, but because they somehow know that the rules are set for their own benefit. Religion can begin to promote this new model of the family *now*.

Notes

1. The literature on religion and marriage contains many references to "submission" of wives and warnings that a good wife should "submit" to her husband, always supported by quotations from scriptures. These familiar messages of subordination and submission encourage women to remain passive, suffering victims in their relationships with authoritarian husbands. According to the second author, submission must be studied in light of the example of Christ. Submission must not be confused with weakness as it often is: submission is possible *only* when one *has power to surrender.* Jesus set aside his power and glory, *choosing* to submit to the will of his

Father. In an abusive situation, with the victim rendered powerless through fear or confusion, submission is not even possible. The victim without options, trapped by economic circumstances and fear of injury or psychological abuse, is not submitting to that husband. She is enduring the relationship from a position of weakness. It is only when a victim has options, real choices, that she can surrender those options and choose to be submissive.

2. Traditional ideology includes the patriarchy but it is more than just patriarchy. It is a set of beliefs and attitudes that is a fundamental part of the way some persons evaluate life and circumstances and serves to guide and motivate their behavior. Traditional ideology is the configuration of all the conservative wisdom passed down through the ages as the "natural" order of things.

References

Bowker, L. H. 1982. Battered women and the clergy: An evaluation. *The Journal of Pastoral Care* 34(4):226–235.

Bullough, V. L. 1974. *The subordinate sex: A history of attitudes toward women.* New York: Penguin.

Bussert, J. M. K. 1986. *Battered women: From a theology of suffering to an ethic of empowerment.* New York: Division for Mission in North America, Lutheran Church in America.

Clarke, R.-L. 1986. *Pastoral care of battered women.* Philadelphia: The Westminster Press.

Daly, M. 1973. *Beyond God the father.* Boston: Beacon Press.

Davidson, T. 1977. Wifebeating: A recurring phenomenon throughout history. In *Battered women: A psychosociological study of domestic violence,* ed. Maria Roy. New York: Van Nostrand Reinhold.

Davidson, T. 1978. *Conjugal crime: Understanding and changing the wifebeating pattern.* New York: Hawthorn.

Davis, E. 1971. *The first sex.* New York: Penguin.

DeMause, L. 1975. Our forebears made childhood a nightmare. *Psychology Today,* April, 85–88.

Dobash, R. E., and R. P. Dobash. 1978. Wives: The "appropriate" victims of marital violence. *Victimology* 2(3/4):426–42.

———. 1979. *Violence against wives: A case against the patriarchy.* New York: Free Press.

Finkelhor, D. 1979. *Sexually victimized children.* New York: Free Press.

Frieze, I. H. 1980. Causes and consequences of marital rape. Paper presented at the annual meeting of the American Psychological Association, Montreal, Canada.

Gardner, J. A. E. 1977. Varieties of discontent: female response to religious misogyny. Paper presented at the annual meeting of the American Psychological Association, San Francisco, CA.

Hays, H. R. 1964. *The dangerous sex: The myth of feminine evil.* New York: G P Putnam's Sons.

Ingram, K. Violence in Christian marriages. *Virtue,* October 1985, 30–32.

National Center on Child Abuse and Neglect, U.S. Department of Health and Human Services. 1982. *Executive summary: National study of the incidence and severity of child abuse and neglect.* Washington, D.C.: Government Printing Office.

O'Faolain, J., and L. Martines. 1973. *Not in God's image: Women in history from the Greek to the Victorians.* New York: Harper and Row.

Pagelow, M. D. 1981a. *Woman-battering: Victims and their experiences.* Beverly Hills: Sage.

———. 1981b. Sex roles, power, and woman battering. In *Women and crime in America,* ed. Lee H. Bowker. New York: Macmillan.

———. 1984. *Family Violence.* New York: Praeger.

———. 1988. The criminal abuse of other family members. In *Family violence as a criminal justice issue,* ed. Lloyd Ohlin and Michael Tonry. Chicago: University of Chicago Press.

Pfohl, S. J. 1977. The "discovery" of child abuse. *Social Problems* 24(3):310–311.

Radbill, S. X. 1968. A history of child abuse and infanticide. In *The battered child,* 1st ed., eds. Ray E. Helfer and C. Henry Kempe. Chicago: University of Chicago Press.

———. 1974. A history of child abuse and infanticide. In *The battered child,* 2d ed., eds. Ray E. Helfer and C. Henry Kempe. Chicago: University of Chicago Press.

Richardson, H. W. 1974. *Nun, witch, playmate: The Americanization of sex.* New York: Harper and Row.

Russell, D. E. H. 1982. *Rape in marriage.* New York: Macmillan.

Schulman, M. A. 1979. *A survey of violence against women in Kentucky.* Washington, D.C.: Government Printing Office.

Stark, R., and J. McEvoy, III. 1970. Middle-class violence. *Psychology Today,* November, 552–54; 110–112.

Straus, M., R. Gelles, and S. Steinmetz. 1980. *Behind closed doors: Violence in the American family.* New York: Doubleday.

Travis, L. 1981. Are there battered women in your pews? *Eternity Magazine,* November, 32–34.

Virtue Magazine. October 3, 1985.

2
Spouse Abuse: A Basic Profile

Lenore E. Walker

When most of us think of the marriage vows, we believe the promise to love and cherish our spouse includes the key to a blissful relationship designed to meet the needs of the family. Unfortunately, the statistics indicate that for a significant number of women, perhaps anywhere between one-third and one-half, those vows bring with them exposure to a life filled with physical, sexual, and psychological abuse rather than the expected dreams.[1] Too often, clerics, like many other members of our society, have ignored this reality and instead pretend that spouse abuse does not exist. We have only recently begun to address the problem and bring it out from behind closed doors.

Spouse abuse, or more specifically woman abuse, since the data suggest that the overwhelming number of victims are women rather than men, has existed for as long as we have historical records. The literature frequently has placed the blame on the introduction of patriarchal religion for the support of men's belief in their right to use physical, sexual, or psychological coercion to force women into doing whatever it is they want done, without regard for women's rights (see Davidson, 1978 for a more complete discussion). Others have demonstrated that the Bible has given at least as many messages to treat a woman kindly and with respect (Fortune, 1987). Regardless of the role of religion, however, it has always been seen as women's lot in life to expect to be harmed in some way if unable to meet some standard, usually set by men.

Why Abuse Occurs

Most of the earlier writings suggest that if a woman develops a better character, she will be less likely to be abused by her husband. If she misbehaves, she must take the consequences. In some cases, her misbehavior is simply inferred from the abuse, even without credible evidence that she has done something wrong. Even today, it is often believed that spouse abuse will stop when the woman develops better character or behaves better. Often it is not understood that the man controls whether or not there will be abuse in the home. Misbehavior on the part of the woman, however, should not justify the use of violence. There are other resources available to men and women to resolve conflict, and if those of us who are called upon to pass judgment on people's behavior are able to state this clearly, the rate of spouse abuse will quickly be lowered. Unfortunately, the lack of serious consequences for men who batter women whom they also love reinforces their behavior.

There have also been theories suggesting that the women or the men involved in domestic violence, as spouse or woman abuse is often called, have serious psychological problems that somehow contribute to their abusive lifestyles. It used to be commonly believed that battered women were really masochists who provoked their men to beat them because of some deep-seated psychological need. Recent research has demonstrated the falsity of this belief (Walker, 1984). Men who batter women have also been labeled psychopathic, as though their abusive nature were due to lack of conscience rather than the sense of entitlement to use forceful behavior which the recent research demonstrates (Sonkin, Martin, and Walker, 1985). Although some who are abused or use abusive behavior also have serious psychological problems, those problems are not the cause of the violence.

Identifying Abusive Relationships

The epidemiological research demonstrates that spouse abuse exists in homes across every demographic level measured (Straus, Gelles, and Steinmetz, 1980). It occurs among the poor as well as the rich, the uneducated as well as the educated, the unskilled as well as the professional worker, the pious as well as the less religious. Wife battering has been found to occur proportionately across racial and ethnic groups. It is often so well hidden that it is impossible for an outsider to know what is happening inside the abusive home. Family members contribute to the silence out of fear that the abuse will get worse if someone else knows. But frequently cues are given which, if correctly interpreted by the concerned helper, can assist that family to become free of abuse.

The goal of any helper, including clergy, is to protect each person in the family from further harm or death. Keeping the family together at the risk of continuing the harm to its individual members will not stop the violence. Furthermore, the research shows that it places children who witness or experience the violence at a 700 times greater risk of becoming a batterer or battered woman in their own marital relationship (Kalmus, 1984). Thus, taking no action really means to perpetuate the abuse into the next generation.

Patterns in Abusive Relationships

There are some patterns found in abusive relationships that are inconsistent with our common-sense notions. One such pattern is in the reporting of the violence. It is generally thought that truth usually can be estimated to be somewhere in the middle of two different stories. However, in battering relationships the truth is always worse than what either the man or woman reports. A man generally denies that he has been abusive or, if he admits it, he blames the woman for what she made him do. Often he explains any visible bruises by blaming her clumsiness, overmedication, or other accidental causation. Even when he takes responsibility for causing the injuries, he is apt to minimize the impact.

A woman also minimizes and denies the seriousness of the abuse and frequently does not challenge the man's inadequate or inaccurate explanations. As might be expected, this is an attempt to keep the peace and reduce the likelihood of further harm. Abusive men are more likely to give details of what the women did or did not do to lead up to the abusive incident. Women are more likely to explain the details of who did what to whom during the abusive incident. However, women will cover up and deny the truth when they believe that the listener will not believe them or will not be helpful in keeping them safe.

Battered women have developed a sensitivity to cues of further violence and can sense an incident is beginning even before others might recognize the signs. If they share these perceptions with others who cannot recognize those early warning signs, they are likely to be ignored and their perceptions invalidated. Some women stop trying to tell others. They become silenced into passivity. Others become more frantic in trying to get someone else to hear them and may be erroneously labeled as "hysterical." Still others may take matters into their own hands and "fight back," using verbal or physical violence themselves.

The variety of responses to battering sometimes makes it confusing to discern whether or not abuse is occurring in a relationship. This difficulty is further compounded by the ability of men who abuse women to demonstrate socially acceptable behavior. Women often describe them as having two personalities, like a Dr. Jekyll and Mr. Hyde. This integration of both mean and good-natured personalities is a pattern in many violent men. Others do not demonstrate any behaviors that could be interpreted as positive; they may have done so at an earlier time in their lives, or might simply be cruel people. Frequently, men who abuse women do not demonstrate their "bad" side until after they are married. During the courtship period, they are kind, generous, and very loving. Occasional glimpses of a bad temper, unfounded jealousy, intrusive behavior, and unreasonable expectations may appear, but these are quickly glossed over by the more salient loving-kindness. It is difficult to identify a batterer from other nonabusive men; given their heterogeneity, it is expected that they will be just like others in many areas.

Defining Physically and Sexually Abusive Behaviors

Battering behaviors are not so difficult to recognize if they are being looked for. Physical abuse ranges from less serious acts such as slapping to life-threatening acts such as choking, drowning, and threatening or actually using knives, guns, or other lethal weapons.

It is often difficult for religious leaders to understand how sexual abuse can occur in a marital relationship, in which there are vows to be sexual with one another. However, violent sex is often used as a powerful form of control by abusive men in a way that has nothing to do with the kind of sexual relationship that expresses love and affection within the marriage bond (see Chapter 6 for further clarification).

Psychological Battering (Also Known As Psychological Torture)

It has been more difficult to determine the difference between psychological abuse in a battering relationship and other forms of psychological distress that occur in dysfunctional marriages. In our research project, we decided to use the definition of psychological torture that has been agreed upon by Amnesty International as the way to define a psychologically abusive relationship. A part of this definition includes creating a situation in which the family is isolated and the man's opinions and points of view are the only ones to which family members are exposed.

Sometimes the woman supports the isolation as a way to avoid situations that might precipitate more battering incidents. Or she may be so embarrassed by the violence in her family that she avoids contact with others. In other cases, the man actually keeps that woman as a psychological prisoner in her own home. He may not allow her to use the car or telephone without his permission. He may accompany her everywhere she needs to go, including standing outside the women's restroom while she is inside, or call her so many times a day that she literally has no time away from him.

Some women hide their embarrassment by behaving as though they think they are better than others. The abusive family may appear to be a close-knit family to others, especially when they attend religious services, but often use that tight outer shell as a defense against anyone's seeing what is really going on.

Another form of psychological torture common in battering relationships is the man's accusations against the woman for supposed infidelity, usually sexual, but sometimes only of personal disloyalty to him. He is jealous, over-possessive, and extremely intrusive into her life. The woman is thus afraid of making any commitment for herself without first getting his permission. Church- or temple-related activities might be an easier place than others for these women to begin to make individual contact with the outside world. However, male clerics must be careful not to place themselves in a compromising position with this woman, or the man will be likely to accuse him of a sexual liaison. These jealous accusations have frequently happened to male psychologists who have seen battered women in individual psychotherapy and have helped the women explore a decision to leave an abusive relationship.

Women therapists are sometimes accused by the abusive husband of being lesbians and wanting sex with their wives, too. The batterer is jealous of the transference relationship which normally occurs in psychotherapy because he views it as a threat to his exclusive hold on the woman's decision-making ability. Clerics, who might have a similar caring relationship with female congregants, need to avoid any appearance of impropriety that could neutralize their efforts on behalf of the battered woman. It goes without saying that any romantic involvement is both inappropriate and dangerous.

Psychological battering is also expressed in the numerous derogatory comments frequently made about all women and also those specific to a particular woman. Denigration of women's power and ability, including setting up high expectations that cannot be met by any human being and then berating a woman for not being competent enough to do so, is typical. Name calling and use of curse words is frequent, although there are batterers who can make a sentence of ordinary language sound obscene.

Some batterers yell while their partners are quieter, but in other cases it is the woman who yells while the man is more soft-spoken. Tone of voice does not always convey the danger of its content. In many cases it takes only a look to convey the meaning, and frequently the signal is missed by everyone but those directly involved. Do not assume the violence is not dangerous just because it has not been observed by others.

Just like prisoners of war or other hostages, battered women are forced to undergo debilitating experiences that make them too weary to fight back. It is quite common for women to describe their abusive mates waking them in the middle of the night, or even preventing them from going to sleep, by the demands to listen to what the men have to say. These harangues are filled with angry diatribes against themselves, the victim, or others. Often they are drunken ramblings that make no sense or simply desperate attempts by the man to obtain some companionship but without any participation by the woman (Walker, 1979). Battered women may also eat improperly, resulting in physical debilitation. Numerous medical complaints may result from the wear and tear on the victim's body due to all of the tension under which she lives.

Battering relationships are more lethal, even to the batterer, than other relationships (Jones, 1980). It is entirely possible that someone, usually the woman, will die. Sometimes it is the man or the children. The most likely time for a homicide or suicide to occur is at the point of separation (Browne, 1987). Fear that a man might kill her, her children, or himself is one reason that a woman is reluctant to terminate the relationship. Threats to kill are frequently made during the abusive incidents. The man's fear of abandonment is often so great that he believes if he cannot have her, no one else can.

If a woman leaves, he is likely to stalk her until he finds her and persuades her to return either through sweet talk or threats of more violence. It is totally inappropriate for clergy to collude with the abuser by helping to persuade a woman to return to the relationship and try to work things out when she has the courage to leave. It is best to work on stopping the violence when they are apart for a number of reasons, including the potential for someone to die. Clerics need to think about offering the women and children sanctuary, as they do for victims of nonfamily violence, rather than sending them back into the home which has become a war zone.

Cycle Theory of Violence

The unanswered question about family violence in most people's minds is why women stay and "take it." In my research, I have learned that there are complex psychological reasons why both partners want to keep a marriage together in addition to the typical reasons such as love, the sake of the children, religious reasons, economics, fear, and status (Walker, 1984). After listening to the stories of hundreds of battered women, it became clear that the battering frequently, although not always, occurred in a pattern.

This pattern typically has three phases: the tension-building period, the acute battering incident, and loving/contrition. Although most couples do not realize they are behaving in this pattern, it is obvious to an outsider who obtains details of several battering incidents. The pattern may change over time in the same relationship due to outside influences. The abuse generally gets worse over time, but some events can cause it to slow down or speed up; for example, the abuse escalates in frequency and severity when the woman is pregnant or when there is an infant in the home. It has been found that the teaching of their own pattern to couples may help them recognize the abuse early enough in the cycle to take some action to stop it from escalating.

Phase I: Tension Building

The first phase, or tension-building period, has multiple incidents that stop before they get out of hand. The woman can control the frequency and severity of these incidents by trying to please the batterer and keep his world calm.

At this point the battered woman's behavior does make a difference in how rapidly the abuse progresses into the more serious type of incident (phase two). It gives her and others the false impression that she can stop the battering if only she behaves better. In fact, all she can do is set the timing for when the acute battering incident in phase two will occur. Sometimes she can also influence where it occurs by speeding it up and misbehaving. At times women do this to protect themselves by minimizing the abuse, not because they like to provoke or experience being beaten.

Phase II: The Crisis

The second phase is when the worst injuries may occur, although visible injuries occur in only about one-half of the incidents. If the police are called at all, which happens in only a minority of cases, this phase is what they are most likely to witness. Those who try to evaluate the battering relationship based only on this phase miss the essence of what has happened. To analyze only the discrete events, even if they are the most serious ones, minimizes the repetitive and escalating danger. Battering relationships that do not terminate in divorce are at high risk to be terminated due to someone's untimely death.

Phase III: The Aftermath

The third phase, loving/contrition, is not always observable in battering relationships and indeed was present in only two-thirds of the 1600 incidents my research project studied (Walker, 1984). In many cases where it was difficult to find any positive behavior, there was at least an absence of tension reported during this third phase. (After living with so much tension, its absence—even if only for a short period of time—can be reinforcing.) Acceptance of the gifts and pleas for forgiveness may simply perpetuate the man's abusive behavior. This third period provides most of the rewards for this couple if they stay together. No matter how sincere the man is at this time or how eager he is to start over with a clean slate, however, most women cannot forget their terror that they might be beaten for doing or saying something wrong, something they could not have identified prior to the explosion.

Conclusion

In this article I have tried to demonstrate that there is no one identifying psychological characteristic nor are there magical ways of learning who is and who is not engaged in spouse abuse. However, it is clear that there are many types of psychological torture that can produce learned helplessness and the three-phase cycle. Although there is no one profile of spouse abuse, there are some patterns of violence which can be detected by the trained observer. Clergy who can recognize spouse abuse will be able to provide assistance to help family members stop the abuse and begin the healing process.

References

Browne, A. 1987. *When battered women kill.* New York: Free Press.

Davidson, T. 1978. *Conjugal crime: Understanding and changing the wifebeating pattern.* New York: Hawthorne.

Fortune, M. 1987. *Keeping the faith: Questions and answers for abused women.* New York: Harper & Row.

Jones, A. 1980. *Women who kill.* New York: Holt, Rinehart.

Kalmus, D. 1984. The intergenerational transmission of marital aggression. *Journal of Marriage and the Family* 51(4):11–19.

Sonkin, D. J., D. Martin, and L. Walker. 1985. *The male batterer.* New York: Springer.

Straus, M., R. Gelles, and S. Steinmetz. 1980. *Behind closed doors: Violence in the American family.* Garden City, NY: Anchor/Doubleday.

Walker, L. E. A. 1979. *The male batterer.* New York: Harper & Row.

Walker, L. E. A. 1984. *The battered woman syndrome.* New York: Springer.

3
Child Physical Abuse:
Assessment and Reporting Guidelines

Penny Tokarski

Throughout history, childhood has been unsafe. It has been marked by injury, emotional deprivation, and sometimes death. Maltreatment of children under the guise of discipline has been an accepted norm. Supposedly, such behavior has also been backed by the Biblical dictum of "spare the rod, spoil the child." Children have been said to require "severe discipline" to rid them of their fiendish ways. In this country, cruelty to children was not truly recognized nor was any positive action taken until the late nineteenth century.

Recognition of Child Maltreatment

Child maltreatment crosses not only socioeconomic lines, but also generations. Morbidity and mortality of the child-abuse syndrome includes all age groups of children, although two-thirds of abused children in the United States are less than six years of age (Rosenberg and Bottenfield, 1982; Fontana, 1984). Because of the vulnerability of this age group, including their difficulty in sheltering or defending themselves, the physical problems suffered as a result of maltreatment can be significant and life-threatening. Since almost one million children are reported as abused each year in the United States (Helfer, 1984), a sizable number of infants, toddlers, and preschoolers are at risk.

Males and females are almost equally subjected to child abuse, and whites much more than other racial groups (Suski, 1986). Premature infants deserve special attention since they have a threefold greater risk of abuse (Rosenberg and Bottenfield, 1982). Large families, families with twins, the poor, and the unemployed have been shown to have a higher risk for abuse (Bergman, Larsen, and Mueller, 1986; Groothuis, Altemeier, and Robarge, 1982).

For children in abusive families, "discipline" is neither educational nor constructive. It does not teach proper behavior or attitudes. It simply produces an injury—either physical or emotional—that frequently requires some sort of medical intervention (Schmitt and Kempe, 1983). "Disciplinary" actions that leave marks are abusive actions. More subtle indicators include abandonment, neglect of medical or physical needs, verbal abuse, or "scapegoating."

But is an inflicted injury always easily differentiated from an accidental one? Professionals today have come to realize that the problem is far more complex and varied. In one case the parent and the child may not be acting "on the same wavelength." In another the child may be the "target child" in the family—singled out for physical and verbal abuse. In still another a victim may crave attention to the point of misbehaving in order to receive it (Rosenberg and Bottenfield, 1982).

In just as much need of nurturing, the abusing caretaker may see the child as a reflection of himself or herself, or believe the child deliberately misbehaves to defy authority. It has been shown that abusing parents are frequently treating their children as they were treated during childhood. Although they may be "regular people," and not psychopaths, they may still be socially detached or depressed, have a poor self-concept, and be stressed with marital problems, financial difficulties, or substance abuse. Placing such an adult with such a child in a situation of stress or crisis often results in injuries.

Skin Injuries

The most common manifestations of physical abuse are skin injuries—bruises, scratches or scrapes, and lacerations. Presence of any of these indicators after "disciplinary action" implies that too much force was used by a disciplinarian who could not control his or her emotions. Bruises inflicted usually have the appearance of the object used, such as a belt or switch. A review of the literature by Wilson (1977) provides useful guidelines for estimating the age of bruises. Bruises twenty-four to forty-eight hours old are generally reddish purple; one week old, brownish; ten to fourteen days old, yellowish to yellow-brown. In a dark-skinned child, such bruises may become deeply pigmented on healing. If the skin was broken and a scab has formed, the new skin will be lighter or depigmented in the pattern of the injury after healing.

Regardless of the number of bruises or injuries seen, the presence of marks after discipline indicates that too much force was used, and the medical diagnosis would be child abuse. Routine childhood bumps and bruises are generally distinguishable from inflicted injuries. They appear on exposed bony surfaces of the body—forehead, elbows, knees, and shins—and should raise no concern (Kerns, 1979; Tokarski, 1982). Children should be directly and emphatically questioned about any suspicious injury. In almost all cases they will truthfully state whether a bruise, scratch, or injury was accidental and explain the details about the incident. In any infant or nonverbal child (including a retarded or handicapped child), the caretaker should be able to provide a plausible explanation for any injury. Histories that do not fit the appearance of the injury must be considered suspicious for child abuse until proven otherwise (Schmitt and Kempe, 1983). With multiple injuries (e.g., fractures, bruises) or with several in different stages of healing, abuse must be considered (Kottmeier, 1987).

One of the more easily recognizable manifestations of inflicted injury is a human bite mark. Bites are most commonly scattered over the cheeks, abdomen skin, arms, and legs (Bernat, 1981; Trube-Becker, 1977). They may be seen in conjunction with other injuries (e.g., bruises, lacerations) and may be single or multiple. Two types of patterns have been identified. The first is a "suck mark" injury with central bruising and scratches surrounding it such that it has a "sunburst" appearance. More commonly this is seen in homicides with sex crimes. The second, more likely to indicate child abuse, has mirror-image crescents of bruises or abrasions where the teeth have injured the skin (Levine, 1977).

Burns

Burns constitute in some professionals' minds a more serious type of abuse, since these injuries are more deliberate. In a study conducted by Moritz and Henriques (1947), it has been shown that a 70 second exposure to water at 125.6° F will cause first- or second-degree burns (see also Feldman, Scholler, and Feldman, 1978). Since gas water heaters are preset at 140° F (Feldman et al., 1978), there is an obvious threat to the child any time an abusive or unconcerned caretaker bathes a child. Resultant "dunking" or "bath water" burns usually are apparent from the waist down and on the lower forearms and hands.

Splash burns or burns from objects such as irons and hair-curling equipment are frequently accidental. However, if a burn is severe or has received no medical attention, or if home remedies are not sufficient and the parent seeks no further care, the parent is neglecting his or her responsibility to the child.

Other "object" burns, such as that from a stove burner, are often intentional. Burns such as these have specific patterns—rod-shaped (curling iron), parallel lines (space heaters), concentric circles (electric stove burners). In order to teach the child not to touch hot objects, especially the stove, parents may deliberately force the child's hand down on the hot coil. Splash burns may have a large area of injury with one or more surrounding smaller burns from the splash.

Cigarette burns are usually one of the more visible and identifiable types of burns. They are often implanted on palms and soles for "disciplinary purposes." Allegedly this "teaches children," frequently toddlers, not to disobey parents or to touch hot objects. Burns from cigarettes are round with a central indentation and are all of the same size (Schmitt and Kempe, 1983). Children abused by burning have bruises, fractures, or other stigmata of the child-abuse syndrome (Watkins, Gagan, and Cupoli, 1985). Although all burns are not deliberately inflicted, all those that seem suspicious should be reported.

Head and Nervous System Injuries

Any injury to the head or neck should be considered worrisome, regardless of the external appearance. A slap or hit to the head or face is an inappropriate action with potentially life-threatening results. Forty to seventy percent of abused children with injuries to the brain will have external evidence of injury to the head (Klein, 1981). A bruise on the scalp or face or a skull fracture indicates that the force of a blow to the head was dissipated by these external structures. Some children, especially infants, present comatose or stuporous after an injury without any superficial evidence. In many cases these are "whiplash" injuries in which the infant's head or neck has been shaken by the caretaker. An infant cannot tolerate the excessive whiplike forces of being shaken; the result is brain injury and swelling. Caffey, a radiologist, first noted in 1946 the association between bleeding within the skull and multiple long-bone fractures in children (Fontana, 1984). His observation was a landmark in the history of recognition of the syndrome of child abuse and neglect.

Head trauma in small infants can be especially elusive because the "soft spots" or growth areas of their skulls allow some degree of expansion or pressure build-up through swelling of the brain following injury or bleeding inside the skull. The brain and its coverings, including the skull, are quite soft. In addition, a disproportionately large amount of blood is contained within the vessels of the skull and brain in the infant. These physical factors, plus a rapid physiologic response by the young brain, can quickly lead to brain swelling and death. "Simple" falls and injuries do not generally result in significant trauma to the brains of younger children and infants. One particular study revealed that only 3% of infants falling from a height of 35 inches or less sustained fractures, and none had injuries to the brain (Helfer, Slovis, and Black, 1977). Therefore, a fall by an infant from a couch or bed two feet or less from the floor does not usually produce significant nervous system injuries or even skull fractures.

More "minor" common injuries to the face and head include slap marks on the face (linear purplish marks, usually on the cheeks), small round bruises near the corner of the lips (where the child was pinched to quiet him), and small bruises inside the ear flaps (where the child was grabbed by the ear). Black eye(s) or bruises around the ears often signify a special type of skull fracture. Some children are also punched by the caretaker in the eye or on the side of the head.

Other less visible injuries to the child's mouth may occur when the infant has been forcefully fed. Whitish scarring of the undersurface of the tongue is present when the spoon or bottle has injured the soft, moist tissue of the floor of the mouth. In older children teeth may be missing, or there may be bleeding or bruising of the gums or tongue. There may be little or no explanation for such findings, or the child himself may simply state he was hit in the mouth. Any injury to the face, head, or neck, however, should be considered serious or out of the ordinary.

Chemical Abuse

Changes in children's behavior, either acutely or over time, may indicate that the child is being neglected, traumatized at home, or being exposed to drugs or chemicals. Psychotropic drugs such as major tranquilizers may cause excess sleepiness, dizziness, difficulty in walking, or confusion (Shnaps et al., 1981; Meadow, 1977). The literature cites several examples, including intentional poisoning of children with antidiarrheals and antivomiting medications (Fleisher and Ament, 1977), by anticlotting drugs (White, Voter, and Perry, 1985; Hvizdala and Gellady, 1978), by injection of bacteria into the blood (Hodge et al., 1982), by aspirin (Pickering, 1976), and even by sodium chloride (table salt) (Rogers et al., 1976). A parent or caretaker may willfully administer such agents to an infant or child. Since these children generally require hospitalization, some speculate that the parent, burdened with emotional, marital, and social problems sees this hospitalization as an escape from their problems (Shnaps et al., 1981; Meadow, 1977; Hvizdala and Gellady, 1978).

Emotional Abuse

The trauma of derogatory remarks toward the child also may cause alterations in the child's behavior. A significant "disciplinary action" or constant abuse may make the child chronically withdrawn, depressed, submissive, and fearful. He may act more infantile or more mature than his chronological age. This range of behaviors is symptomatic of emotional abuse.

In many custody disputes similar situations exist. A well-meaning parent may persistently allege abuse or neglect of the child by the spouse. Although no physical or behavioral evidence is found by professionals, the parent repeatedly subjects the child to physical examinations, especially in cases of sexual abuse. The child begins to see himself or herself as a pawn. In a broken family, where identities and feelings may be confusing to a child, he begins to question his own self-worth. This may not be termed emotional abuse by some professionals, but in many cases it produces the same results.

The Future

The effect of child maltreatment on society is significant. It is well known that if a child is abused, he may well be an abuser as an adult. Injuries to the child may produce physical scarring, and the parental rejection involved in child abuse cases results in psycho-emotional scarring. Disturbed children thus grow into disturbed adolescents, with a resultant increase in juvenile delinquency among this population (McCord, 1983). Education regarding proper disciplinary techniques and child-rearing practices can be of some help in preventing further abuse. Individual psychotherapy, however, has not been shown to be cost-effective (Rosenfeld and Levine, 1987).

The greatest immediate need, however, is the recognition of suspicious injuries. As soon as such injuries are reported, involvement of other professionals can take place. Without such recognition and reporting, the parent may receive counseling, but the child never receives a guarantee of safety or self-worth. Child maltreatment is not a one-sided problem, and neither are its recognition and management.

References

Bergman, B., R. M. Larsen, and B. D. Mueller. 1986. Changing spectrum of serious child abuse. *Pediatrics* 77(1):113–116.

Bernat, J. E. 1981. Bite marks and oral manifestations of child abuse and neglect. In *Child abuse and neglect: A medical reference,* ed. N. S. Ellerstein. New York: Wiley, p. 162.

Feldman, K. W., R. T. Scholler, and J. A. Feldman et al. 1978. Tap water scald burns in children. *Pediatrics* 62(1):6.

Fleisher, D., and M. Ament. 1977. Diarrhea, red diapers, and child abuse. *Clinical Pediatrics* 17(9):820–824.

Fontana, V. J. 1984. The maltreatment syndrome of children. *Pediatric Annals* 13(10):736–744.

Groothuis, J., W. A. Altemeier, and J. P. Robarge. 1982. Increased child abuse in families with twins. *Pediatrics* 70(5):769–773.

Helfer, R. E. 1984. The epidemiology of child abuse and neglect. *Pediatric Annals* 13(10):745–751.

Helfer, R. E., T. L. Slovis, and M. Black. 1977. Injuries resulting when small children fall out of bed. *Pediatrics* 60:533.

Hodge, D., W. Schwartz, et al. 1982. The bacteriologically battered baby: Another case of Munchausen by proxy. *Annals of Emergency Medicine.* 11(4):205/77–207/79.

Hvizdala, E., and A. M. Gellady. 1978. Intentional poisoning of two siblings by prescription drug. *Clinical Pediatrics* 17(6):480–482.

Klein, D. M. 1981. Central nervous system injuries. In *Child abuse and neglect: A medical reference,* ed. N. S. Ellerstein. New York: Wiley, pp. 73–76.

Kottmeier, P. K. 1987. The battered child. *Pediatric Annals* 16(4):344–345.

Levine, L. J. 1977. Bite mark evidence. *Dental Clinics of North America* 21(1):146.

McCord, J. 1983. A forty year perspective on effects of child abuse and neglect. *Child Abuse and Neglect* 7(3):270.

Meadow, R. 1977. Munchausen syndrome by proxy: The hinterland of child abuse. *Lancet* 2:343.

Moritz, A. R., and F. C. Henriques. 1947. Studies of thermal injury. *American Journal of Pathology* 23:695.

Pickering, D. 1976. Salicylate poisoning as a manifestation of the battered child syndrome. *American Journal of Diseases of Children* 130:674.

Rogers, D., J. Tripp, A. Bentovim, et al. 1976. Non-accidental poisoning: An extended syndrome of child abuse. *British Medical Journal* 1:793.

Rosenberg, N., and G. Bottenfield. 1982. Fractures in infants: A sign of child abuse. *Annals of Emergency Medicine* 11(4):100.

Schmitt, B. D., and C. H. Kempe. 1983. Abuse and neglect of children. In *Nelson's Textbook of Pediatrics,* 12th ed., eds. R. E. Behrman and V. C. Vaughan. Philadelphia: W. B. Saunders.

Shnaps, Y., M. Frand, Y. Rotem and M. Tirosh. 1981. The chemically abused child. *Pediatrics* 68(1):119–121.

Tokarski, P. A. 1982. Management of child abuse, in Warner, C., and Brain, G. R. (eds), *Topics in Emergency Medicine: Human Violence* 3(4):24–29, Aspen Systems Corporation.

Trube-Becker, E. 1977. Bitemarks on battered children. *Zeitschrift Fuer Rechtsmedizin* Rechtsmedizin–Journal of Legal Medicine 79:73.

Watkins, A. H., J. Gagan, and J. M. Cupoli. 1985. Child abuse by burning. *Journal of the Florida Medical Association* 72(7):499.

White, S. T., K. Voter, and J. Perry. 1985. Surreptitious warfare in ingestion. *Child Abuse and Neglect* 9(3):349–352.

Wilson, E. F. 1977. Estimating of the age of cutaneous contusions in child abuse. *Pediatrics* 60(5):751.

4
Abuse of the Elderly in the Home

Mildred Daley Pagelow

I ntrafamily victims and abusers about whom much less is known than those discussed in earlier chapters are the elderly abused by their in-home caretakers. Following Congressional hearings in 1980, some predicted that elder abuse would become the issue of the 1980s. But after the first few research reports and some media interest, the topic has again become almost as invisible as many of the aged victims, who are ignored as long as they remain in the home.

Public interest in crimes against the elderly is aroused when the crimes are committed by strangers or when the elderly are maltreated in nursing homes, though only about 6 percent of the elderly are institutionalized. The vast majority of the elderly either live alone (30 percent), or live in families (63 percent); *these* are the people at risk of abuse by family members (U.S. Bureau of the Census, 1979). In the privacy of their homes, the elderly may suffer the same kinds of abuse children and wives receive, but in addition they are often victims of financial exploitation (Shell, 1982).

This chapter addresses what is probably the least visible type of abuse in the family. We will explore research findings to identify groups at highest risk for abuse, the persons most likely to be abusers, the types of abuse the elderly most frequently suffer and their causes, and from all that we will devise methods for identification and prevention. For reasons that will be made clear later in this chapter, there is no professional group in a better position to help the abused elderly than the clergy.

Defining the Problem of Elder Abuse

The term *elderly* is defined on the basis of chronological age, arbitrarily referring to persons aged sixty-five or older (Pagelow, 1984), although some research includes persons under sixty-five (Block and Sinnott, 1979; Lau and Kosberg, 1979). Defining *abuse* presents serious problems (Pagelow, 1984; Pedrick-Cornell and Gelles, 1982). A report for the state by the California

Department of Social Services (CDPSS, 1985) defines adult abuse in the following terms.

Physical Abuse: willful infliction of corporal punishment or injury. It includes, but is not limited to, direct beatings, sexual assault, unreasonable physical constraints, or prolonged deprivation of food or water.

Fiduciary abuse: when a person in a position of trust willfully steals money or property, or secretes or appropriates money or property not in keeping with that trust.

Neglect: failure to exercise the degree of care a reasonable person would exercise. Neglect includes, but is not limited to, the failure to assist in personal hygiene, provide food and clothing, provide medical care for physical and mental health needs, protect from health and safety hazards, and prevent malnutrition.

Abandonment: unreasonably deserting or willfully forsaking an elder.

Mental suffering: deliberately causing fear, agitation, confusion, severe depression, or severe emotional depression through threats, harassment, or intimidation.

The lack of a common definition of abuse is one of the most serious problems in estimating how much and what kinds of crimes against the elderly occur in this country. This becomes obvious when comparing findings from the few published research reports. Most researchers agree that acts must be intentional to be considered abuse (Block and Sinnott, 1979; O'Malley et al., 1979), but in one study (Douglass, 1983) neglect was categorized into "passive" or "active" (deliberate).[1] Passive neglect was defined as "Elderly dependent is ignored, left alone, or not supplied with essential foods, clothing, medications because of ineptness or inability of the caregiver" (Douglass, 1983, p. 398). More cases of passive neglect were reported by 228 professionals in this study than of any other type of maltreatment.

The following acts are categorized differently or not included in various studies of elder abuse: withholding food and water from nonambulatory elders, infantilization, overmedicating or undermedicating, not providing medical care, threatening abandonment, being slow to change clothing or bedding when the elder is incontinent, locking elderlies in their room, or tying them to their beds (Beck and Ferguson, 1981; Gentry and Nelson, 1980; Oliveira, 1981). Depending on researchers' definitions, the same acts may be categorized differently, which drastically affects research findings.

The Scope of the Problem of Elder Abuse

Witnesses at Congressional hearings on domestic abuse of the elderly estimated that between 500,000 and 2.5 million persons over the age of sixty-five are abused by their caretakers (U.S. Congress, 1980), although there had been very few studies on which to base these ideas. Percentage estimates ranged from 4 to 10 percent (Lau and Kosberg, 1979; Block and Sinnott, 1979). If the lower rate of four percent is correct, there are over a million abused elders in this country—meaning there are about the same number of abuse victims at both ends of the life span: the young and the old. It is possible that aged victims of family violence will soon outnumber child victims because of the growth of the aged population.

There is no way of knowing how many elderly persons are abused, but evidence shows that abuse of the aged by their in-home caretakers is a widespread problem, and the problem will continue to grow as the number of persons at risk continues to grow.

Characteristics of Abused Elders and Their Abusers

The elderly most likely to be abused are white women between the ages of seventy-five and eighty-five, middle- to lower-middle-class, Protestant, and suffering physical and/or mental impairment (Oliveira, 1981; Sengstock and Liang, 1983). Their abusers are most likely to be family members who live with them, usually the victims' own children who are in the over-forty "sandwich generation."

Age and Sex of Victims

Victims are mostly in the "old old" category, and the vast majority (from 69 to 81 percent) are female (CDPSS, 1985; Sengstock and Liang, 1983). Their ages range from seventy-five years and beyond; their median ages are about seventy-five to seventy-eight years (Block and Sinnott, 1979; CDPSS, 1985; Sengstock and Liang, 1983; Shell, 1982). Persons at higher risk of abuse are the dependent elderly, and dependency increases with age; after age seventy-five, impairments increase and people begin to become the "frail elderly" (Cazenave, 1981).

There are two major reasons that approximately three out of four abused elders are female: their greater longevity and dependency. More than 28 million Americans are over the age of sixty-five (an increase of four million in five years). By the end of this century, "The greatest increase, 53 percent, will occur among those seventy-five and older which has important implications since this group is most vulnerable to physical, mental, and financial crises requiring the care of their family and society" (Steinmetz, 1981, p. 6). In the United States in 1984 there was a ratio of ten women to seven men (U.S. Bureau of the Census, 1986), and this ratio is growing. On the average, women outlive men by seven years; the proportion of women in the population increases with age.

Women are more likely to become dependent as they age because of widowhood and economics. One reason there are more widows is that women tend to marry men older than themselves (Rawlings, 1978), and widowers are seven times more likely to remarry than widows. Most elderly men (77 percent) live with their wives, whereas only 36 percent of elderly women live with husbands. Thus, two out of three older women have a choice of living with others, usually relatives, or living alone, which is more expensive.

Health and Socioeconomic Status

While only 26 percent of elderly persons are limited in their activities because of health reasons, and even fewer (16 percent) are unable to carry on major activities of daily living, a formidable 81 percent of persons over sixty-five have one or more chronic diseases or conditions (Schaie, 1982).

Dependency increases as persons lose the ability to function independently. The more losses they suffer, physical or mental, the greater the burden they become to their caretakers. The greater the burden they are, the more stress they cause (Steinmetz, 1981), and the more stress they cause, the greater the likelihood of abuse (Sengstock, Barrett, and Graham, 1984).

People with money stay healthier longer and obtain better medical care than the poor. The highest medical expenses occur in the last few years of life, and chronic or acute illnesses can drain lifetime savings very quickly.

Even if elderlies are in relatively good health, financial problems due to limited incomes may cause them to share housing with their children. Older women are much more likely to be poor than older men or younger women, and many must give up their independence to stretch their limited budgets. Older minority women are even more likely to be poor, but reports show that the majority of abuse victims are white (Block and Sinnott, 1979; CDPSS, 1985).

Poverty alone does not cause elder abuse. One study reports that 58 percent of the abuse cases were middle-class (Block and Sinnott, 1979). Probably abuse of elders is more likely to occur among middle-class families than either the upper or lower classes. The upper class can provide in-home nursing and services, spacious homes with greater privacy for other family members, and access to the finest nursing home care. Lower-class homes often lack privacy even before an old person moves in, so the impact can be less traumatic. The lower class usually has greater contact with social services and may know where to turn for help when needed. And when poor, old persons require full nursing care, they are more likely to qualify for admittance to public institutions.

The middle class, on the other hand, may not be able to afford in-home maintenance and respite care, and may lack the option to institutionalize the elderly because they cannot afford quality care homes and would fail the means test for public nursing homes. They may also be unaware of social services in the community, or be unable to qualify for them. Even if their homes are sufficient for the nuclear family, the strain of cramped quarters causes stress and friction, which in turn can be directed against the elders. The process is described by one expert:

> Families grudgingly accept the burden of keeping elderly relatives in their homes because of lack of alternatives, but they resent the intrusion into their lives . . . the stage is set for overt or covert hostility . . . teenagers may refuse to vacate the bathroom for anxious grandparents.[2] Because of physiological changes, old people must use the bathroom more frequently, often causing several trips at night, and they also require less sleep. Frequently, since they are excluded from family activities, they retire early and awaken at three or four in the morning, only to disturb the rest of the family by rattling utensils in the kitchen, getting their own breakfasts. This is the "Pots and Pans Syndrome." It is interpreted by the others as a sure sign of disorientation and the onset of senility, and soon they are presented to physicians or mental health workers who quickly diagnose them as "confused" or "disturbed," whereupon they are prescribed unneeded medication. We *hook* the elderly into abusing drugs! When they fight back, they are seen as "difficult" and medication is increased. (Oliveira, 1981)

Sharing living quarters out of economic necessity may begin with good intentions but can lead to friction and stress. When older parents live with their children and become physically or mentally handicapped, the difference between abuse and good care can depend on the ability to hire professionals or sitters, or to put the parents in good nursing homes (Pagelow, 1984).

Abusers and the Ways They Abuse

An abuser most commonly is an involuntary caregiver (usually a relative) living with the victim, who lacks resources to live elsewhere; the abuser often feels trapped and may be abusing drugs or alcohol (Fulmer, Street, and Carr, 1984). Research shows that a majority of the abusers live in the same households as those they abuse (Sengstock and Liang, 1983; Shell, 1982). One study found that 36 percent were over sixty years old, about half of whom were between sixty and sixty-nine (Shell, 1982). Abusers most frequently are the sons and daughters of the victims, and the second largest abuser category is spouses (Sengstock and Liang, 1983; CDPSS, 1985; Shell, 1982). Perpetrators are also likely to be substance abusers (O'Malley et al., 1983). Most researchers report finding multiple types of abuse.

There are indications that the type of abuse in a given case may depend on the age and sex of the perpetrators (Pagelow, 1988). For example, older caretakers, well-meaning but inept and over-stressed, could be more likely to neglect or psychologically abuse their charges than younger, able-bodied caretakers, who may be more likely to abuse physically. Caretakers of the "old old" elderly are themselves likely to be in the "young old" category. Soon it may not be unusual for seventy-year-old "children" to be caring for their frail ninety-year-old parents (Douglass, 1983). "This is the century not only of old age, but of multi-generational families, often composed of several generations of near elderly, elderly, and frail elderly women. About half of those over sixty-five who have living children are members of a four-generation family" (Steinmetz, 1981, p. 6).

Types of maltreatment may also differ according to the sex of the caretaker. Female caretakers may be more likely to maltreat their elderly charges through psychological abuse/neglect and physical neglect; all are forms of passive resistance. Males may be more likely to physically abuse the elderly, which is deliberate and purposive. Males and females may be equally likely to financially exploit the elderly (Sengstock and Liang, 1983).

At first it was thought that most abusers were females, as 78 percent of caretakers are female, most often daughters or daughters-in-law (Pagelow, 1984), but the data gathered from over 400 cases in each of the studies show that the abuser is slightly more likely to be male (CDPSS, 1985; Shell, 1982). Physical and financial abuse were the types most frequently found in two official reports, and the majority of abusers in these reports were males (CDPSS, 1985; Shell, 1982). Pillemer's study (1985) showed a mutual dependency between physical abusers and their victims, but the greatest dependency was the financial dependency of the abusers, and almost all abusers were male.

Horror stories of physical abuse and neglect are the cases that get publicized, but these are easy to identify and represent only the tip of the iceberg. Most experts believe these are relatively rare (Sengstock and Liang, 1983; Shell, 1982). Oliveira (1981) says that physical battery is the *least* common kind of abuse, occurring in only 19 percent of all cases, but that half of the abuse is psychological. Most abuses in the home are those that can go undetected until their effects are so extreme they are unmistakable to outsiders. Psychological abuse and neglect are probably the most damaging to the victims' mental health and may shorten their lives by reducing their will to live. But these abuses are the *least* likely to be detected.

Invisible Victims

Detection often depends on in-home visitors such as other relatives, social workers, visiting nurses, or empathetic persons who spend time building rapport and trust, such as the clergy. But what can they look for? Signs of maltreatment of old people are similar in many ways to indicators of child maltreatment, but they are more difficult to isolate from the normal aging process. For example, physical abuse may be indicated by the types and locations of physical trauma and how well the injuries and explanation match. Neglect is indicated by evidence of dehydration, malnutrition, bed sores, over- or undermedication, and household conditions and odors. Psychological abuse or neglect may be detected by how the elders respond to their caretakers and whether their demeanor changes as their caretakers come and go.

There are specific problems in intervention for elderly victims that are not present in child abuse and neglect cases. The most important difference is that the law protects adults' rights to privacy; no one can interfere without their permission. In many cases, overwhelming evidence is present that adults have been victims of crimes in their homes, but without their cooperation, little or nothing can be done. Victims do not ask for help and may refuse assistance: "In fact, abused elders and their abusers *almost invariably* deny it" (Galbraith and Zdorkowski, 1984). Elderly victims refuse to ask for help because of their fear of losing independence; fear of retaliation; embarrassment over their state of health, hygiene, or family relationships; and fear of forced relocation and institutionalization (O'Malley et al., 1983). In addition, many still *love* their abusers.

Intervention and Prevention

Although state laws on mandatory or advisory reporting vary considerably (Haggerty, 1981; O'Malley et al., 1983), an important first step is to educate the public to recognize symptoms and report suspicions. Many professionals have little patience for the desire of victims to protect their abusers or to remain in conditions that, to them, are clearly substandard. They do not understand victims' strong ties both to their abusers and to their familiar surroundings. Their greatest fear is losing their homes and being institutionalized which, "All too often . . . is the intervention of choice of well-meaning professionals" (Anderson and Thobaden, 1984, p. 9).

No professional group is in a better position to help abuse victims and prevent abuse of the elderly than the clergy. No other type of intrafamily abuse than elder abuse is more amenable to reduction or prevention through intervention by religious groups. From the pulpit, the clergy can alert the faithful to this invisible problem, calling on congregations to visit elderly members and inviting caretakers to seek help from their pastors. Volunteer organizations can be urged to offer respite care for the elderly to reduce caretakers' heavy burdens.

The traditional mission of the clergy has been to offer solace to the sick and infirm, which has most often been accomplished by home visits. Who has better entree to homes of the dependent elderly? Neighbors, nurses, social workers, police: all can be denied entry with greater ease than priests, ministers, and rabbis. What old person, admittedly nearing death, who has been faithful all his or her life, will deliberately lie to a cleric's gently inquiry about bruises or emaciation? Whereas an older person can lie to another outsider for the "greater good" of protecting a loved one, a lifetime of cherished values prevents that person from fabrication to the clergy.

The cleric does not face the same problem of building trust that other professionals have; the trust of the faithful elderly may be taken as a given. Informed with the truth, the cleric can then offer assurances of confidentiality and assistance, calling upon members of the congregation to assist. It may take only sporadic relief from the burden of caretaking, and the knowledge that the caretaker is not solely responsible for the well-being of the dependent elder, for the psychological abuse and neglect or physical neglect to cease. If the abuse is financial or deliberate, authorities should be notified. Religious groups and their leaders should network with appropriate professional groups.

Public and private agencies are beginning to offer services nationally, such as a combination of health care, day-care supervision, housekeeping services, counseling, meal deliveries, transportation, visits from friendly companions, home repairs, and more (Rosenblatt and Peterson, 1986). Senior centers are springing up around the country, providing meals, counseling, recreation, and day care. They charge on a sliding scale for day care, which provides respite from twenty-four-hour-a-day caretaking. One senior center in Los Angeles served over 19,000 persons in 1985 (Rosenblatt and Peterson, 1986). Some agencies even provide emergency housing (JAMA, 1980).

Some professionals are offering suggestions for political activism to push for more government services to the elderly (Giordano and Giordano, 1984; Haggerty, 1981). Medical professionals are also trying to educate their peers about this "new" problem (Ferguson and Beck, 1983; Rathbone-McCuan and Goodstein, 1985; O'Malley et al., 1983).

One professional group—the clergy—has remained almost universally silent on the topic of elder abuse, yet they can no longer ignore a problem of silent suffering that will grow over time. Religious leaders must become sensitized and begin to lead their followers to the forgotten and invisible dependent elderly. They must use their special talents and privileges to help both the abused and their abusers.

Notes

1. When Douglass divides neglect into two types—passive and active—his definition for passive neglect includes both physical neglect (not providing food, clothing, and medication) and psychological neglect (ignoring and leaving alone). Neglect is usually divided by researchers into only two categories: physical and psychological.

2. When I listened to Oliveira describe the middle-class family's response to the intrusion in their lives, memories of a doctor's family surfaced. The doctor's aged mother and father moved in with his nuclear family. His teenage daughter and son complained but generally ignored the more crowded living conditions of their modest home. However, they adamantly refused to yield the bathroom to their diabetic grandfather, whereupon the old man would go to another room and urinate in the fireplace! Needless to say, all members of the family were very upset, and the old man was usually scolded at length. His embarrassment was obvious, but he said nothing to defend himself.

References

Anderson, L., and M. Thobaden. 1984. Clients in crisis. *Journal of Gerontological Nursing* 10(12):6–10.

Beck, C., and D. Ferguson. 1981. Aged abuse. *Journal of Gerontological Nursing* 7(6):333–336.

Block, M. R., and J. D. Sinnott, eds. 1979. *The battered elder syndrome: An exploratory study.* Division of Human and Community Resources. College Park: University of Maryland.

California Department of Social Services. 1985. *Dependent adult and elder abuse: Report to the legislature, report year 1984.* Sacramento.

Cazenave, N. A. 1981. Stress management and coping alternatives for families of the frail elderly. Paper presented at the National Conference for Family Violence Researchers, Durham, NH.

Douglass, R. L. 1983. Domestic neglect and abuse of the elderly: Implications for research and service. *Family Relations* 32(3):395–402.

Ferguson, D., and C. Beck. 1983. H.A.L.F.—A tool to assess elder abuse within the family. *Geriatric Nursing,* September/October, 301–304.

Fulmer, T., S. Street, and K. Carr. 1984. Abuse of the elderly: Screening and detection. *Journal of Emergency Nursing* 10(3):131–133.

Galbraith, M. W., and R. T. Zdorkowski. 1984. Teaching the investigation of elder abuse. *Journal of Gerontological Nursing* 10(12):21–25.

Gentry, C. E., and B. D. Nelson. 1980. Developmental patterns for abuse programs: Application to the aging. In *Abuse of Older Persons,* ed. D. F. Holden and P. L. Carey. Knoxville: University of Tennessee, School of Social Work.

Giordano, N. H., and J. A. Giordano. 1984. Elder abuse: A review of the literature. *Social Work,* May-June, 236.

Haggerty, M. 1981. Elder abuse: Who is the victim? *Gray Panther Network,* January-February, 4–5.

Journal of the American Medical Association. 1980. The elderly: Newest victims of familial abuse. 243(12):1221–1222.

Lau, E., and J. I. Kosberg. 1979. Abuse of the elderly by informal care providers. *Aging,* September/October, 10–15.

Oliveira, O. H. 1981. Psychological and physical factors of abuse of older people. Excerpts from his speech at the Multidisciplinary Conference on Family Violence, June 11, Long Beach, CA.

O'Malley, H., H. Segars, R. Perez, V. Mitchell, and G. N. Knuepfel. 1979. *Elder abuse in Massachusetts.* Boston: Legal Research for the Elderly.

O'Malley, T. A., D. E. Everitt, H. C. O'Malley, and E. Campion. 1983. Identifying and preventing family-mediated abuse and neglect of elderly persons. *Annals of Internal Medicine* 98(6):998–1005.

Pagelow, M. D. 1984. *Family violence.* New York: Praeger.

———. 1988. The criminal abuse of other family members. In *Family violence as a criminal justice issue,* ed. L. Ohlin and M. Tonry. Chicago: University of Chicago Press.

Pedrick-Cornell, C., and R. J. Gelles. 1982. Elder abuse: The status of current knowledge. *Family Relations* 31(3):457–465.

Pillemer, K. 1985. The dangers of dependency: New findings on domestic violence against the elderly. *Social Problems* 33(2):146–158.

Rathbone-McCuan, E., and R. K. Goodstein. 1985. Elder abuse: Clinical considerations. *Psychiatric Annals* 15(5):331–339.

Rawlings, S. W. 1978. *Perspectives on American Husbands and Wives.* Department of Commerce, Bureau of the Census. Washington, D.C.: Government Printing Office.

Rosenblatt, R. A., and J. Peterson. 1986. New mix of services: A little help lets elderly live at home. *Los Angeles Times,* 6/25/86, I:1–14.

Schaie, K. Warner. 1982. America's elderly in the coming decade. In *Adult development and aging,* ed. K. W. Schaie and J. Geiwitz. Boston: Little, Brown.

Sengstock, M. C., S. Barrett, and R. Graham. 1984. Abused elders: Victims of villains or of circumstances? *Journal of Gerontological Social Work* 9(1/2):101–111.

Sengstock, M. C., and J. Liang. 1983. Domestic abuse of the aged: Assessing some dimensions of the problem. *Interdisciplinary Topics Gerontology* 17:58–68.

Shell, D. J. 1982. *Protection of the elderly: A study of elder abuse.* Winnipeg, Manitoba: Manitoba Council on Aging.

Steinmetz, S. K. 1981. Elder abuse. *Aging,* January/February, 6–10.

U.S. Bureau of the Census, Department of Commerce. 1979. *Social and Economic Characteristics of the Older Population: 1978.* Series P-23, No. 85. Washington, D.C.: Government Printing Office.

———. 1986. *Statistical Abstracts in the U.S.: 1986. National Data Book and Guide to Sources.* Washington, D.C.: Government Printing Office.

U.S. Congress. 1980. Select Committee on Aging, Subcommittee on Human Services. *Domestic Abuse of the Elderly.* Washington, D.C.: Government Printing Office.

5
Identifying Sexual Abuse in Families and Engaging Them in Professional Treatment

Robert J. Kelly

C hild sexual abuse has become one of the most widely publicized social problems of the 1980s. With few subcultural exceptions, sex between adults and children has always been taboo. Yet it has been taboo not only to engage in adult-child sex, but also to speak about the existence of such deviant behavior. Only recently have we been able to break down the irrational fear we have had about examining and discussing this unpleasant topic. We have realized that the tragedy of this behavior will not disappear simply by denying its existence or choosing not to discuss it.

This chapter seeks to help pastoral counselors, clergy members, and other religious leaders effectively identify and respond to cases of child sexual abuse of an incestuous nature. Let us hope and pray that all types of child sexual abuse will remain taboo, but let us meanwhile confront our fears by acknowledging the existence of this behavior while learning how we might constructively respond to the tragic cases we encounter.

Identifying Incest

There are three ways that we usually learn about a case of incest: (1) we are told directly by a family member; (2) we are told by someone else who "knows" or strongly suspects that incest is occurring in some family; or (3) we "know" or strongly suspect it ourselves from our conversations with, or observations of, a family. Our course of action depends upon which of the three sources we are dealing with and the degree of confidence we have in the correctness of that particular source. It is imperative that we are able to open our eyes and identify true cases of incest, but we should also keep in mind the hardships that can occur when a family is falsely accused of incest. For this reason, we must carefully examine our suspicions of incest before proceeding with a response.

Disclosure by a Family Member

If we are told directly by a family member about the existence of incest, we should almost always believe that incest is actually occurring in that family. As recent studies have shown, people generally do not lie about incest, unless it is to deny its existence (Jones and McGraw, 1987). We should consider the motives and general reliability of the disclosing family member. But we must not assume that incest is not occurring just because this family member is generally unstable or has possible motives for falsely accusing another family member.

An unstable family member may be unstable because of the very dysfunctional, incestuous family situation that he or she is reporting. Also, although a person may have a motive for falsely accusing another family member, this rarely occurs. The Jones and McGraw study showed that even when the possible motives of denying child custody or visitation were involved, very few false allegations of incest were reported.

Moreover, we can sometimes find ourselves erroneously discrediting a family member because the accusation is taking place at a time when that discloser is angry at the accused family member for other visible reasons; or because the disclosure is taking place years after the incest first started and we cannot believe that it could be kept a secret for so long if it were truly occurring; or because the discloser lacks the emotional conviction we would expect in a true incest victim.

With regard to these last points, I encourage readers to become aware of what Roland Summit has deftly described as the "accommodation syndrome" (Summit, 1983). As Summit mentions, many children respond to the powerlessness and secrecy inherent in acts of incest by psychologically adapting, or accommodating, to the abuse. Children cannot cognitively accept that a trusted family member, who they want to believe is "all good," can actually be doing wrongful acts with them. These victims accommodate in different ways, perhaps by accepting all the blame for these acts or by some type of escape, such as emotional withdrawal, running away from home, using drugs, or in some severe cases, regressing into a dissociative state.

Most children will keep incest a secret, either to hold onto the image of that family member as "all good" or because of the threats made by that abuser. Threats may involve physical harm, but more often they are threats involving the loss of love or loss of family togetherness, such as "Don't tell Mommy or she'll get mad at me and I'll have to leave home forever," or "If you tell Mommy she'll be so mad at you that she will never speak to you again." Faced with the apparent choice between "destroying the family" by disclosing the abuse and "saving the family" by keeping the incest a secret, most children will decide that the only good choice is to maintain the secret.

Some children will never disclose this secret, even as adults. For example, in a therapy group I currently co-lead for men who were sexually abused as children, thirteen of the first fourteen men who came to the group had kept their sexual abuse experiences a secret for at least nine years, with one man having kept it secret for forty years.

As Summit explains, an incest victim's disclosure is often delayed and unconvincing. The victim may disclose the secret only at a time when he or she has matured enough to gain some personal power (which explains the delay in disclosure), and that disclosure may seem unconvincing if it occurs at a time when the victim is angry at the abuser for other reasons. Thus, for example, we might not believe an adolescent girl who discloses incest when she is angry at her father for his not giving her permission to go to a party. We might erroneously assume that this is just a rebellious teenager, and we may in fact sympathize with this father for having to deal with this adolescent phase.

Once a child discloses incest, much family upheaval occurs. Family members tend to blame the victim at least in part for this upheaval. The new pressure the child feels may lead him or her to recant the disclosure so that the family can be reunited. It is important to recognize that such recantations may actually be the last stage of accommodations syndrome (i.e., the child's way of adapting to the incest experience). Although it is possible that a recantation may be valid, we should not automatically assume that incest has not occurred simply because a child withdraws a previous allegation.

Allegation by a Non-Family Member

When we are told by people about their suspicions of incest in another family, we should be careful in assessing the credibility of their report also. They may have other motives for accusing a family of incest, or they may just be drawing incorrect conclusions. Nevertheless, any allegation of incest must be considered seriously. Most people do not make false allegations about their neighbors, especially ones as potentially damaging as incest. We need to take a calm, rational look at the reasons for these suspicions before deciding upon a response.

Once you are convinced that the allegations are valid, you must decide how your response will involve the people making the allegation. For example, you may need to tell those people that you will handle any further investigation and then encourage them to remain quiet about their suspicions. In many cases the people disclosing their suspicions will need to be reassured that they did the right thing. They may need this reassurance not only at the time of disclosure, but throughout the long ordeal that will inevitably follow any valid allegation of incest. The disclosers will need to be supported in a way that lets them know they are not responsible for the disruption of this family. Although they may have precipitated the disruption, they are not to blame for the family dysfunction. In fact, in most cases they will have helped the family take an important, though painful, step toward a healthier family environment.

Personal Suspicions

We, too, can be incorrect in our suspicions about an incestuous family. Our hunches and our other possible motives must be carefully considered before we forge ahead with a direct accusation. Whenever possible, it is a good policy to have a confidential consultation with another professional who has had experience identifying incest and dealing with the entire process of family confrontation.

To increase our ability to identify incest, we should be aware of current literature on behavioral and emotional risk factors and indicators of incest. For example, David Finkelhor, one of the leading researchers in the field, has proposed that certain variables make child sexual abuse more likely in a given family. In comparing the families of college students who were sexually abused with families of those who were not sexually abused, he was able to identify a variety of risk factors. Sexual abuse was more likely to occur in families in which a stepfather was present, the mother was emotionally distant, the mother held a less powerful role than the father, and repressive attitudes and messages existed within the family (Finkelhor, 1979).

Finkelhor and his colleague Angela Browne have also conceptualized a model to describe the effects of child sexual abuse (Finkelhor and Browne, 1986). Within this model, psychological effects are perceived more accurately as mere symptoms rather than definite signs that a child is abused. Nevertheless, awareness of the presence of these effects may help us identify abuse. The model postulates that psychological effects arise from four traumatic elements inherent in an abuse experience: (1) early sexualization; (2) stigmatization; (3) powerlessness; and (4) betrayal.

These four elements, or traumagenic dynamics, may lead to a variety of emotional and behavioral manifestations. For example, the sexualization dynamic may lead to precocious sexualized behavior or later sexual dysfunction. The stigmatization aspect may cause feelings of alienation and lead to social withdrawal and isolation. The powerlessness dynamic may lead to a loss of self-efficacy and the existence of fears and helplessness. Finally, the betrayal component may hinder a victim's ability to trust and form appropriate peer relationships.

It is of critical importance that we realize that the presence of these risk factors or indicators is not positive proof that incest has occurred. Our suspicions are more easily confirmed with some indicators, such as a child's contracting venereal disease or becoming pregnant. But a variety of causes can be found for other indicators. For example, a child may be depressed or withdrawn for many reasons, only one of which is incest. Moreover, most stepfathers do not abuse their stepchildren; thus the presence of a stepfather should not be interpreted as a sign of abuse. On the other hand, the absence of typical risk factors or indicators does not preclude the possibility that incest has occurred. Thus, even if 30–40 percent of female incest victims exhibit social withdrawal, there are still 60–70 percent who have been abused and are not exhibiting this withdrawal.

A Pastoral Response to the Incestuous Family

Identifying incest is in itself an important task, but it should be followed by an appropriate pastoral response to the incestuous family. The effectiveness of this response usually depends upon the preparation that the pastoral counselor has done before working with the family as well as on the contact itself. The last part of this chapter will provide an outline of issues and suggestions associated with these two phases of pastoral response.

Preparation before Working with the Family

1. *Become aware of personal feelings toward incest.* Most of us have a very strong negative reaction to any mention of incest. We need to examine our beliefs, stereotypes, and any emotional reactions that are elicited by a case of incest we encounter. Are we disgusted to the point of not being able to deal with the family? Does this case remind us of other difficult abuse situations in which we became emotionally involved? Are we aware of feelings toward our own family members which we may be transferring onto these family members? We must honestly confront our feelings about incest and sex in general so that we can more comfortably deal with actual cases. We also need to be able to talk openly and comfortably about sexuality.

2. *Become aware of personal feelings about psychotherapy.* The best response a pastoral counselor can make to cases of incest is one that helps the family move into psychotherapy. To do so, that counselor must be aware of any personal biases he or she may have against such therapy. Some pastoral counselors may feel that their own competence is threatened if they need to refer to a family to another professional. Pastoral counselors should recognize that, on the contrary, their ability to wisely refer such cases to specialized treatment agencies is a sign of their competence. Other pastoral counselors may share the widespread feelings of prejudice toward people who seek psychotherapy. They may shy away from referring families because they do not want the family to feel this stigma. These counselors must realize that this attitude not only hinders families from gaining the therapy they need, but

also perpetuates the feelings of stigmatization previously described in Finkelhor and Browne's traumagenic model.

3. *Become aware of the professional resources available.* The quantity and quality of professional resources for dealing with incest vary greatly throughout different parts of this country. Pastoral counselors should attempt to build a resource network with diagnostic agencies, therapists, the local Department of Children's Services, and the relevant law enforcement divisions. Families can be spared from much trauma if the response from these resources is coordinated and cooperative. One highly regarded treatment approach is that of Parents United, which has many chapters throughout the country. The Parents United treatment model uses a combination of individual, marital, group, and family therapy specifically designed for incestuous families, as is the case with its auxiliary chapters of Daughters and Sons United and Adults Molested As Children United. Information on these and other resources can be obtained in most locales by dialing the local Child Abuse Hotline. Additional information can be obtained from regional and state child-abuse agencies, or by contacting the National Center on Child Abuse and Neglect in Washington, D.C.

4. *Clearly decide upon your role.* If there are appropriate psychotherapeutic resources for dealing with incest in your community, your major role should be to help the family seek this aid. Prepare to be supportive but firm in advising the family to enter therapy. You must also decide exactly what your additional role will and will not entail. Most clerics will maintain some contact with the family, continuing their important work as spiritual leaders. Your role should be discussed with the primary therapist so that the support you give the family will be consistent with the overall therapeutic plan.

5. *Become aware of confidentiality and legal issues.* You need to become aware of the legal and ethical issues involved in working with incest cases. The laws regarding the clergy-penitent privilege in cases of incest vary from state to state. Of primary concern is whether you will make a child-abuse report to the local Department of Children's Services or law enforcement agency. Even if you are not required by your particular state's law to file a child-abuse report, you may still feel an ethical duty to make this response in order to minimize the chances that the incest will continue.

Pastoral counselors may feel some sense of betrayal when reporting families or when referring them to a therapist who is then legally mandated to make such a report. Indeed, the families may actually report feelings of betrayal, especially if they have disclosed directly to the counselor about the abuse. Pastoral counselors may feel less disloyal if they realize that most cases of incest do not stop by themselves. In fact, recent studies have shown that people who commit incestuous acts often molest other children outside of the family (Abel et al., 1987). Moreover, we know that without adequate therapy, some children who are molested will themselves molest other children as they grow older. For these reasons, the involvement of legal and therapeutic agencies that can work with and monitor the activities of these families is imperative.

6. *Become aware of what will happen in the legal and protective service system.* The response of the legal and protective service systems will also vary from region to region. Find out what can be expected in your community once a child-abuse report has been filed. In many cases a social worker will visit the home. If there exists a reasonable suspicion that incest has occurred, the victim(s) or the perpetrator may then be removed from the home. Eventually the family may end up in dependency court, or less frequently, civil or criminal court. Therapy is often mandated, with future court decisions being based partly on the progress that can be demonstrated in therapy. In most cases, a good deal of family upheaval will occur and should be anticipated.

7. *Accept the necessity for family upheaval.* Pastoral counselors usually hold high regard for the sanctity of the family. It may be difficult to reconcile this belief with a pastoral response that precipitates family upheaval. There may be a tendency to deny the pathology within an incestuous family, to focus on the strengths of that family, and to hope that the family can work out its own problems, especially with the help of prayer. But as the title of this book implies, praying for incest to go away is simply not enough.

Perhaps the most helpful psychological model for understanding the need for familial upheaval is the family systems model (see Minuchin, 1974; Waterman, 1986). According to a family systems model, family members take on various roles in relation to one another. These roles become quite stable as the family system reaches a balanced state known as homeostasis. Once this balanced state has developed, it is very difficult for the system to adopt a new set of roles unless a major shift in the family occurs.

Incestuous families develop homeostasis, but the roles that members have adopted are pathological. For example, a teenage daughter who is having sex with her father may have been forced into the role usually assumed by the wife/mother. The pain resulting from the pathological schism or rigid boundary between husband and wife is not dealt with directly because functional family roles are assumed by other family members. Thus, the husband now looks to his daughter for sexual gratification, and that daughter takes on the role of wife and mother as she feels the responsibility for keeping the family together.

Family systems theory suggests that changes in this type of pathological homeostasis will not occur unless the family system is disrupted, as usually takes place when incest is reported to local authorities. The opportunities for a return to the old pathological system need to be blocked if more appropriate roles are to be learned and adopted. Without such a change, the pathological system may cause devastating psychological consequences for all family members.

Working with the Family

As mentioned previously, the pastoral counselor should rarely be the primary therapist for the family. However, he or she needs to adopt a role that is consistent with the overall therapeutic plan for that family. The details and timing of this response should be coordinated with the primary therapist. However, some general issues should be kept in mind.

1. *Balance care with firmness in responding to emotional reactions.* Once an incestuous family is confronted, family members will experience a myriad of emotional reactions, including shock, denial, fear, outrage, grief, and despair. Pastoral counselors must continue to show sincere concern for the family, although this concern should be balanced with firmness in moving the family toward therapy. Do not feed into a family's attempts to deny the seriousness of the incest by telling family members that everything is all right. Be honest in helping them accept that a great deal of family disruption will have to occur.

2. *Educate family members about what they can expect.* In your preparation for dealing with the incestuous family, you will have learned a great deal about the resources available and what can be expected in the legal and protective service systems' response to the case. Help the family cope with the inevitable upheaval by communicating what you have learned, including the confidence that you may have gained from consulting with the professionals who will become involved. Explain to the family that you and/or the therapist will be filing a child abuse report, as required by law.

3. *Help family overcome stigmata associated with psychotherapy.* The best way you can help a family overcome their prejudice about therapy is to show them that you do not feel negatively toward people who seek therapy, and that you do feel positively about the many people who have found help through therapy. Having a referral source ready for them can be very helpful, since families that are confronted with incest will not have the presence of mind to take the steps toward finding an appropriate therapist. Communicating your confidence in a particular therapist can smooth the transition into therapy.

4. *Clearly communicate your role.* Some families may feel that you have betrayed them by accusing them of incest, and these families may not want any future contact with you. Other families may look to you for support, especially if you have been a direct source of support in the past. You will need to explain clearly to the family what your role will be, in accordance

with the overall therapeutic plan you have coordinated with the primary therapist.

5. *Support the person who disclosed the incest.* If you discovered the incest through a family member's disclosure, be particularly careful in explaining to that person that you are not abandoning him or her simply because you are making a referral to another therapist. Explain that you will continue to care for that person whether or not you have future meetings together. Since the family will probably be angry with that family member for disclosing the abuse, the discloser will need to be assured of your support. You may also be able to help other family members examine their tendency to blame this discloser for the family disruption that will occur.

6. *Care for the entire family.* Incest and its aftermath affects the entire family. Do not focus your support solely on the family members who were involved sexually. Pay attention to siblings, even if they were not sexually involved. Siblings will undoubtedly experience many emotional reactions about the incest and the family disruption that follows, yet they often do not receive adequate support.

7. *Be aware of sociocultural issues.* The sociocultural aspects of incest are usually grossly neglected. Factors such as income, attitudes toward sexuality, language barriers, and racial prejudice within community service agencies will affect a family's ability to use community resources in dealing with the incest. For example, the threat of losing an abusing husband's income may make it extremely difficult for a mother to accept his being taken from the home. In some subcultures, a mother may have such a fear of being perceived as a failure in her roles as wife and mother that she is not able to acknowledge the incest. Pastoral counselors may benefit from becoming aware of how such sociocultural factors may affect cases of incest (see Kelly and McCurry-Scott, 1986).

8. *Lead an appropriate response by the religious community.* The religious community of which this family is a member will need assistance in understanding how to react to the incest and to the family. Most pastoral counselors may feel responsibility to keep the incest confidential except for cooperation with the appropriate community agencies. However, when the religious community is already aware of the incest, the clergy member may need to take a more direct stand in helping the community develop a caring response to the family. The community will need to be educated in a way that fosters neither self-righteousness nor paranoia, but is sensitive to the fact that there may be other incestuous families yet to be discovered in the community. Arranging lectures focusing on prevention of sexual abuse can also help the community gain confidence in its ability to confront the problem of incest.

As a final note, pastoral counselors should be mindful of the fact that many adult women and men have experienced incest as children. Indeed, for some victims this abuse continues well into adulthood! The complexity of incest dynamics must never be underestimated if pastoral counselors are to succeed in making an effective multifaceted response.

References

Abel, G. G., J. V. Becker, M. Mittelman, J. Cunningham-Rathner, J. L. Rouleau, and W. D. Murphy. 1987. Self-reported sex crimes of nonincarcerated paraphiliacs. *Journal of Interpersonal Violence* 2:3–25.

Finkelhor, D. 1979. *Sexually victimized children.* New York: Free Press.

Finkelhor, D., and A. Browne. 1986. The traumatic impact of child sexual abuse: A conceptualization. *American Journal of Orthopsychiatry* 55:530–541.

Jones, D. P. H., and J. M. McGraw. 1987. Reliable and fictitious accounts of sexual abuse to children. *Journal of Interpersonal Violence* 2:27–45.

Kelly, R. J., and M. McCurry-Scott. 1986. Sociocultural considerations in child sexual abuse. In *Sexual Abuse of Young Children* eds. K. MacFarlane, J. M. Waterman, et al. New York: Guilford.

Minuchin, S. 1974. *Families and family therapy.* Cambridge, MA: Harvard University Press.

Summit, R. 1983. The child sexual abuse accommodation syndrome. *Child Abuse and Neglect* 7:177–193.

Waterman, J. M. 1986. Family dynamics of incest with young children. In *Sexual Abuse of Young Children,* eds. K. MacFarlane, J. M. Waterman, et al. New York: Guilford.

6
Marital Rape

Kersti Yllo
Donna LeClerc

S exual violence is, first and foremost, an act of violence, hatred, and aggression. Whether it is viewed clinically or legally, objectively or subjectively, violence is the common denominator. Like other acts of violence (assault and battery, murder, nuclear war), there is a violation of and injury to victims. The injuries may be psychological or physical. In acts of sexual violence, usually the injuries are both (Marie Fortune, 1984:5).

When individuals suffer injuries, they search their environment for support. They look to family and friends for nurturance and healing, and to representatives of their belief system for answers. The psychological damage to self-esteem and self-worth caused by such acts of violence has victims questioning their responsibility for or in the crime. They want to know that it was not their wrongdoing that brought violence into their lives. Unfortunately, much religious belief, doctrine, and dogma have not given the victim the reassurance she seeks because the dogma and doctrine are based on androcentric interpretations that do not bring a healing or liberating messages.

The purpose of this chapter is to 1) explore Judeo-Christian ideology regarding sexuality, particularly in respect to marital rape; 2) provide data on marital rape which reveal the realities of sexual abuse in marriage; and 3) offer ways in which clergy and secular counselors can better help victims who come to them.

Judeo-Christian Ideology

Theological history, like any specific history, reflects the experiences of people and cultures at certain stages of development. To fully understand the Judeo-Christian ideology, one must understand the cultural, psychological, and sociological conditions of the times and places that generated it.

The originators of monotheistic thought, which is the basis of Judaism, Christianity, and Islam, brought with them attitudes about sexuality and roles of men and women that were shaped by their forbearers. These attitudes included mythology that had been produced by the surrounding poly-theistic cultures. This mythology included beliefs about women, their repro-ductive abilities, and their roles in the individual societies.

The early writers of the Hebrew scriptures were developing ideas that reflected a change in social mores of their time; rather than defining for women a subordinate role, they were attempting to provide a level of protec-tion. Theirs was a society seeking to free itself as a fledgling nation from what is identified as injustice (Exodus 6:1–8). Later androcentric assump-tions, whether they came from later Hebraic scholars or Christian theolo-gians, have read male dominance and female subordination into that specific situation.

There can be no question that this emerging nation, Israel, brought with it sexual mythology, but confusion about sexuality and male power appears to have been a recurring theme among early societies. Pagan superstition is now unknown to modern man, but often myths—both ancient and mod-ern—become part of societal attitudes, laws, and behaviors. Therefore, it is important for theologians to be able to look at the writings that form modern religious thought and be able to separate cultural, psychological, sociologi-cal, and historical information from the basic precepts of faith.

Rather than accepting the inerrancy of scripture as integral to preserva-tion of faith or using Western thought to understand Near Eastern develop-ment, it is more important to try to understand the struggle of a people to identify their faith and how this identification related to sexuality. Early in the Book of Genesis is found the story of Abraham and Isaac. Abraham is about to offer Isaac as a blood sacrifice, but intervention comes and an ani-mal is offered instead. This is interpreted as the beginning of the idea of substitution; human sacrifice would be replaced by animal sacrifice. The story of Lot and his daughters can be viewed as part of this same theological understanding. The quick intervention by the messengers followed by the destruction of the cities could be read in light of the Abraham story as saying that any violation of human dignity will no longer be acceptable.

Thus, the practice of offering any family member to rape would not be considered part of hospitality. While the laws of hospitality would continue to be important, household members would not be the sacrificial lambs to men's fears. It would be possible to place a new value on women and address the issue of rape.

Rape, murder, and mayhem in the Land of Benjamin (Judges 19–21) are qualified at the end of the story: "In those days there was no king in Israel; every man did that which was right in his own eyes" (Judges 21:25). The writers who recount this story as a part of their theological history neither clean up the story nor express approval of the events. Instead the story is presented as a prelude to the need for a strong moral and ethical system that can be universally applied.

Read this way, a theological history of humanity's search for God would clearly exclude any form of oppression or violence against women. The idealistic motives of the writers are apparent; the ability to ensure this idealism is less clear. Following the conversion of Constantine in about 313, the Pauline School, Augustine, and Aquinas all taught to one degree or another that "inferiority touches the entire nature of woman" (Ruether, 1983, p. 96). Man's need to safeguard family morality was thus interpreted to imply sexual and physical violence were justified and oppressive, invalidating behavior was condoned.

Nevertheless, present-day theologians and clergy are rethinking cultural attitudes toward women and their role in society and are applying different theological definitions to their experience. We cannot go back and change historical events, nor can we read into history what is not there. But we can examine this 4,000 year search for an ethical and moral structure based in theological thought and learn from the errors made within the confines of individual cultures.

In the proceeding, brief discussion of Judeo-Christian ideology regarding sexuality, we have emphasized the importance of the cultural context of theological thinking. As clergy and pastoral counselors are increasingly called upon to mediate marital problems, special efforts must be made to recognize how sexism—particularly regarding our contemporary understanding of sexuality, wife abuse, and marital rape—has been entwined with basic religious values.

Understanding Rape in Marriage

In our society, the notion of marital rape has been largely regarded as a contradiction in terms. Within our cultural, legal, and religious traditions, the wife is seen as "becoming one" with the husband. The loss of the wife's identity to her husband (symbolized by her name change) is accompanied by the expectation that she has given her body to him as well. The vow "I do" has been interpreted as a statement of permanent consent to sex.

While everyone assumes that sexuality will be part of marriage, the question of permanent consent is far more controversial. Religious teachings often instruct the wife to do her "wifely duty." The legal system lends support to this structure by explicitly exempting husbands from the rape laws in nearly half of the United States. But does wifely duty include submission to forced or even violent sex whenever and wherever the husband chooses? What are the cultural values that lead religious and legal systems to condone coercion, abuse, and rape? We suggest that those values are rooted in misogyny rather than a higher Being.

The Incidence of Rape in Marriage

Diana Russell (1982) has gathered some of the first direct evidence about the prevalence of marital rape experiences in the population at large. Russell surveyed a random sample of 930 women residents of San Francisco, eighteen years and older, about any incident of sexual assault they had had at any time throughout their lives. Fourteen percent of the 644 married women in the sample had been forced to have intercourse and 2 percent had experienced other types of forced sex. Sexual assaults by husbands were the most common kinds of sexual assault reported, occurring over twice as often as sexual assaults by a stranger.

It is important in evaluating Russell's findings to realize that she did not ask any of her respondents whether they had been *raped,* a stigmatizing term that many women are reluctant to use to describe sexual assault. Instead, she asked women to describe any kind of unwanted sexual experience with a husband or ex-husband, and then included in her tally only those women who described encounters that met the legal definition of rape: forced intercourse, or intercourse obtained by physical threat(s), or intercourse completed while a woman was drugged, unconscious, asleep, or otherwise totally helpless and hence unable to consent.

Russell's findings that marital rape is the most common kind of rape cannot, then, be ascribed to semantics. She used the same definition of sexual assault in tabulating the experiences with husbands that she used in the case of strangers.

The findings from Russell's study are bolstered by the results from a survey recently completed in Boston (Finkelhor and Yllo, 1985). In a study on the related subject of childhood sexual abuse, a representative sample of 326 women were asked whether a spouse or a person they were living with as a couple had ever used physical force or threat of force to have sex with them. Ten percent of the women who had been married (or coupled) answered yes. These women, too, reported more sexual assaults by husbands than assaults by strangers (10 percent versus 3 percent). Forced sex in marriage is a frequent—perhaps the most frequent—type of sexual assault.

Given these survey findings about the high incidence of marital rape, it is very likely that anyone who provides marital counseling will come into contact with the problem. However, because marital rape has traditionally been viewed as a contradiction in terms, counselors, along with the general public, have not *seen* the problem or tried to deal with it.

The Trauma of Marital Rape

Many people fail to get alarmed about the problem of marital rape because they think it is a rather less traumatic form of rape. Being jumped by a stranger in the street, they imagine, must be much more damaging than having sex with someone you have had sex with several times before.

Seeing rape primarily in sexual terms, however, leads to failure to understand the real violation involved in rape. The most salient features of rape for victims are most often the violence, the loss of control, and the betrayal of trust.

Women raped by strangers often go through a long period of being afraid, especially about their physical safety. They become very cautious about where they go and whom they go with (Burgess and Holmstrom, 1974). Women raped by their husbands, however, are often traumatized at an even more basic level: their ability to trust. The kind of violation they have experienced is much harder to guard against, short of a refusal to trust any man. Marital rape touches a woman's basic confidence in forming relationships and trusting intimates. It can leave a woman feeling much more powerless and isolated than if she were raped by a stranger. Moreover, a woman raped by her husband has to live with her rapist, not just a frightening memory of a stranger's attack. Being trapped in an abusive marriage leaves many women vulnerable to repeated sexual assaults by their husbands.

Many women suffer additionally because they cannot get the help they need to end their victimization. The emotional and economic entrapment they experience in marriage and the community silence surrounding the problem of marital rape are, for many, a formidable barrier to freedom from violence.

There are many community institutions tht must become more sensitive to the many forms of wife abuse. Our state legislatures and courts should criminalize rape in marriage. Our criminal justice system should be trained to respond. Our medical practitioners need to become aware of the problem and learn to deal with it in a way that empowers women rather than victimizes them further (Yllo and Bogard, 1987).

Our churches too much respond. Too many women turn to their source of spiritual strength and guidance only to be turned away, intentionally or unintentionally, by clergy and pastoral counselors who are unaware of the scope and nature of the problem. Enlightened individuals in these important roles can make a positive difference.

Types of Marital Rape

In order to understand the experience of marital rape, it is essential to listen to the victims themselves. The authors draw on the interviews with fifty women (Finkelhor and Yllo, 1985) whose partners used force or threat of force to try to have sex with them related their experiences. The women do not make up a representative sample. However, they do represent a wide spectrum. They are homemakers, secretaries, nurses, factory workers, social workers, and so on. Some were married to wealthy businessmen or lawyers; others had wed professors, farmers, truck drivers, or laborers; some were married to men who were unemployed. In other words, these women are from a broad range of backgrounds typical of the area in northern New England where the original study was conducted. The women were contacted through family planning agencies, health centers, battered women's shelters, and through the media.

While the popular image of marital rape may be that it is not a very serious event, the testimony of the victims who discussed their experiences with forced sex speak of degradation and trauma. While we may envision Rhett Butler sweeping Scarlett O'Hara upstairs struggling, only to be subdued and beaming the next morning, the victims describe violation and violence. The analysis of in-depth interviews with victims revealed three basic types of rape in marriage, each with a distinct dynamic and all with painful consequences.

Battering Rapes

Women who were the victims of *battering rapes* were also subjected to extensive physical and verbal abuse, much of it unrelated to sex. The husbands were frequently angry with and belligerent to them and often had alcohol or drug problems. The sexual violence in these relationships appeared to be just another aspect of the physical abuse. Following are excerpts from a case study of one of these battering rapes:

> The interviewee was a twenty-four-year-old woman from an affluent background. Her husband was a big man, over six feet tall, compared to her 5' 2", he drank heavily and often attacked her physically. The beatings occurred at night after they had a fight and she had gone to bed.
>
> Their sexual activities had violent aspects, too. Although they shared the initiative for sex and had no disagreements about its timing or frequency, she often felt that he was brutal in his love-making. She said, "I would often end up crying during intercourse, but it never seemed to bother him."
>
> The most violent sexual episodes occurred at the very end of their relationship. Things had been getting worse between them for some time. They hadn't talked to each other in two weeks. One afternoon she had come home from school, changed into a housecoat and started toward the bathroom. He got up from the couch where he had been lying, grabbed her, and pushed her down on the floor. With her face pressed into a pillow and his hand clamped over her mouth, he proceeded to have anal intercourse with her. She screamed and struggled to no avail. Afterward she was hateful and furious. "It was very violent . . . ," she said, " . . . if I had a gun there, I would have killed him."
>
> Her injuries were painful and extensive. She had a torn muscle in her rectum so that for three months she had to go to the bathroom standing up.

The assault left her with hemorrhoids and a susceptibility to aneurisms that took five years to heal.

Force-Only Rapes

The second group of women have somewhat different relationships. These relationships are by no means conflict-free, but on the whole there is little physical violence. For this group, the forced sex grew out of more specifically sexual conflicts. There were long-standing disagreements over some sexual issue, such as how often to have sex or what were appropriate sexual activities. The following is an excerpt from a case study of a force-only rape.

> The interviewee was a thirty-three-year-old woman with a young son. Both she and her husband of ten years are college graduates and professionals. She is a teacher and he is a graduate counselor. Their marriage, from her report, seems to be of a modern sort in most respects. There have been two violent episodes in their relationship, but in those instances, the violence appears to have been mutual.
>
> There is a long-standing tension in the relationship about sex. She prefers sex about three times a week, but feels under considerable pressure to have more. She says that she is afraid that if she refuses him that he will leave her or that he will force her.
>
> He did force her about two years ago. Their lovemaking on this occasion started out pleasantly enough, but he tried to get her to have anal intercourse with him. She refused, he persisted. She kicked and pushed him away. Still he persisted. They ended up having vaginal intercourse. The force he used was mostly that of his weight on top of her. At 220 pounds, he weighs twice as much as she.
>
> "It was horrible," she said. She was sick to her stomach afterward. She cried and felt angry and disgusted. He showed little guilt. "He felt like he won something."

Additional Forms of Marital Rape

In addition to the sexual assaults classified as battering and force-only, there were a handful that defied such categorization. These rapes were sometimes connected to battering and sometimes not. All, however, involved bizarre sexual obsessions in the husbands that were not evident in other cases. Husbands who made up this group were heavily involved in pornography. They tried to get their wives to participate in making or imitating it. They sometimes had a history of sexual problems, such as difficulty in getting aroused or guilt about earlier homosexual experiences. Sometimes these men needed force or highly structured rituals of sexual behavior in order to become aroused. A case study of one of these obsessive rapes is illustrative:

The interviewee was a thirty-one-year-old marketing analyst for a large corporation. She met her husband in high school and was attracted to his intelligence. They were married right after graduation because she was pregnant.

After the baby was born, he grew more and more demanding sexually. "I was really just his masturbating machine," she recalls. He was very rough sexually and would hold a pillow over her face to stifle her screams. He would also tie her up and insert objects into her vagina and take pictures which he shared with his friends.

There were also brutal "blitz" attacks. One night, for example, they were in bed having sex when they heard a commotion outside. They went out to investigate to discover it was just a cat fight. She began to head back to the house when her husband stopped her and told her to wait. She was standing in the darkness wondering what he was up to when, suddenly, he attacked her from behind. "He grabbed my arms behind me and tied them together. He pushed me over a log and raped me," she said. As in similar previous assaults, he penetrated her anally.

The interviewee later discovered a file in her husband's desk which sickened her. On the card, he had written a list of dates, dates that corresponded to the forced sex episodes of the past months. Next to each date was a complicated coding system which seemed to indicate the type of sex act and a ranking of how much he enjoyed it. (Finkelhor and Yllo, 1985)

Pastoral Counseling of Marital Rape Victims

Clerics who are requested to provide support or counseling should first examine their own feelings and understand how these feelings could be the result of conditioning derived originally from myth. Dealing with abuse and rape means dealing with traditional attitudes toward women, marriage, and husband-wife power relationships. The combination of traditional attitudes and religion has led to the development of belief systems that are more likely to blame the victim than the offender. Often the basic question is simply whether a woman has a right to decide what she does with her own body.

The clergy must first be willing to ask about sexual abuse. Most women do not know that they can or should disclose this information. A victim can conceal this for years, always suffering self-doubt and self-blame because of the experience and because no one took the time to inquire. It is best if time is taken to let the woman know that violence can take different forms but that no matter what form it takes, it is still an act of violence and therefore not sanctioned.

Words should be used that will validate the woman's feelings. Statements such as "It's all right to feel hurt, angry, betrayed, or confused" will help the woman to feel confident in discussing her problem. Here is a sample: "Some women in the course of violence have felt that they have been made to engage in sexual activities that were not comfortable for them. This is seen as an act of power. Have you ever felt this way?"

This approach will allow the woman to share her feelings by knowing that she is not alone in her experience and that she also has a sympathetic listener. A woman can recover from marital violence; she can learn that no one should be abused and that she is an important person who should be treated with respect. To help in this recovery process, each counselor needs to be sensitive and careful, never responding to the person seeking support in a way that is accusatory or threatening.

Marital rape results in the loss of trust and in feelings of confusion that can paralyze the victim. Religious leaders who are well informed can begin to disrupt this pattern before the effects disable the woman and destroy her relationship with her clergy and her faith in the church as an institution.

References

Burgess, A., and L. Holmstrom. 1974. *Rape: Victims of crisis.* Bowie, MD: Brady.

Finkelhor, D., and K. Yllo. 1985. *License to rape: Sexual abuse and wives.* New York: Holt, Rinehart & Winston.

Fortune, Marie M. 1984. *Sexual Violence: The Unmentionable Sin.* N.Y.: Pilgrim Press.

Ruether, R. 1983. *Sexism and God-talk.* Boston: Beacon Press.

Russell, D. 1982. *Rape in marriage.* New York: MacMillan.

Yllo, K., and M. Bogard, eds. (forthcoming). *Feminist perspectives on wife abuse.* Beverly Hills, CA: Sage Publications.

7
Crisis Intervention: A Practical Guide to Immediate Help for Victim Families

Albert R. Roberts

When a battered woman calls the police or a shelter hot line, she may be in crisis—a state precipitated by a particularly severe beating or other abusive situation. A woman in this situation has feelings of vulnerability and helplessness accompanied by intense fear, anger, terror, anxiety, or sleep disturbances. Because of the extreme emotional distress, the victim is usually willing to reach out for help; at this point she may be especially responsive to immediate crisis intervention.

The children of battered women may also be in crisis, but their plight has often been overlooked as domestic violence treatment programs have focused their efforts on emergency intervention for the women. Progressive programs now incorporate crisis intervention for children into their treatment plans. This chapter will describe the following areas of crisis intervention: early intervention by victim assistance programs, assessment in the hospital emergency room, specific intervention techniques used by hot lines and battered women's shelters, and treatment of the children.

Crisis Intervention by Victim Assistance Programs

In the mid-1970s a new type of intervention model emerged, in which a crisis intervention team (working in cooperation with the police department) arrives at the scene simultaneously with the police or shortly thereafter and remains to help the victim after the police have completed their work. The significant advantage of that type of crisis intervention model over other types is its ability to provide immediate, on-the-scene assistance twenty-four hours a day.

These programs were developed to serve *all* victims of violent crime; they are not limited to helping battered women. But since violence in the home constitutes a considerable percentage of police calls, abused women are frequent beneficiaries of this innovative system. The Pima County Victim Witness Program (serving Tucson, Arizona) has received national recognition for providing immediate crisis intervention to battered women and other crime victims. It has served as a model for similar programs in other cities. Located in the Pima County Attorney's office, the program was initiated in 1975 with a grant from the Law Enforcement Assistance Administration (LEAA). The crisis-intervention staff use two police vehicles (unmarked and radio-equipped) to travel to the crime scene. The mobile crisis teams are on patrol every night between 6:00 P.M. and 3:00 A.M. At all other times they are contacted using a "beeper" system.

Domestic violence cases are potentially the most dangerous for the crisis counselors. The staff work in pairs, generally in a male/female team. They are given intensive training in self-defense, escape driving, and police-radio use as well as crisis-intervention techniques.

Assessment and Intervention in the Emergency Room

At a growing number of large hospitals in urban areas, crisis intervention is being provided by emergency room staff. A recommended way for emergency rooms to detect and assess batterment is through the use of an "adult abuse protocol." Two pioneers in the development of these protocols are Klingbeil and Boyd of Seattle who, in 1976, initiated plans for emergency room intervention with abused women. Using a set procedure serves two purposes: 1) it alerts the hospital staff to provide the appropriate clinical care; and 2) it documents the violent incident so that if the woman decides to file a legal complaint, "reliable, court-admissible evidence" (including photographs) is available.[1]

Although this procedure was developed for use by emergency room social workers, it can easily be adapted for use by other health care personnel. The following hypothetical case describes the way in which the adult abuse protocol has been used successfully.

Mrs. J was admitted to the emergency room accompanied by her sister. This was the second visit within the month for Mrs. J and the emergency room triage nurse and social worker realized that her physical injuries were much more severe on the second visit. Mrs. J was crying, appeared frightened, and in spite of the pain, she constantly glanced over her shoulder. She indicated that her husband would follow her to the emergency room and that she feared for her life. The social worker immediately notified security.

Mrs. J indicated that she just wanted to rest briefly and then leave through another entrance. She was four months pregnant and concerned about her unborn child. She reported that this had been the first time Mr. J had struck her in the abdomen. The social worker spent considerable time calming Mrs. J in order to obtain a history of the assaultive event. Consent for photography was obtained and Mrs. J indicated that she *would* press charges. "The attack on my child" seemed to be a turning point in her perception of the gravity of her situation, even though Mr. J had beaten her at least a dozen times over the previous two years.

With Mrs. J's permission, an interview was conducted with her sister who agreed to let Mrs. J stay with her and also agreed to participate in the police reporting. When Mrs. J felt able, the social worker and victim's sister helped her complete the necessary forms for the police who had been called to the emergency room.

Although the physician had carefully explained the procedures and rationale to Mrs. J, the social worker repeated this information and also informed her of the lethality of the battering, tracing from her chart her last three emergency room visits. Mrs. J was quick to minimize the assaults but when the social worker showed her photographs from those visits, documenting bruises around her face and neck, she shook her head and said, "No more, not any more." Her sister provided excellent support and additional family members were on their way to the emergency room to be with Mrs. J. When the police arrived Mrs. J was able to give an accurate report of the day's events. She realized there would be difficult decisions to make and readily accepted a follow-up counseling appointment for a battered women's group.

It should be noted that not all cases are handled as easily as the one cited above. The two aspects of Mrs. J's situation which led to a positive resolution were (1) the immediate involvement of emergency room staff and their discussion with the patient of her history and injuries; and (2) the availability of supportive relatives.

Intervention Techniques Used by Telephone Hot Lines and Battered Women's Shelter

When a battered woman in crisis calls a hot line, it is *essential* that she talk immediately to a trained crisis counselor—not be put on hold or confronted with an answering machine. If she is not able to talk to a caring and knowledgeable crisis counselor, she may just give up, and valuable opportunity for intervening in the cycle of violence will have been lost.

The overriding immediate goal of crisis intervention in the battering syndrome is ensuring the safety of the woman and her children. To determine whether a call is a crisis call, the worker asks such questions as these:

"Are you or your children in danger now?"

"Is the abuser there now?"

"Do you want me to call the police?"

"Do you want to leave and can you do so safely?"

"Do you need medical attention?"

The Marital Abuse Project of Delaware County in Pennsylvania encourages battered women to call the police themselves, but there are circumstances in which they cannot. In those cases, shelter workers call the police (with the woman's permission) and then contact the woman again. If the facility has two phone lines, it may be advisable for the worker to keep the woman on one line while the police are contacted on the other. Staff are advised to follow up on the woman's call to law enforcement by waiting a few minutes and then also calling the police to find out where they will be taking her (to the police station, hospital, or wherever). If it is too soon for the police to have this information, the worker asks the officer to call back. If thirty minutes elapse without a call from the police, the worker contacts the police department again.

Following is a step-by-step guide to intervention with battered women which is included in the training manual developed by the Abuse Counseling and Treatment, Inc. (ACT) program in Ft. Myers, Florida. It is referred to as the ABC Process of Crisis Management—the *A* referring to "achieving contact," the *B* to "boiling down the problem," and the *C* to "coping." This approach is useful to any professional who comes in contact with an abuse victim in crisis.

A. *Achieving Contact*
   1. Introduce yourself: name, role and purpose.
   2. If the contact is over the phone, ask the client if she is safe and protected now.
      If the contact is in person, assure the client that she is safe and protected now.
   3. Ask the client how she would like to be addressed: first name, surname, or nickname; this helps her regain control.
   4. Collect client data. This breaks the ice and allows the client and counselor to get to know each other and develop trust.
   5. Ask the client if she has a counselor or if she is taking medication.
   6. Identify client's feelings and check for perceptions. How realistic is her assessment of her situation?

B. *Boiling Down the Problem*
   1. Ask the client to describe briefly what has just happened.
   2. Encourage the client to talk about the here and now.
   3. Ask the client what is the most pressing problem.

4. Ask the client if it were not for the stated problem, would she feel better right now?
5. Ask the client if she has been confronted with a similar type of problem before, and if so, how did she handle it then? What worked and what didn't?
6. Review with the client what you heard as the primary problem.

C. *Coping with the Problem*
1. What does the client want to happen?
2. What is the most important need—"the bottom line"?
3. Explore what the client feels is the best solution.
4. Find out what the client is willing to do to meet her needs.
5. Help the client formulate a plan of action: her use of available resources, current activities and use of time.
6. Arrange follow-up contact with client.[2]

Careful recruitment and thorough training of crisis-intervention staff is essential to a program's success. It is also necessary for an experienced clinician to be on call at all times for consultation in difficult cases. In addition to learning what to say, the workers need to learn about the tone of voice and attitude to be used while handling crisis calls. Crisis workers are advised to speak in a steady, calm voice, to ask open-ended questions, and to refrain from being judgmental.

A shelter's policies and procedures manual should include guidelines for crisis staff. For example, the ACT program has developed a forty-five page training manual which includes sections on shelter policies and procedures, referral procedures, and background information on domestic violence, including discussions of both the victims and the abusers.

Abused women who are under the influence of drugs or alcohol or who have psychiatric symptoms pose a dilemma for shelter staff. The women are victims of batterment, but they also have a significant problem which the staff are not trained to treat. Shelter policy generally requires crisis counselors to screen out battered women who are under the influence of alcohol or drugs, but there are exceptions. At Womanspace (in central New Jersey) women with drug or alcohol problems are accepted, provided that they are simultaneously enrolled in a drug or alcohol treatment program.[3] Likewise, it is the crisis counselor's responsibility to determine if a woman's behavior is excessively irrational or bizarre or if she is likely to be a danger to herself or others. If a woman is suspected of having psychiatric problems, she is generally referred to the psychiatric screening unit of a local hospital or to a mental health center for an evaluation.

Telephone Log

Battered women's shelters usually maintain a written record of all phone calls, whether or not they are crisis calls. In addition to seeking such routine information as name, address, phone number, marital status, and ages of children, the log form may also include the following: questions (Are you in immediate danger? Do you want me to call the police? How did you get our number?), action taken by crisis worker, and follow-up action. Shelters that are often overcrowded may also have a space on the form where the counselor can indicate if the family can be housed immediately, is to be referred to another shelter or safe home, or needs to be put on a waiting list.

Womanspace developed a one-page telephone log form that asks questions on the front and, on the reverse side, contains further screening questions and an explanation of shelter policies. An example is the following printed statement which explains the program's policy on weapons:

> We do not allow weapons in the shelter.
> We ask that you not bring a weapon or anything
> that may be used as a weapon with you.
> Do you own a weapon? _____
> If yes, do you agree to let us keep it in a
> safe place for you? _____ [4]

Printing this and other procedural statements on every telephone form ensures that all crisis workers impart the same basic information to clients.

At the bottom of each form is a list of nine of the most frequently used telephone numbers, including those of three area police departments. The advantage of having those phone numbers on every form is that those numbers are always readily available and valuable time will not be lost during a crisis searching for them.

Group Therapy

Once the woman and her children have arrived at a shelter or other safe place and the immediate danger of further violence has passed, group counseling can be initiated. Rhodes and Zelman[5] have developed group therapy sessions based on a crisis-intervention model which are *intended for mothers as well as their children.* The sessions are provided for current and former residents of a spouse-abuse shelter in White Plains, New York and are led by staff from a local mental health clinic. The clinic staff believe that the families who come to the shelter are in crisis; therefore, group treatment focuses on crisis-intervention principles. The group sessions emphasize (1) relieving feelings of isolation and alienation of persons in crisis; and (2) strengthening the relationship between the mother and children, who are viewed as the "natural support group."

When a woman comes to the shelter, the group leader talks to her individually and develops a treatment plan for the woman and her children. Group sessions are one component of this treatment plan. The group leader is careful not to overlook the needs of the children during group sessions. As a result of the children's presence, special types of intervention are included: play therapy, educating parents, modeling appropriate parent-child interactions, and encouraging the children to exchange ideas and feelings.

Treatment for the Children

Battered women who seek temporary shelter to escape from the violence at home generally have children who come to the shelter with them. The children often feel confused, afraid, and angry. They miss their father and do not know if or when they will see him again. It is not uncommon for children to be misinformed or uninformed about the reason that they were suddenly uprooted from their home, leaving their personal possessions, friends, and school to stay at a crowded shelter. Similarly, the children may not realize that all the other children have come to the shelter for the same reason. Moreover, large numbers of these children have, at one time or another, also been victims of physical abuse. The 1986 Annual Report from the Family Violence Center, Inc. in Green Bay, Wisconsin reported that close to half (seventy-three) of the 148 abusive partners had also beaten their children.[6]

The majority of shelters offer only basic child-care service; they do not provide the crisis counseling needed to help the children deal with the turmoil of recent events. Too often the child's crisis is unrecognized and the opportunity for intervention ignored. However, some innovative techniques for helping children have been incorporated into the programs at some shelters. Group therapy for mothers and children was discussed in the previous section. Two other methods—coloring books and children's groups—are described below.

Coloring Books as Part of an Individualized Treatment Approach

Some shelters use specially designed coloring books that discuss domestic violence in terms children can understand. Laura Prato of the Jersey Battered Woman's Service, Inc. (JBWS) in Morristown, New Jersey has created two coloring books: one for children age three to five entitled "What is a Shelter?" (26 pages), and another for six- to eleven-year-olds called, "Let's Talk It Over" (22 pages).[7] In addition to the children's books, Prato has also written two manuals for shelter workers to serve as discussion guides for the counselors. The coloring books contain realistic, sensitive illustrations that depict the confused, sad, and angry emotions that the children are feeling. They are illustrated in black and white so that the children can color the pictures if they wish.

The purpose of the coloring books, and the way in which they are to be used, is explained in the introduction to the counselor's manuals. The manuals state that the books are used as part of the "Intake and Orientation process" for all children who stay at the JBWS shelter. The stated objectives of the books are as follows:

To provide assurances of the child's continued care and safety.

To encourage children to identify and express their feelings.

To provide information needed for children to understand what is happening in their families.

To provide information that will improve each child's ability to adapt to the shelter setting.

To begin to assess the individual child's needs and concerns.[8]

The counselor's manuals stress the importance of the way in which the book is presented to the child, as shown in the following passage:

The process surrounding the use of the orientation books is extremely important. It is likely to be the initial contact between the counselor and the newly arrived family and one that will set the tone for future interactions. Consistent with JBWS Children's Program philosophy, this initial meeting communicates respect for mother and child and acceptance of their feelings.[9]

Before meeting with the child, the counselor meets privately with the mother to show her the book, explain its purpose, and ask for her permission to read the book to her child. The books have been prepared in a way that encourages the child's active participation. Throughout both books are several places where the children are encouraged to write their own thoughts on the page.

Group Treatment for Children

Another way to help children cope is through therapeutic groups; an example is the approach developed at Haven House, a shelter for battered women and their children in Buffalo, New York. Intervention is provided through groups for children age eight to sixteen. The two group leaders established a six-session treatment program covering the following topics: (1) the identification and expression of feelings; (2) violence; (3) unhealthy ways to solve problems; (4) healthy ways to solve problems; (5) sex, love, and sexuality; and (6) termination and saying goodbye.

The children are always given homework to "keep the session alive" between meetings. For example, after the discussion on violence they are asked to develop a minidrama on family violence to be presented the next week. Following the session on healthy problem solving, they are asked to prepare a list of healthy ways of coping with their problems.[10]

Conclusion

Police officers, victim advocates, hospital emergency room staff, and counselors at areawide hot lines and battered women's shelters often come in contact with beaten women who are experiencing crisis. Effective crisis intervention requires an understanding of the value and methods of crisis intervention as well as the community resources to which referrals should be made.

Battered women are often motivated to change their lifestyles only during the crisis or postcrisis stage. Therefore, it is important for all service providers at community agencies to offer immediate assistance to battered women in crisis.

This chapter has examined the techniques and process of crisis intervention on the part of victim assistance programs, emergency rooms, and hot lines and shelters serving battered women and their children. Emphasis was placed on treatment for children of violent families who are also experiencing a crisis and whose needs are often overlooked.

Knowledge of referral sources is essential. It is just as important for the police, hospitals, and human service agencies to know about and refer women to programs that help battered women and their children as it is for staff at domestic violence programs to refer clients to the victim assistance program, drug or alcohol treatment programs, the hospital psychiatric screening unit, and so on. However, merely referring a client to another community program does not end the counselor's responsibility. The counselor should follow up to ascertain whether the woman called to obtain the needed services and, if so, whether or not the services were provided. Unfortunately, there are too many cases in which, for one reason or another, the client who sought help remains unserved. Particularly when counseling abused women who are involved in a potentially life-threatening relationship, the counselor needs to follow up to ensure that appropriate services are delivered.

Notes

1. See K. S. Klingbeil and V. D. Boyd, 1984, "Emergency Room Intervention: Detection, Assessment and Treatment," in A. R. Roberts, ed., *Battered Women and Their Families: Intervention Strategies and Treatment Programs* (New York: Springer), 7–32.

2. S. Houston, "Abuse Counseling and Treatment, Inc. (ACT) Manual," Ft. Myers, FL.

3. R. Podhorin. February 12, 1987. Director, Womanspace, Inc., Lawrenceville, NJ, Personal Communication.

4. *Ibid.*

5. See R. M. Rhodes and A. B. Zelman, January 1986, "An Ongoing Multifamily Group in a Women's Shelter," *American Journal of Orthopsychiatry,* 56:120–130.

6. S. Prelipp. February 13, 1987. Director, Family Violence Center, Green Bay, Wisconsin, Personal Communication.

7. See L. Prato, "What is a Shelter?", "Let's Talk It Over", "What is a Shelter?: A Shelter Worker's Manual", and "Let's Talk It Over: A Shelter Worker's Manual," Morristown, NJ: Jersey Battered Women's Service, Inc., undated; and D. Arbour, February 12, 1987, Director, Jersey Battered Women's Shelter, Morristown, NJ, Personal Communication.

8. See L. Prato, "What is a Shelter?: A Shelter Worker's Manual," *op. cit.*

9. *Ibid.*

10. See J. J. Alessi and K. Hearn, "Group Treatment of Children in Shelters for Battered Women," in A. R. Roberts, ed., *Battered Women and Their Families* (New York: Springer Publishing Co., 1981).

8

Legal Remedies and the Role of Law Enforcement Concerning Spouse Abuse

Ellen Pence

T he criminal justice system has received a great deal of criticism for its unwillingness to take an active stand on spouse abuse. One example of a pioneer effort to make reforms in police and court practices is the Duluth Domestic Abuse Intervention Project (DAIP). This project secured interagency policy agreement with all the key agencies that intervene in domestic assault cases. This chapter examines their efforts and observations.

The development of interagency policies that protect victims, hold abusers solely accountable for their choice to use violence, and simultaneously keep an eye toward the goal of reducing community and cultural supports of battering necessitates a theoretical framework that helps in understanding the dynamics of battering and that goes beyond psychological explanations. Duluth's intervention project was designed with the philosophy that there are four fundamental cultural facilitators of woman abuse: the belief in the natural rightness of hierarchy, the widespread objectification of women in our society, the ability of batterers to force women's submission to their will, and the pervasive institutional practice of blaming the victim.

Challenging Cultural Facilitators of Battering

The combination of a belief in male authority within adult relationships, objectification of women, a socioeconomic system which forces submission of women to men, and the ability of batterers to use physical force with relatively few consequences allows battering to continue for long periods of time against specific victims and explains the disproportionate number of women as victims. Experience in Duluth, Minnesota shows that law enforcement and criminal justice systems can be a crucial part of an effort to undermine the cultural supports for physical battering. Effective intervention requires two fundamental changes in police and court practices. First the responsibility of using violence must be seen as lying solely with the assailant. Second, a consistent response to control assailants' violence must be secured through coordination and interagency policy development.

Currently the criminal justice system's response to battering is ineffective. Police argue that the problem rests with prosecutors, who too often fail to convict; prosecutors charge that police seldom arrest, and judges claim that sentencing alternatives fail to include effective rehabilitation services. Underneath it all, everybody implies that battered women are somehow to blame. The most important aspect of changing the criminal justice system's response to battering is the need to coordinate the many actors to secure a consistent and uniform response. Policies which promote arrest, increase convictions, place legal sanctions on assailants, require education or some form of restitution for violent behavior, and when necessary, protect women from further contact with the assailant are effective only when they are uniformly and consistently applied. Uniformity in enforcement is not a problem unique to domestic assault cases, but the probability that violence in these cases will escalate in severity and frequency warrants a rigorous effort toward achieving consistency.

The purpose of battering is to establish and maintain control over the victim. The assailant will use the control he has established to protect himself from the legal system. The officer who throws up his hands in frustration when a woman refuses to press charges after a brutal beating is witnessing the extent to which she is physically and psychologically controlled by her assailant. The prosecutor who receives the phone call or letter asking that the charges be dropped must understand that the victim is acting as her abuser's emissary to the court. She stands between him and the prosecutor, not because it is in her best interest, but because it is in his best interest. The nature of the relationship between the abuser and his victim is one in which the abuser imposes his will upon the victim.

The development of policies must distinguish between taking responsibility for placing controls on the assailant and imposing new prescribed behaviors on battered women. Incarcerating women for failing to testify against their abusers is an inappropriate measure against victims. Public policy directed toward enforcement of assault laws should clearly distinguish between the role of the community and the role of the woman who has been assaulted in such an effort.

The criminal justice system must not, like the abuser, dictate the women's behavior. If the traditional responses to battering are changed, and policies and procedures are developed to impede the facilitators of battering, women can be protected from continued acts of violence, and the community can begin the process of presenting a general deterrence to violent behavior.

Domestic Abuse Intervention Project

The goal of many criminal justice reform projects, such as the DAIP, is to protect the victim by bringing an end to the violence. In Duluth, four objectives of the intervention process have been identified to achieve this goal:

1. To bring cases into the courts for resolution and to reduce the screening out of cases.

2. To impose and enforce legal sanctions on the assailant to deter him from committing further acts of violence.

3. To provide safe emergency housing, education, and legal advocacy for victims of assault.

4. To coordinate interagency information flow and monitor responses to individual cases to prevent assailants from getting lost or manipulating the justice system.

Protecting the Victim by Bringing the Assailant
into the Justice System and Reducing Case Attrition

The use of mandatory arrest policy, new advocacy procedures, prosecution guidelines, jail holds, improved bail procedures, new civil protection order procedures, and written protocols have all served to substantially increase the number of assault cases coming into and being resolved in the court system.

Law enforcement is the community agency most likely to deal initially with assault cases. Reducing the number of cases screened out of the criminal justice system by police requires limiting the discretion of individual officers through administrative policy requiring or at least encouraging arrest under defined conditions. Several police policies were used in Duluth to increase arrests of abusers. The first effort was to provide training to police officers and encourage arrest, but not to limit the arrest discretion of line officers. The policy now in use requires an arrest when probable cause exists, there is an injury, and the victim and alleged assailant are former or current cohabitants.

After three years of testing, police administrators found that arrests were most consistent when the options of mediation or separation were eliminated in cases involving sign of physical injury and that police injuries were the lowest during the time period of mandated arrest policy.

In addition to arrest, follow-up by women's shelter advocates is used to avoid screening cases away from the courts. Police officers are required to file reports on all calls involving a complaint of an assault. Within two days of a nonarrest case and two hours of an arrest call, shelter advocates contact the victim to provide information regarding a civil protection order and procedures for filing criminal charges. In addition, transportation and emergency housing are offered. Letters are sent to victims if the officer's report indicates a threat of an assault but does not indicate that an assault occurred.

Protecting the Victim by Imposing and Enforcing Legal Sanctions

The court must use specific legal definitions regarding alleged acts in establishing guilt or innocence, but sentencing requires a broader understanding of battering as controlling behavior used by one family member against another. Much of the clinical literature on battering examines personality characteristics and profiles of abusers to better understand the assailant. What is far more helpful to those in the justice system is a profile of the abuse itself. The more fully the court understands the nature of the assailant's violence and use of coercive controls, the more effective the court will be in determining the best legal sanctions to protect the victim. Battering is a system of behaviors used by the assailant to establish control or dominance over the victim. Understanding the entire system is as important to the judge, probation officer, prosecutor, and therapist as knowledge of the specific criminal behavior which brought the assailant into the court system.

The impact of a shove against a wall or a slap in the face cannot be understood outside the context in which it occurred. If police and probation officers, social workers, or judges are forced to measure the danger or impact of the battering on the victim solely by the severity of her injuries, effective intervention is impossible. In the past police, probation officers, and prosecuting attorneys often concentrated on gathering information about issues related to the events immediately preceding the assault ("What were you arguing about?") or relationship issues ("Do you want to stay together?"). They understood the specific act of violence as a symptom of a bad relationship rather than a part of a system of dominance and even terror being illegally imposed by one person upon another.

As a result of this policy, police have often mediated disputes rather than arrest assailants; city attorneys have dismissed charges due to a reluctant witness rather than building a good case and working with an advocacy program to lessen the impact of the assailant's control on the witness, and probation officers have recommended fines or restitution rather than strict court sanctions to protect the victim.

Some specific legal sanctions now being used include the following:

1. Pre-sentence investigation. A probation officer has access to information from the victim provided by the shelter advocate. This information will

contain not only a history of the abuse, but a history of all pertinent information regarding the assailant.

2. Sentencing guidelines. Suggested sentencing guidelines have been developed and are informally followed. A first offense usually results in a stayed jail sentence and one-year probation. Although terms of the probation may vary, it would typically include a requirement to participate in the DAIP counseling and education program.

3. Jail time. A jail sentence is sometimes ordered on the first offense if the assailant has previously participated in counseling, is resistant to rehabilitation, and/or has previously violated the terms of a court order for protection.

4. Order of protection. Often this order is attainable without the assistance of an attorney. The order is granted or denied based upon the victim's allegations and the perpetrator's oral response to them.

5. Formalized hearing. Court orders ceased to be issued merely by establishing that a problem existed. The court makes an attempt to determine if abuse does or does not exist. In the event the abuse allegation is denied, a civil trial is held. In most cases the respondent has admitted to some use of physical abuse threats.

DAIP staff are present at hearings. They not only coordinate all intervening agencies but may become involved with both the assailant and victim throughout treatment. Typically, DAIP will contract with the assailant for a twenty-week counseling and education program. In some cases the person may also be required to participate in individual therapy, seek psychiatric help, or participate in an outpatient chemical dependency program.

The assailant is given an opportunity to request a review hearing prior to signing any counseling agreement with DAIP. DAIP is appointed as an interested third party in the case and may request a review hearing or ask the court to initiate a contempt of court action if necessary. DAIP is also responsible for reporting attendance at counseling sessions and repeat offenses to the court. Victims are encouraged by the court, DAIP, shelter advocates, and the assailant's counselor to attend the education groups held by the Women's Coalition. Violation of a civil order for protection can result in either a civil contempt of court charge or a misdemeanor charge.

The program's effectiveness, and therefore women's safety, depends on the willingness of all parts of the system to implement the policies and procedures of their respective agencies and to enforce court orders. In Duluth, enforcement means that police will arrest when witnessing a violation or having probable cause to believe the alleged assailant violated a court order, that prosecutors will avoid dropping cases involving a reluctant witness at the pretrial and will make the attempt to obtain convictions in order to secure maximum influence of the court over the assailant. Enforcement also means that probation officers will request revocation of probation in cases involving re-offenses or failure to adhere to conditions of probation involving the harassment of victims or court ordered counseling, that therapists will report re-offenses for court action, and that judges will impose increasingly harsh penalties for repeat offenders. The court should not issue orders it is unable or unwilling to enforce. The enforcement of court orders and agreed-upon policies and procedures is the backbone of any effective intervention process.

The purpose of bringing cases into the court system is to deter the assailant from continued acts of violence by presenting increasingly harsh penalties on the abuser. The effectiveness of such an effort is highly dependent upon the consistency with which the message of the community is reinforced. Law enforcement and court procedures and policies should be designed to secure maximum court controls while offering tools to change the long-term behavioral patterns of assailants. To be effective, court sanctions must be clear, enforceable, and enforced.

Protecting the Victim by Safe Housing and Advocacy

A comprehensive, integrated community response to domestic assault requires safe housing and advocacy programs for battered women and their children. Demands on the Duluth battered women's shelter changed dramatically as the justice system developed a consistent response to domestic assaults. In 1980 the shelter worked with 269 women; in only 17 percent (45) of the cases, either the victim obtained an order for protection or their partners were convicted of assault. In 1983 the shelter worked with 719 women; 43 percent (312) had either obtained orders for protection or had their partners convicted of assault.

The shelter provides a supportive, safe environment and advocacy. The role of the advocate is to help the women take action, to provide a support system, and to help reduce the women's sense of isolation. Using this approach, the shelter staff have organized neighborhood-based informational classes which not only present facts on all forms of battery and its dynamics, but also present the specifics on how to best utilize the court system. They have also expanded the services to women identified by others in the system (police, courts, social service agencies) as being battered.

Some abusers will attack their victims regardless of any threat of jail or punishment. The intervention process must always keep the women's safety as a first consideration and resist tendencies to minimize the danger. The need for advocacy services and shelter for battered women is essential in effective intervention. The court and law enforcement system, as well as traditional social service relationships, cannot provide the peer support system women need to counterbalance the effects of battering. From some women, court intervention is not adequate protection and safe housing for themselves and their children is necessary.

Coordinating Information Flow

Securing consistent response from several independent agencies requires close coordination and sharing of information. Coordinating and monitoring communication flow are the essential ingredients added to existing agency services by the DAIP staff.

The power of a coordinated response is that from the moment of the arrest or the service of an order for protection, the assailant receives a consistent message that regardless of his stress level, his economic or family situation, or the action of his partner, he cannot assault, threaten, or sexually abuse her. A comprehensive communication network is complex, but the essential features of the Duluth system are summarized as follows.

1. Police officers file reports on all cases of domestic abuse. The reports are reviewed by the police inspector to determine compliance with the mandatory arrest policy. Copies of police reports are shared with the shelter advocate for follow-up with the victim and with DAIP staff for preparation of a case file.

2. Jailers contact the shelter to notify advocates of the arrest and the release time of any assailant arrested on a charge related to domestic abuse.

3. All complaints of lack of police officers' compliance with arrest policy are reported to the inspector of the patrol division for investigation. The patrol division inspector reports back to the DAIP and original reporter on disposition of the investigation.

4. Information on the advocate's visits with victims are, with the woman's permission, called to probation officers conducting the presentence investigation.

5. All assailants are court mandated to DAIP rather than individual counseling agencies in order to coordinate cases. Probation officers and clerks of court forward probation agreements and orders for protection to the DAIP immediately following the court order.

6. DAIP assigns assailants to groups in four agencies and receives attendance reports weekly from agency counselors on all referred assailants.

7. Assailants are allowed two absences in the first twelve counseling groups and two in the second twelve education groups before being brought back to court for noncompliance.

8. Any woman who reports a second offense to her advocate or a counselor is encouraged to report that violation to the DAIP staff or the court for follow-up if reporting will not further endanger her.

9. DAIP staff, counselors, representatives of the shelter, and probation department staff meet every two weeks to discuss problems in cases and to evaluate procedures.

10. Representatives from each participating agency meet on a biyearly basis to review the entire system.

11. Computerized updates on any police or court action are sent to the probation officer, the clerk of court, the counselor, the victim's advocate, the arresting officer, and the sentencing judge on a regular basis.

12. Monthly calendars listing education groups are sent to all women. For the first month after police contact or the order for protection hearing, women are called by a shelter advocate each week and invited to the education group. Child care and transportation are provided as needed.

This extensive system of communications rarely permits a deviation from procedures to go unnoticed. DAIP staff follow up on all breakdowns in the system. Some flexibility in the system is needed, but most objections that individuals have made to the procedures have resulted from the manipulation of people in the system by their assailants and from failure to communicate with others in the system.

Difficulties and Pitfalls

The process outlined in this chapter is described by many as a model program. However, it is complex and fraught with difficulties and pitfalls. In some states the process is undermined by inadequate or nonexistent laws. Laws which reserve the process for obtaining civil protection orders for people who are legally married and living together leave unprotected fully one-half of the women who are the potential victims of battering. The laws and court practices of some states make it almost impossible to secure a protection order without an attorney and thus make the courts inaccessible to thousands of poor women.

Efforts to implement such a program are thwarted in many states by the absence of laws that provide police with the ability to arrest and jailers with the option of temporarily holding arrested assailants while victims seek safety. The failure of many state legislatures to recognize the need for adequate state funding for emergency shelter services for battered women and their children strips some communities of the most fundamental resource needed to organize a community-wide protection process.

In addition, other key factors may impede these efforts. These factors include the attitudes of community leaders, inertia or the collective apprehension of change, a failure to understand the role community institutions play in causing and perpetuating battering, and finally, lack of adequate resources to do the job.

Perhaps the most vehemently resisted concept was the notion that all cases were subject to review, that all responses need to be justified. Each policy enacted in Duluth was accompanied by a process for monitoring individuals in the system to ensure their compliance with new protocol and procedures.

Conclusion

The legal system is not *the* solution, but only one part of a complex problem. To be effective, laws and law enforcement need broad community support. The responsibility of advocating these changes, if left to battered women and shelter or advocacy programs with no support from the broader community agreements, will be tenuous at best. Ministers, church groups, counselors, therapists, community groups, and supportive individuals in the court and law enforcement systems can all work with their local shelter or advocacy programs to effect these changes. It is a long, time-consuming effort, but in the end it puts into motion a process that begins to undermine all of the cultural facilitators of violence against women.

References

Dobash, R. E., and R. P. Dobash. 1979. *Violence against wives.* New York: Free Press.

Galbraith, J. 1983. *The anatomy of power.* New York: Houghton Mifflin.

Ganley, A. 1981. *Court mandated counseling for men who batter: A three-day workshop for mental health professionals* (Washington, D.C.: Center for Women Policy Studies.)

Neidig, P. 1984. Spouse abuse: Mutual combat or wife battering? Paper presented at Conference on Family Violence Research, University of New Hampshire.

Ptacek, J. 1984. A clinical literature review of men who batter. Paper presented at Conference on Family Violence Research, University of New Hampshire.

Walker, L. 1979. *The battered woman.* New York: Harper and Row.

9

Child Protective Services and Treatment Options for Children and Youth

Carol C. Haase
Gail Ryan

C hild abuse is a very complex problem, a symptom of family distress that manifests itself in a dysfunctional relationship between child and parent. It is a problem that requires intervention from the community. Lack of appropriate physical and emotional care in childhood has long-term consequences for the child and the community, and it becomes the community's responsibility to intervene on behalf of the unprotected child who is being damaged (Steele, 1986).

For purposes of this chapter, abuse is defined as any nonaccidental injury that results in physical, psychological, or sexual injury to a child. Neglect includes any omission of care, including deprivation of food, shelter, medical care, supervision, or nurturance. Abuse and neglect jeopardize a child's health, safety, and development. In most states, the community's intervention in child abuse is implemented by a Child Protective Services agency (CPS). This agency is legally mandated to intervene on behalf of the child for the child's protection.

The Role of Child Protective Services

In the broadest sense, the role of child protective services can be divided into four major functions: (1) intake, or the investigation and assessment of a child at risk for abuse; (2) child placement services, which may be called foster care or alternative care services; (3) ongoing protective services supervision of child and family; and (4) adoption services for children who cannot safely return home. In this chapter, we will discuss the role of the CPS worker in intake services, some aspects of child placement services, and protective services supervision.

The Four Major Functions of Child Protective Services

The community CPS agencies generally operate within the state or county Department of Social Services. (Depending upon the state or county, these agencies may be referred to by a variety of different titles, such as Department of Rehabilitation Service, Health and Human Services or Human Resources, Public or Social Welfare Department, Division of Youth and Family Services, or Social Services.) CPS is a highly specialized unit within an agency which responds to reports of suspected child abuse and neglect. It is this unit's responsibility to protect children and to rehabilitate families through the process of investigation, assessment, treatment, and coordination of services.

CPS workers are expected to fill a variety of roles in their response to reports of child abuse: screening referrals to determine which are valid and are providing timely response to these referrals; investigating reports of abuse by contacting the alleged abused child, family, and abuser; determining the child's need for medical attention; contacting appropriate law enforcement personnel; assessing and mediating family problems; establishing a therapeutic relationship with family members; advocating for the child and family; coordinating services; providing treatment; drafting reports for the court; and arranging a variety of rehabilitative services. All too frequently CPS is misconstrued as having sole responsibility in managing child abuse cases. These are unrealistic expectations frequently placed upon CPS without provision for adequate training, funding, resources, or support from administration and community.

Child Protection Teams

It has been recognized that no one person, agency, or profession can be solely responsible for addressing the complexities of child abuse. A multidisciplinary, interagency approach is most successful in the management of these cases. Over the past twenty-five years, child protection teams have been developed in many communities. These teams may be established within a social services department or hospital; they consist of a composite of professionals and laypersons from various community agencies and different disciplines.

The team's function is to coordinate a comprehensive, interdisciplinary approach to the intervention and resolution of child protection cases. The child protection team shares the burden of proof and responsibility with the CPS worker through consultation and recommendation. Team members include representatives from the public and private sectors in the fields of social work, law, mental health, religion, and education.

Intake: The Child Protective Investigation

Reports of suspected child abuse and neglect originate from sources such as neighbors, relatives, schools, police, hospitals, other agencies, parents, or children themselves. It is the intake workers' responsibility to screen the referral, gather as much information as possible regarding the suspected abuse or neglect, and respond in a timely manner. They must determine whether the investigation should begin immediately or within the next twenty-four hours and whether the child is in immediate danger. The purpose of the investigation is to determine the following:

1. That a child has been abused, neglected, or is in imminent danger.
2. The potential risk for further injury to children if they remain in the home (safety of the home).
3. The degree of risk to other siblings in the home.
4. The amount of dysfunction in the parent-child relationship and throughout the family.
5. The parents' attitudes, emotional stability, motivation to change, ability to use services, and prognosis.

During this investigation by the CPS worker, the child and siblings are observed and interviewed, usually separately from other family members. Parents or alleged abusers are interviewed, and family interactions are observed. As many data as possible are gathered to understand the child's *and* parents' status and needs. The investigation explores the following questions.

1. Is the injury consistent with the explanation?
2. Is the injury the result of abuse, failure to protect, or an accident?
3. Does the parent accept or deny a role in the incident?
4. What are the precipitating circumstances surrounding the abuse?
5. Is there a history of previous abusive incidents to the child or other siblings?
6. What are the disciplinary beliefs and history of the parent(s)? Were the parents abused in their own childhood?
7. Do the parents have a supportive network?
8. Do the child and siblings have support systems and safeguards?
9. Is there substance abuse by parent(s) or caregiver(s)?
10. Is the family relationship one of harmony or disharmony? Is there spouse abuse in the home?
11. Are there histories of violence, breaking the law, and police involvement?
12. Are there positive relationships with extended family members and essential others?
13. What are the placement options for the child? Remain in the home? Placement with relatives? Placement in shelter or foster care?

14. Is the family responsive to therapy?

15. Does the parent exhibit levels of emotional instability, depression, or other emotional or psychiatric problems that interfere with consistent, safe parenting? (Carroll and Haase, in press).

The CPS intake investigation may be done in several hours or take up to thirty days. During this process, information is gathered not only from family members, but from other available sources such as schools, police, neighbors, employers, extended family members, public and private agencies and organizations, hospitals, clinics, doctor's offices, and central abuse registries.

Placement Services

When a child is removed from the home during a crisis or following a report of abuse and is then taken into protective custody and placed in emergency shelter (a "receiving" home or temporary foster home), the task of the CPS agency is to gather all available information and complete the initial investigation as swiftly as possible. During this phase, the juvenile court is involved, and the judge makes the ultimate decision on placement of the child. Not all abused children are removed from their parents' home. In many cases the family can recognize the inappropriateness of the abusive incident and their need for help. The child may remain in the home with supervision from CPS while the family is engaged in treatment and support services are made available to reduce the family's stress.

If the child is placed in foster care, the judge will decide when it is safe for the child to return to the parents' home. The judge's decisions are based on the information provided by the CPS workers and other professionals involved with the family are in accordance with the following guidelines for removing a child from the home.

1. Severe physical or sexual abuse.
   a. Physical abuse that requires hospitalization, nonaccidental death of a sibling or other child, life-threatening abuse to head or abdomen, large burns, fractures, sadistic abuse, beating with a weapon or instrument, or multiple bruises in various stages of healing.
   b. Severe malnutrition (nonorganic failure to thrive).
   c. Deliberate poisoning with intent to kill.
   d. Sexual abuse (incest), if the perpetrator has not left the home.
2. Evidence of repeated abuse by history, physical examination, or X-ray, even though not reported.
3. Re-abuse after initial report and intervention.
4. Severe emotional abuse (child emotionally disturbed or totally rejected or unwanted by parents).

5. Child less than one year old with any physical abuse or moderate to severe failure to thrive.
6. Parents can describe child's behavior only as unduly provocative or obnoxious to the parents.
7. Child is extremely fearful to return home.
8. Adolescent refuses to return home or is beyond control.
9. Mental health or law enforcement indicates parent is dangerous.
10. Nonperpetrator parent is not protective (for example, stood by while abuse occurred).
11. Parent wants child *after* appropriate counseling.
12. Parents persistently refuse intervention and treatment services from onset.
    a. Parents persistently deny abuse diagnosis.
    b. Parents persistently state that physical abuse is necessary and justified to correct misbehavior.
    c. Parents refuse treatment services with open hostility, passive-aggressiveness, or total indifference.
13. Multiple, ongoing crises (Schmitt and Loy, 1978, pp. 193–194).

When a child is in an out-of-home placement, the role of CPS is to design, implement, supervise, and provide treatment and support services to the parents, the child, and the caregivers who are fostering the child. Every effort is made to help the parents develop adequate skills and create a safe environment to which the child can return.

The return of children to their own homes is as critically important as removal from potentially dangerous ones. The following suggestions from *The Child Protection Team Handbook* constitute an excellent set of criteria for determining whether the child should return home.

Prerequisites:
1. If either parent was diagnosed as severely disturbed on a previous evaluation, this person is permanently out of the home; or a recent evaluation has been done and finds the parent no longer dangerous.
2. If the child provoked the abuse, behavior has improved.
3. A team conference has been held regarding this decision.
4. Follow-up services by CPS will be continued for at least one year and preferably until school age.
5. Telephone lifelines with several resources (including provisions for crisis child care) will remain available, and the parents have a phone.

Note: The contract with the parents should make clear from the beginning that the child's return is not going to be based on any time schedule, but relates strictly to the attainment of the following behavioral changes.

A. Parents are utilizing therapy (for example, they keep appointments, keep contracts, talk freely, consider therapy valuable, and no longer use denial).

B. Child management has improved. The CPS worker or other professionals have documented many specific improvements in the parents' ability to cope with their child.

1. Parents can talk about alternative ways of dealing with anger.
2. Parents have demonstrated impulse control.
3. Parents can tolerate the child's expression of some negative feelings toward them (for example, "I hate you").
4. Parents use disciplinary techniques that are fair, nonpunitive and consistent.
5. Parents have asked for advice regarding child rearing and have been able to implement some of this advice.
6. Parents have recognized and solved specific problems of child rearing.
7. Parents are beginning to recognize the child as an individual with needs, desires, and rights of his own, and have reasonable expectations.
8. Parents speak in positive terms about the child.
9. Parents keep all scheduled visits with child.
10. Child is no longer fearful of parents.
11. Perpetrator has shown the most improvement in these skills.
12. Perpetrator can recognize potentially dangerous situations and knows how to remove himself or herself from the child at these times.
13. Nonperpetrator understands responsibility to protect child and has demonstrated an ability to intervene on child's behalf.

C. Crisis management is improved. The CPS worker or other professionals have documented specific improvements in the parents' ability to cope with crises.

1. Parents no longer live in the chaos of multiple, overwhelming, ongoing crises (for example, one parent has a stable job).
2. Marriage is stable. The parents are supportive of each other and can relieve each other in child care or housework.
3. Parents can talk about alternatives to dealing with crises.
4. Parents have solved specific crises.
5. Parents have asked for help during crises and have been able to use it.
6. Parents have recognized and solved specific stresses before these turned into major crises.
7. Interpersonal relationships have increased; isolation has decreased. The parents have friends who are supportive and available (Schmitt and Loy, pp. 193–194).

Ongoing Protective Services: Supervision and Treatment

CPS workers are usually the primary providers of treatment services to these confused and troubled families. When the investigation is completed and there is a determination that abuse exists and ongoing services are necessary, the intake worker transfers the case to an ongoing CPS worker, who arranges and/or provides treatment and other services to the family.

The intake phase may be therapeutic for the family; however, this phase is not always possible because of the nature of the "investigative process" and because the first concern of the intake worker must be the *protection of the child*. The second concern during the investigative process must be to support and reassure the child, minimizing further trauma or confusion during the crisis intervention and investigative process. The intake worker should use an honest and empathetic approach to the parents during the intake process to facilitate the parents' ability to trust the ongoing CPS worker, who will need to establish a therapeutic alliance with the family. This therapeutic relationship is an essential part of the treatment process.

The treatment plan should be designed to meet the needs of each individual family member and, wherever possible, the family as a whole. Treatment may consist of the following:

1. Counseling: Individual, family groups (play therapy, dyads or triads, i.e., mother-child or parents-and-child) or marital counseling (frequently these services are referred by CPS to other agencies such as mental health centers, private psychiatrists, psychologists).

2. Lay therapy: Involvement of trained parent aides who befriend the family and are available, supportive, noncritical, and patient while modeling an empathetic relationship to the abusive parents.

3. Homemaker services: To assist mothers with the various demands of caring for children and organizing a household. Frequently, homemakers are used in families to keep the family together, or when a child is initially returned to the home (Kempe and Helfer, 1972).

4. Crisis nurseries: Short-term foster or shelter care is a place where children can be left for several hours or several days during a family crisis.

5. Day care: CPS may contract with day-care providers to keep children. Some of these homes or centers provide a therapeutic environment for the child. Others simply provide relief or respite from the responsibility of child care or enable parents to pursue employment or education.

6. Parenting classes: Parents may be required to attend classes provided by CPS or other agencies to learn parenting skills, child development, stress management, and so on.

7. Emergency services: Assistance may be available for housing, food, clothing, transportation to and from essential appointments, and so on (Carroll, 1972).

8. Referral services: Visiting nurses from public health departments, Big Brothers/Sisters programs, after-school activities for children, Parents

Anonymous, or Parents United programs may be available for family members.

Treatment cannot focus solely on the parents but must also address the needs of the child. Children may have developmental delays or emotional disturbances as a result of the abusive environment. Parent-child relationships may need repair if reunification is to succeed. The treatment and service needs of these families are often extensive and may require long-term intervention. Because CPS workers who have large caseloads are often unable to allocate the time necessary to meet these needs, other resources need to be available for these families in the community. In many cases, the CPS staff assumes the role of case manager and refers, coordinates, and monitors services provided to the family by other agencies.

The goal of treatment is to help the parents develop a better sense of self-esteem, experience pleasure in being a parent, improve coping skills, develop appropriate expectations in the role of parenting, and become responsible, competent caregivers.

Conclusion

Child abuse is a symptom of disturbed parent-child relationships. It can be prevented, identified, and treated. Children can be protected and abusive parents can be rehabilitated.

Because of the long-term needs of many abusive families, CPS units may become overloaded with ongoing cases. It is essential that review, monitoring, and follow-up of cases be a part of the CPS system. A variety of disciplines and agencies is needed to respond to the multiproblem family in which children have been abused or neglected. A multidisciplinary team is essential in each community, not to supplant the services of individual agencies, but to function as adjuncts with CPS and other community professionals, to improve coordination of services to these families, to avoid duplication of services, and to share in decision making and treatment planning.

Each community must identify and develop the resources necessary to support the protection of children. It is the responsibility of all of us in our special ways to reach out and provide a positive and meaningful assistance to abused children and their families.

References

Carroll, C. A. 1972. The function of protective services. In *Helping the Battered Child and his Family,* eds. C. H. Kempe and R. E. Helfer. Philadelphia: J B Lippincott, p. 283.

Carroll, C., and C. Haase. In press. The function of protective services. In *The Battered Child,* eds. C. H. Kempe and R. E. Helfer. Philadelphia: J B Lippincott.

Kempe, C. H., and R. E. Helfer. 1972. Innovative therapeutic approaches, In *Helping the Battered Child and his Family,* eds. C. H. Kempe and R. E. Helfer. Philadelphia: J B Lippincott, p. 47.

Schmitt, B. D., and L. L. Loy. 1978. Team decisions on case management." In *The Child Protection Team Handbook,* ed. B. D. Schmitt. New York: Garland Publishing, pp. 193–194.

Steele, B. F. 1986. Notes on the lasting effects of early child abuse throughout the life cycle. In *Child Abuse and Neglect.* Pergamon Journals Ltd. 10:283–291.

10

Practical Guidelines for Professionals Working with Religious Spouse Abuse Victims

Anne L. Horton

C urrently, domestic abuse is the focus of many disciplines and helping professions, yet the complexity of the problem defies any one agency, institution, or discipline to meet single-handedly all the needs of these families. While the initial purpose of seeking help may be physical, most victims have long-term psychological and spiritual needs as well, and success in treatment and prevention will ultimately depend on a coordination of services and a better understanding of the total needs of clients. Such coordination of services and ideologies needs to evolve from a cooperative perspective rather than a competitive or antagonistic one.

Because shelter and advocacy groups initially defined traditional beliefs and values as dysfunctional and philosophically opposed to their positions, religious victims have often been ill-served and misunderstood by the treatment (secular) community as well as inadequately provided for by an untrained religious community (see Chapter 26). Thus, the purpose of this chapter is threefold: (1) to identify a common purpose that is sensitive to religious values and consistent with good clinical practice—a merger of ecclesiastical and secular concerns about spouse abuse; (2) to offer basic practical counseling guidelines for assessment and treatment of battered women, which reflect both safety goals and the spiritual values of religious spouse abuse victims; and (3) to offer secular clinicians a few suggestions for developing sensitivity to, and advocacy for, religious clients.

A Common Purpose

Today, clerics—with their religious perspective, ecclesiastical positions of leadership, social awareness, clinical skills, and family focus—are the counselors of choice for an increasingly large number of spouse abuse victims. However, this area of concern has developed so rapidly that these leaders often lack awareness and substantive knowledge about abuse and appropriate treatment approaches. Meanwhile, religious women have been identified by many secular helping professionals, particularly those in the early movement to end violence in the home, as having cultural beliefs that foster the patriarchal order and perpetuate discrimination against women. Many religious victims were told that their religion, in fact, caused the abuse.

To address today's multiplicity of needs, as well as the spiritual concerns of victims, an integrated perspective on family violence must be dynamic and change-oriented. However, to achieve this high level of intervention, religious advisors must be willing to coordinate their services with those of other caretakers in a common commitment. To enlarge upon their helping abilities, clerics need to learn as much about the abuse field as possible, know what other services are available, acknowledge their own limitations as abuse experts, and determine how agencies might enhance the clergy's services and vice versa. Without this cooperation, clergy, agency clinicians, and policymakers will continue to be at odds with their members (clients), with one another, and with the goals of both the religious and secular communities.

Meanwhile, the secular community also continues to foster a limited view of strengths that the religious community can offer. Because professional counselors are usually less involved religiously than most of society (Marx and Spray, 1969), they have little appreciation for and understanding of the meaning of religion in many people's lives. Religion is considered to be the "most important thing" in the lives of 31 percent of the population and "very important" to 55 percent, but when it is considered a therapeutic influence at all by secular counselors, they often view it as dysfunctional or problematic (Bergin, 1983).

Today, many churches and religious leaders are offering financial and practical support as well as free services to religious and nonreligious spouse abuse victims and their families. The church as an institution offers a rich community of potential service providers and additional untapped victim support networks. By extending professional expertise, training, respect, and cultural acceptance to this large population of religious victims and their spiritual leaders, the secular agency can more than double its effectiveness in reaching all abuse victims. The joint commitment of both groups—the commitment to change and enhance the human condition and to save lives—can be sizably increased by combining these two potent resources.

Like money, religion is not the root of all evil; its influence depends on its use. Physical abuse is a form of human behavior and is a very temporal choice indeed. Even though a person may continue to have certain essential values, his immoral act of willfully and knowingly harming another should not ever find sanction within any ethical or treatment framework. When religion is distorted to explain or excuse inhumane treatment of one man or woman against another it is just that—a distortion.

Therefore, the truly moral individual accepts a personal responsibility to be a worthy partner in a marital association. This commitment to basic equality, the end of oppression, and respect for humankind is the essence of most counseling professions, as well as the basic charge of the world's major religions. Just as the clergy must recognize that battering, not divorce, destroys abusive marriages, secular counselors must recognize that abuse, not religion, degrades women. A bond of respect and worthy common cause must unite these two humanitarian institutions toward saving lives and ending injustice.

Basic Assessment and Treatment Considerations

At the outset it is important that religious leaders and clinicians alike understand that all family violence has five things in common: (1) it is interactional, (2) it is learned, (3) it is a *choice,* (4) it is *always* inappropriate in family relations, and (5) it can be treated. It is also critical to understand the order in which violence must be treated: (1) ensure personal safety *first,* (2) treat the violent behavior, (3) pursue relationship concerns once safety is firmly established, and (4) resolve and mourn issues of separation and loss if reconstitution is not possible (Fortune, 1987).

Where, when, how, and with *whom* a counselor intervenes *may* have an enormous impact on outcome. In working with violence, timing is a critical factor. The earlier the diagnosis, the more likely is change. This fact alone must urge the religious leader or counselor to early identification (see Chapter 2). The longer one waits, the more likely abuse is to recur and escalate, establishing a pattern that becomes harder to break with each repetition. The very knowledge that an outside party is involved often serves as a deterrent as well as a resource.

The following guidelines were drawn up following a study of needs expressed by religious abuse victims (see Chapter 26) and will be helpful to ecclesiastical leaders and secular counselors alike. Many of these needs are generic to all abuse victims, but others arise specifically from a population committed to spiritual values. Many victims operate from a dual perspective that emphasizes both an external power and an internal responsibility toward life. Abuse is, therefore, often not easily understood by victims who assume that the violence is either the Lord's will or their own fault. They fail to recognize a third explanation for this behavior—that the abuser, and no one else, is directly responsible for his violence. These people are especially vulnerable as they attempt to explain temporal, unrighteous behavior within a religious framework. Both secular and religious leaders can help them understand this difference.

Desirable Helping Skills

Religious victims desire counselors who

1. Are sensitive and empathetic, innovative and flexible.

2. Listen, respect, and validate, rather than minimize or discredit.

3. Are creative providers, developers, and pathfinders.

4. Offer practical, specific suggestions suited to their particular needs, not just platitudes or idealism.

5. Possess good decision-making skills and judgment without being judgmental. Child abuse and spouse abuse by nature demand strong crisis-intervention skills: an ability to act quickly and to think about total treatment of all family members with a particular focus on safety first.

6. Do not preach, challenge, or blame. Victims need explicit education, information, and awareness, not indoctrination. Common areas of misinformation or voids involve developmental behavior of children and leadership skills in the family. Working with these families as a partner and an involved advisor is usually most effective.

7. Acknowledge the importance of maintaining the family without making its preservation the only alternative.

8. Possess a large range of experience in multiple settings with a variety of clients.

9. Do not assume, stereotype, or make blanket statements concerning religious leaders, religious victims, or religious beliefs.

10. Work with these clients to strengthen common goals rather than focus on the differences in their belief systems.

11. Can see the entire scope of these clients' consequences.

12. Employ a strong advocacy position in working with the institutional system that a client must satisfy in order to satisfy her value system.

Basic Counseling Guidelines

1. Counselors need to *ask about abuse.* They should never assume victims will offer information. In fact, most clients will *not* identify themselves. The clergy and secular professionals must develop a personal comfort level in approaching this topic and not ignore it. In addition, they should be very direct and specific, avoiding vagueness, clarifying the answers, and exploring details. Appropriate questions include (1) does your partner ever hit you? (2) does he allow you to come and go where you want to? (3) have you ever had to call the police or get medical attention for abuse? (4) are you afraid your husband might hurt you if _____? Victims will speak freely if the climate is right and they feel accepted. It is better to overinvestigate than to underinvestigate. This investigative work often requires counselors to gain new skills, especially in interviewing child victims.

2. *Counselors need to validate a victim's experience and validate a vic-*

tim's religious beliefs as important. Many religious victims have basic belief systems that reflect a set of personal values and a cultural lifestyle which must be respected and considered as an integral part of their identity. Religious beliefs are *not* "notions," idiosyncrasies, disorders, or mental illnesses. Nor are they the presenting problems.

The NASW Code of Ethics assures all clients of dignity, respect, and self-worth. Other professions have similar mandates regarding discriminatory practices. Secular counselors: Does your attitude toward "religious" people interfere with your ability to be accepting toward these clients? Do you respect their differences and try to understand why their differences are important to them? Religious leaders: Do you support the victim in her pain and acknowledge the inequity of the abuse? Or do you accuse her of causing it?

3. All counselors need to *be aware of their own value systems.* Therapist values alone must not define the victims' problems or the desired treatment outcome. There is no such thing as a value-free counselor, but there is value-sensitive therapy. If your values interfere with the helping process, make an early and honest referral, admitting those differences. Clerics often appear to have the advantage of sharing a value system with their clients, but do not always hear the fear and pain of the person involved; nor do they explore differences in religious interpretation. Just as secular counselors may not see the similarities between religious victims and other clients, religious counselors often make assumptions about church members which reflect their own expectations but not necessarily the victim's desires.

4. *Listen* to a victim's concerns and requests carefully and attend to *all* that is said. Give explicit education and advise the victim of *all* choices. Explore her particular options and encourage her to protect herself.

5. Religious victims, like all clients, are entitled to *self-determination,* but may need a great deal of guidance in sorting out their own problems, alternatives, and goals. If a secular counselor is the primary therapist, involving a religious leader may be helpful, *with* client approval. Not all victims will want to involve their religious community. Clergy are also encouraged to seek outside expertise for an effective treatment partnership.

6. Religious victims must be allowed to *move at their own pace,* not to a therapist's timetable. Reframe options to suit the clients' needs; advise the client that staying with the abuse and leaving permanently are not the only choices. She may have to leave for safety, but not forever. Religious victims often confuse leaving the violence with leaving the relationship, but this need not be the case. If a victim's situation is life-threatening, then safety needs must be attended to initially and treatment sought so that relationship concerns may be approached as the situation becomes less explosive. This first phase may take months or years, but for some victims waiting is an acceptable alternative, whereas separation or divorce may not be. Explain to the client that it is not a spiritual favor to the abuser to allow him to continue

torturing her and be faced with a potential murder or manslaughter charge. Such short-term reasoning will sacrifice long-term relationship values. To remain under such circumstances truly places all family members at risk. Putting her life, and the lives and well-being of the children, on the line cannot be considered virtuous because she is then a co-conspirator in allowing her partner to risk his position in this life and hereafter.

7. Because a religious victim tends to feel helpless, hopeless, and abandoned, one of the most helpful things a worker can do is reassure her that it is possible to *reestablish control over her life.* Advise her that she is only one of millions of women who have struggled with this painful situation. There are many options for the victim. By having realistic choices rationally and patiently suggested to her, the victim can rebuild hope in solving this crisis.

8. Allow the victim *to tell her story.* Storytelling is an important part of the healing process for all battered women. It is not easy for religious women to reach the point where she can "complain" or denigrate any aspect of her marriage publicly. This revelation is critical to her recovery and her ability to move on.

9. The victim needs to know she is *not alone.* Others have had similar experiences, and getting her involved with an appropriate support group will be very helpful during this initial stage. Guilt issues will be addressed also.

10. Being long-suffering is not to be confused with *being actively engaged in change.* Most religions do acknowledge the need for an individual to contribute actively to her own salvation as well as pray. Suggesting prayer, scripture reading, or singing hymns instead of practical suggestions as a means of change is resented by victims. Also, though most religions discourage divorce, it is not always forbidden.

A victim's perceptions are often limited by the abuser's extent of the knowledge and rationale. Distortions of doctrine are common in religious abusers who justify violence. Scriptural twisting is often used to rationalize abuse under the rubric of biblical or religious references.

11. Religious victims need to understand that *violent behavior toward them is never appropriate or deserved,* and it will not be legally or socially tolerated regardless of cultural beliefs. Laws must be obeyed by those living in this country.

12. Domestic abuse is *not a recognized, universal diagnosis.* Not all abuse is alike. Family violence can be globally defined as the maltreatment of one family member by another. However, diagnostically it is most helpful to address family violence within five specific conceptual categories: (1) physical mistreatment—slapping, hitting, burning, or strangling; (2) sexual abuse—rape or incest; (3) verbal abuse—threats, insults, or harassment; (4) psychological/emotional abuse—withholding love, sympathy, understanding; and (5) neglect—inadequate physical or emotional care. All counselors should understand these terms, diagnostic criteria, and treatment options.

13. *Clients should not be stereotyped.* Counselors should not assume each victim or batterer falls into a specific diagnostic pattern. Abuse is multi-dimensional and involves a complex scenario of personalities, behaviors, and background (Gelles, 1979). Complete assessments should always be performed to rule out additional contributing factors.

14. Counselors also need to take a *total assessment* of clients' histories, resources, and perceptions. Do not make assumptions based on your own cultural understanding of expected religious norms. Many clinicians do not practice thorough diagnostic skills after religion and abuse have been mentioned. Not all religious women practice what they are preached! Also, women in any one religion do not become generic. When necessary, learn to include a complete cultural/religious assessment as part of an initial interview, one part of which might be "tell me what part, if any, religion and faith have played in your life."

15. Treatment availability should not be contingent upon certain treatment choices of a family or individual. Victims should not be told that they are not serious about getting help if they are unwilling to leave their abuser or that they should not return to counseling until they are ready to leave home. Try to avoid ultimatums since most victims are very vulnerable and indecisive, at least initially. Clients should not be cut off from services by demanding more of them than they can do. Because a client returns once or even many times to an abusive partner does not mean she is not trying. Her alternatives or fear of the unknown may be very hard for her to overcome. Clients who are afraid to leave the house for an hour do not suddenly reverse all fearful behavior.

16. *Use the client's religious experiences* to help you understand her. Find out where her use of religion has been a strength and resource for her. A religious victim will readily identify where she has been helped or hurt by her faith if a listener validates her and does not immediately discredit her belief based on those with bad experiences or interpretations. Victims then must defend their values instead of discussing the problems or explaining the abuse.

17. *Follow usual dictates* and *give basic education* regarding good abuse protection and crisis-intervention guidelines. Focus on *protection,* then *change. Remember,* as with the alcoholic family, the problem must be intolerable enough to produce change. Prior to this commitment to change will be months, perhaps years, of denial and fear. The counselor should not be intolerant of the process.

18. The abuser is the *most isolated family member,* yet he is expected to make the most dramatic initial changes. If his self-esteem were not so low, he would probably not be out of control in the first place. The abuser needs support too. It is critical to note that among couples who end the abuse and

remain together and are satisfied, both partners were usually actively involved in treatment.

19. *Support* is important to all family members, but support must have *change* as its goal and not inadvertently provide secondary gains instead. It must never be perceived as condonation of the abuse.

20. *Build the client's strengths and self-esteem.* Therapists should not foster abuse or contribute to making the role of victim attractive. Being a martyr is not commendable; ending the violence is. Being a "good woman" has in the past been equated with long suffering, but allowing violence in the home is unhealthy and undesirable for all concerned. Do not blame her, but do not allow suffering to be confused with righteousness. No good or virtue can come from putting a life or the lives of one's children in jeopardy.

21. *Abuse is never the entire problem.* The counselor should not allow abuse to sidetrack other problems, which may be treatable. Therapists should not neglect treatment for problems a family is willing to work on while demanding success in respect to abuse. This position may frighten a victim so that she will not return and will feel abandoned. Remember that victims often flee from counselors because the situation or idea of change is too threatening.

22. Religious leaders and counselors should not overlook the fact that *boys and men may be abuse victims.* This reverse sexism is not uncommon in the treatment or religious community.

23. It is best *not to make sweeping statements* to clients about *all* abusers, all victims, or all violent behaviors.

24. *Change is difficult!* Recognize that success with all domestic abuse clients is very limited and outcomes are often less than the client or counselor hoped for. Working with these clients is both painful and frustrating to clinicians. Lack of respect and control are problems in these troubled families. All victims are initially loathe to take a stand against their partners. Gains are slow, and you must be patient to win the client's trust.

25. *Remember:* Treatment lowers the probability of abuse; it does not remove the possibility! No one can make any promises, nor can safety be totally guaranteed. The goal of treatment, therefore, is to lower the odds. To be successful, treatment of abuse, like all marital endeavors, is a partnership. When both partners are committed and sincere, success and recovery can be achieved.

Suggestions for Secular Clinicians in Developing Sensitivity to, and Advocating for, Religious Clients

Sensitivity

1. Read literature that describes the values and cultural differences of reli-

gious victims in your area so that their beliefs and norms are familiar to you.

2. Gain experiential awareness by talking with colleagues, friends, and religious leaders of these faiths with an open mind.

3. Consider spending time in the homes of a specific religious family, attending services and church-related events which will actively involve you in the day-to-day experiences and lifestyle of these populations.

4. Develop a professional network of religious consultants and referral sources that helps you meet the specific needs and understand the value systems of these clients.

5. Attempt to translate religious terms into vernacular. While religious clients often appear to speak a different language, the sensitive therapist can make an appropriate translation. For instance, the religious client may say, "Oh, the Spirit told me to do it," as opposed to such common expressions as "I just had the feeling I ought to go ahead" or "I just knew it was the right thing." By increasing awareness of our own very personal biases and even prejudices, we as professionals can be more open and accepting than we have been previously.

6. Discuss your personal value dilemmas with professional colleagues. Working with abuse clients generally causes a high rate of worker burnout. Add a basic value difference to the worker's stress, and it may be overwhelming. Counselors need to develop a personal repertoire of coping skills.

7. Define early on those clients whose religious values are of such a nature that they violate your own value system to such a degree that referral is necessary, and find the most appropriate resource available. It is ethically far better to do this than to disadvantage the client. No social worker can work with every client equally well. Know your limits.

Advocacy

1. Identify a secular and religious partnership as a desirable means of offering more resource, support, advocacy, and change. Provide in-service training to sensitize your agency colleagues about the needs of religious victims. Do active outreach to clergy and religious victims as a target population. This aspect of community organization and utilization of untapped resources has been ignored and even scorned by many clinicians. The potential resource pool to be gained is unlimited.

2. Provide accurate material and training packets for clergy. Work as a team to develop information and referral guides. Help religious leaders be aware of resources in the community that their church members can

use with confidence, knowing that they will not be placed on the defensive. Identify agencies that work well with religious victims.

3. Encourage religious leaders to discuss domestic abuse in sermons and raise congregation understanding. Offer to come to the church service, young adult meetings, or Bible study groups and provide educational presentations, workshops, and community information on spotlights of interest.

4. Encourage churches to develop position statements concerning the unrighteous use of force and to put abuse into a framework that does not include vagueness or virtue in respect to the use of physical force.

5. Help clerics develop skills to build self-esteem for victims, perpetrators, and family members as part of their role.

6. Encourage churches to include study of domestic violence in training programs and continuing education. Be familiar with religiously oriented material (*Working Together to Prevent Sexual and Domestic Violence,* Center for the Prevention of Sexual and Domestic Violence, 1914 N. 34th, Suite 105, Seattle Washington, 98103, is a good resource). Marie Fortune has designed helpful training materials on abuse. The National Coalition Against Domestic Violence will have a new booklet by Susan Schechter coming out in the winter of 1988.

7. Churches can help with material resources. Church volunteers can be trained so that they can help other members. A lay counselor who understands a victim and is trusted by her will do more good than a highly knowledgeable but less religiously sensitive person will.

8. It is important to remember that members of the clergy are helping professionals and should be regarded with respect. While clerics may not be as knowledgeable in working with abuse victims, it is critical to understand that they are seen as experts in other areas of major importance to the person seeking advice. If you discount the religious leader for his values or leadership position instead of focusing on the victim's needs, you will risk her trust and raise suspicion since he is seen as God's representative.

9. It is our collective goal to provide for the treatment needs of victims, and this goal will be accomplished only by approaching and gaining the support of institutional religion.

Conclusion

The abusive family is a challenge for any helping person, and value or cultural differences present additional concerns for professionals. The dimensions of religiosity, ethnicity, and ethics are not yet well understood by secular counselors because the variety of backgrounds and beliefs in this country demands constant sensitivity and new knowledge. The same dilemma faces the religious leader who attempts to understand human behavior—particularly undesirable behavior—within a spiritual framework. New knowledge must be continually sought. All counselors are urged to exert this effort. Learn all that is possible about the needs of your members/clients, whether they be safety or spiritual concerns.

The use of many resources, the combined strengths of the religious and treatment community, and the suggestions for working with abuse victims included here should give all helping professionals more awareness in this ongoing process. Value-sensitive counseling requires a common humanitarian commitment which allows all clients to bring their critical identity issues into the helping process and ensures respect, feelings of self-worth, and a fair chance to be heard. Be available. Be knowledgeable. Be charitable. Be an agent of change and a source of comfort. A victim's future and her children's future will continue to be violent unless you help them change the destructive pattern of their lives.

References

Bergin, A. E. 1981. Religiosity and mental health: A critical reevaluation and meta-analysis. *Professional Psychology: Research and Practice* 14(2):170–184.

Fortune, M. February 6, 1987. Resolution of family violence: Appropriate and inappropriate approaches. Unpublished paper. Third Annual Family Violence Conference, Provo, UT.

Gelles, R. J., and J. A. Straus. 1979. Violence in the American family. *Journal of Social Issues* 35(2):15–39.

Gil, D. G. 1970. *Violence against children: Physical child abuse in the United States.* Cambridge, MA: Harvard University Press.

Marx, J. H., and S. L. Spray. 1969. Religious biographies and professional characteristics of psychotherapists. *Journal of Health and Social Behavior* 10:275–288.

11

Dealing with the Abuser: Issues, Options, and Procedures

Edward Gondolf

G radually, the treatment community is learning that wife abuse is not a problem that can be relegated to the experts alone. It requires an active response from the community as a whole, including the church. This chapter discusses the role that the clergy and other counselors can play in changing men who abuse their wives or partners. Several topics to consider in dealing with the abuser are raised and the clergy's direct and indirect contribution to the reform process is discussed.

The Change Process in Abusers

The change process in individual abusers, as well as in men in general, is a long one that requires more than several weeks of counseling or even some time in jail. It is useful to consider the change process of abusive men, which is a series of developmental stages comprising three basic levels: denial, behavioral change, and personal transformation. Recognizing this change process may help the clergy respond more appropriately to the abuser and better guide him in a progressive direction.

The abuser at the *denial* level tends to be markedly egocentric. His world is largely one of objects to be manipulated for his advantage or survival. At this level, intervention that interrupts the violence and confronts the man may be necessary to foster some sense of guilt and responsibility.

At the level of *behavioral change,* the man acknowledges, however tentatively, his abuse and a willingness to change for his own self-interest. Behaviorally oriented treatment, most frequently found in supervised self-help groups, is probably most appropriate at this level.

The man at the level of *personal transformation* is curing the emotional as well as physical abuse. He is beginning to develop a new self-concept that excludes abusiveness and is respectful and supportive of women. At this point, the man needs a new reference group that is supportive of his new self-concept and activities that confirm his ability to live as a different person.

In a sense, this process of change can be likened to a "conversion" process in which the abuser accepts the need to change, his capacity to change, and eventually a new life of change. He ultimately adopts a new self-concept that redefines the way he perceives and relates to the world. The clergy, in this light, is in a position to support and sustain this development. In fact, experience in pastoral counseling and general appreciation for conversion as a spiritual process may enable the clergy to have a profound impact on the abuser.

A cleric faced with an abuser may want to keep in mind the plurality of viewpoints and different orientations to treatment emphasized by various groups. Some programs emphasize the instruction of anger control techniques (Sonkin and Durphy, 1981), while others emphasize resocializing the men to relinquish their tendency to control and dominate women (Gondolf, 1985a). An awareness of these debates may assist religious leaders in interpreting the differences of professional opinion that inevitably emerge and assist them in identifying the shortcomings of various interventions. During assessment, the most appropriate treatment approach can be determined by considering a variety of factors discussed in this chapter.

Level 1: Denial

The first major task of the clergy is to help the man realize that he is abusive and needs help. Accomplishing this vital task, however, can be a challenge in itself, because of the denial or unloading associated with the first level in the change process. The extremes of denial and unloading suggest some underlying characteristics in abusive men.

Denial can take many forms. The most obvious is the man's outright insistence that he has not abused his wife. Many men actually do not perceive their physical shoves, hits, or kicks to be abuse, but *legitimate* them as rightful retaliation or control. If they do concede the battering, they *minimize* it by claiming they did not really hurt her, failing to realize the terror their behavior can cause. They may simply *rationalize* their abuse by noting that the woman had it coming, or *externalize* the responsibility of their abuse by saying "I was drunk (or stressed or angry) when I did it."

Compounding the denial is the Jekyll-and-Hyde behavior that makes abusers generally elusive and difficult to detect (Bernard and Bernard, 1984). As both clinicians and researchers note, many abusers will appear accommodating and responsive in public but act violently behind closed doors. Similarly, there has been much made about the cycle of violence during which the man lapses into a "honeymoon" phase of apologies with his wife (Walker, 1979). Reports of victims confirm that the behaviors of abusers toward them is tremendously contradictory and inconsistent. The men may apologize and attempt to make up one time, then blame the women and threaten to kill them at another (Gondolf, Fisher, and McFerron, 1987).

Confronting Denial

The challenge for the clergy, and for human service workers as well, is to confront the denial in a way that encourages disclosure and acceptance of responsibility. A counselor can often help break through such denial by tactfully noting the discrepancies in the man's story or raising contrary facts from the victim or the police report. In this way, the clergy may present cognitive dissonance for which the abuser has to adjust his version to maintain some consistency.

Another tactic is to ask if specific physical and psychological abuses have been committed: "Have you ever thrown objects or broken things when you are angry?" or "Do you demand a strict account of how your wife manages her money?" While a man might deny being a batterer, he may admit to occasional abusive acts which, when taken overall, amount to extreme abuse.

Also, relating the perceptions of an abused woman might help to break the denial. Abusers overwhelmingly fail to realize the impact of their behaviors. A reformed abuser finally recognized this and was consequently able to take responsibility for all his abuse:

> I made my wife feel like shit. That hurt her more than punching her in the nose. All those years, I thought I was the one being abused. I thought I was right. I didn't have what I wanted: like sexual things, the relationship with a woman that I wanted to have. I never realized that I was the one creating the problems.

Lastly, the pastor or counselor may simply explain to the abuser that he is ultimately responsible for his actions. He is the one who stands behind his fist—no one makes him swing it. Therefore, he ultimately is the one who can stop it. "The bottom line is that you have to decide that you want to do something about the abuse. That can't be forced," said one abuser in an interview. However simplistic this approach may sound, it appeals to the abuser's desire for control and power in a constructive way (Gondolf, 1985b). Listing some of the consequences of continuing the abuse, such as possible jailing or loss of one's family, may in itself bring the point home.

A booklet entitled Man-to-Man on Wife Abuse by Gondolf and Russell (1987) is available to present to abusive men. It discusses many of the arguments suggested here in order to help move abusive men in denial toward treatment.

Unloading and Depression

At the other extreme of denial is the tendency to emotionally unload and even fall into depression. A man may burst forth with an unstoppable stream of feelings long buried or neglected in his denial. Besides serving as a self-indulgent release, an abuser's monologue can be another form of defense in that it allows the speaker to say only what he wants and to avoid answering questions. As important as it is to support this expression, the cleric or counselor must be prepared to interrupt and steer the abuser toward some course of action and away from self-pity.

Part of the challenge lies in the fact that what the men have to unload can be beguilingly pathetic. A typical unloading may include shameful experiences from the batterer's past:

> Growing up was not good for me. My father was a bad drinker, and so was my mother. The two of them would fight almost every weekend. . . . There was screaming and hollering and punching endlessly. I gave up when I was young trying to break it up. I would just lie under the covers and try to detach myself from it all. My younger sisters would all run around crying, but I just hid.

It is not uncommon for an abuser to lapse into depression, especially when his wife and family have left him. In fact, it is often this depression that finally moves the abuser to seek out some sort of help. The man is left to examine himself, which can be a painful and unsettling process. A "What's the use?" attitude consequently appears. Some men will even talk of suicide. An abuser in this condition may require some vigorous assertions from the clergy to break his immobilized spirit, rather than sympathetic listening that may reinforce the depression (Beck et al., 1980). Of course, if there is evidence of chronic or prolonged depression which may be life-threatening, the clergy should refer the man for psychological treatment.

Level 2: Behavioral Changes

Safety and Separation

The clergy also has an obligation to ensure the safety of the wife and children of the abuser. The best first aid, if it has not occurred already, is for the abuser and his wife to separate for a while. For the same reasons that men fall into depression if their wives leave, abusers initially rebel against the prospect of separation: "How dare she leave me!" The abuser may even be inclined to hunt down his victim and threaten her to come back if she has left. Or he may beg her to return home with all sorts of promises that he means to keep but cannot.

The clergy may, therefore, have to do a strong bit of advocacy in order for the abuser to understand the necessity of his wife's going to a women's shelter or to a friend's house, or to have the man move out himself. It may help to propose the separation as a kind of vacation from one another—a time to relax and sort things out. The separation is also a way to prompt the man's letting go of some of the control that underlies the abuse. *Most importantly, it is the only way to ensure safety to the family while the abuser makes some changes.*

The importance of separation is important for therapeutic reasons as well. Nearly 90 percent of the men who join programs join because their wife and children have left them. Most of those who change do so because their wives have stayed at a shelter for a while and received counseling support of their own (Bowker, 1983).

Time Outs

In the meantime, there are some practical steps the clergy can recommend to the abuser. These are designed to interrupt the abuse, at least in the short run. They are not, however, an end in themselves. They are merely a safety precaution, somewhat like putting on handcuffs for the moment.

The most commonly used safety precaution is taking a *time out*. In a *time out,* the abuser signals his wife when he feels abusive and leaves the house to cool off without further discussion. It is an arrangement that should, of course, be discussed between husband and wife ahead of time, and never used as a way to get back at her. Following is a list of time out procedures.

1. Identify a "cue" that trouble is coming (usually a physical sign expressed in a tightening chest, clenching of your hands, or just in a feeling that you *must* control her).

2. Give a *T* sign with your hands to indicate your need to take a time out as soon as you feel that cue.

3. Let your wife know that you need a time out to get control of your behavior. Let her know how much time you need to calm down.

4. Depart without slamming the door and making any further comments.

5. Walk briskly (it's better not to drive), reflecting on the *self-talk* statements (discussed below) or calling a friend to talk with. Don't drink.

6. Return at the end of your stated time limit and admit at least one error you made prior to leaving. (If an argument develops, take another time out or agree on a later time to discuss the matter.)

Self-Talk

Another commonly employed technique is self-talk, in which the abuser affirms to himself positive statements about his capacity for nonviolence and change. Abusers typically repeat defeating things to themselves: "I can never change," "It's not really worth it," "I don't need any help," or "I can't change until she does." His mind rehearses past events and builds mountains out of molehills. This process can amount to a kind of self-hypnosis.

Essentially, self-talk is a matter of the abuser's replacing negative thoughts with positive ones and developing faith that he can be and is better than his thoughts suggest. The abuser might be encouraged to assert a list of statements, such as the "I can's" in the following list, when he gets up in the morning and especially during a time out.

1. I can show my feelings and express my fear in nonabusive ways.
2. I can change and choose the direction of my changes.
3. I can ask for help when I need it and offer help when I think it is needed.
4. I can ask for what I want but know that I cannot always get it.
5. I can tell people when I cannot fulfill their expectations of me.
6. I can consider new ways of thinking, acting, and relating to other people.
7. I can reject stereotypes of how I am supposed to be.
8. I can express my frustrations, disappointments, and anxieties without hurting people.
9. I can take responsibility for my actions and not allow other people to push me into choices I do not want to make.
10. I can show my strength by choosing not to hit someone who does not meet my expectations.

As a religious leader, you may want to recommend a series of Bible or denominational verses on the theme of change for the abuser to ponder. In fact, the "I can's" may appear to be beyond the abuser's reach. The religious verses, on the other hand, may help the abuser to consider spiritual resources that can move him beyond his personal limits.

Options for Treatment

The next major task of the counselor or clergy is to refer the abuser to an appropriate treatment program, to move him toward the behavioral changes of the second level in the change process. In most cases, the clergy is not trained or in a position to offer extensive treatment for the abuser. Therefore, they should direct the abuser towards a specialized program in the community that deals with abusers (Feazell, Mayers, and Deschner, 1984).

Supervised Self-Help Groups. Most of these programs will offer a supervised self-help group that meets weekly to discuss their abuse and how to stop it (Roberts, 1984; Pirog-Good and Stets-Kealey, 1985). In general, they employ a group process that serves to break the social isolation and confront the abusers' denial and resistance to change. Such programs also include some cognitive restructuring, skill building and sex role resocialization organized around a set curriculum lasting from three months to a year (Edelson, 1984; Saunders, 1984).

Individual Counseling. One readily available alternative is individual counseling. Many counselors will discuss the abuser's problems one-on-one. This can be a good start to help get some perspective on the abuse problem. Also, if the abuser is experiencing some long-lasting depression and major changes in functioning (loss of appetite, lowered sex drive, loss of interest in his job or hobbies), individual counseling might be a good idea.

There are many different counseling approaches and techniques, however. The abuser may want to ask specifically for a counselor experienced in dealing with abuse cases. The cleric may want to be sure that the counseling deals with more than just the abuser's anger and how to communicate better.

Marriage Counseling. Marriage counseling is another alternative. The marriage counselor may be helpful in improving the abuser's relationship with his wife, but most abuser programs suggest that such counseling be attempted only after the violence has stopped for at least six months to a year. Several family counselors (Deschner, 1984; Taylor, 1984; Weidman, 1986) from a family perspective advocate treating the abuser and abused together. However, there are cautions and even opposition to this approach (Bogard, 1984). One caution is that the abuser is more likely in couples counseling to displace his responsibility to the woman and continue his denial. Second, it is difficult for a victim to be fully honest about the abuser in couples counseling because of her fear of possible reprisals. Third, the marriage counseling can confuse the marital problems with the problem of abuse.

Alcohol and Drug Programs. Alcohol and drug programs offer an option as well. If the abuser drinks or uses drugs excessively, and a majority do, he could probably use some drug and alcohol counseling (Roy, 1982). Ideally, this kind of counseling should come *in addition* to joining an abuser program, not in place of it. Too often, stopping the alcohol abuse does not necessarily lead to stopping wife abuse; the alcohol is readily used as an excuse for the abuse (Gelles, 1974). Any of these alternatives, however, offers some support to the abuser's attempt to seek help and begin to change.

Pitfalls to Progress

The cleric's work with an abuser should not end with the abuser's participation in treatment. He or she can help address the high dropout rate (as much as 60 percent) in most programs. Two major pitfalls, besides the denial and unloading, contribute to the dropout during treatment: self-pity and self-congratulation. The religious leader can help support the process of change by assisting the abuser to negotiate them.

Self-Pity. Self-pity comes in the form of the abuser's complaining of all sorts of personal problems, hurts, or disappointments. In many cases, the counseling helps to make him more acutely aware of these. Consequently, the abuser feels that no one really understands or appreciates where he is coming from. Some degree of victim blaming may accompany this self-preoccupation. It may simply be in the form of noting that "the women get all the credit, support, or sympathy." The cleric may even be criticized for lending too much support for the wife and be pressed to take one side or another.

Such self-pity, however, may be exposed as another form of denial and excuse. It needs to be exposed for what it is. The cleric, in this case, might appeal to the man's inherent fear of weakness, by noting that self-pity is the ultimate weakness, which says "I have strength to think only of myself and nothing more." Moreover, the pity is dysfunctional, for such preoccupation keeps the abuser from reaching out to others in a way that can help him and the others change for the better.

Self-Congratulation. The other pitfall, self-congratulation, is in a sense the flip side of self-pity; the abuser thinks too much of himself rather than too little. He expects others to praise him, trust him, and reward him for his initial efforts to change. He may ask "Why doesn't she appreciate all the changes I've made?" or "Why doesn't she trust me now that I've stopped abusing her?" or say "She should come back to me now that I have changed."

The fact is that an abuser *has* to congratulate himself for what he has accomplished and realize that he *always* has further to go. He must be reminded, however, that the rewards come as a result of lessening abuse, not simply in the approval of his partner.

The abuser cannot expect his wife suddenly to congratulate him, given what has happened to her. An abused woman has no doubt heard promises about stopping the abuse before, but as is so often the case, the cycle of violence has repeated itself. The woman therefore has to remain cautious for her own sake and her children's.

The cleric might attempt to further convey the woman's point of view. Why should she thank the abuser for stopping the abuse that never should have happened? It is like having someone step on your foot in a subway car; you generally don't say "thank you" when they remove their foot from yours.

Level 3: Sustaining Change

Lastly, the clergy has a role in helping the reforming abuser to sustain his change and adjust to a new way of life. The clergy may in fact be best equipped to assist the reforming abuser at this level of personal transformation. A few abuser programs offer follow-up support groups for this purpose, but even men in a follow-up group report the difficulty in adjusting to a nonviolent living. For instance, reformed abusers note the challenge of living up to their new self-image and not relapsing into the thinking and acting of "the old man." They also talk of the need for an alternative reference group that can support their new set of values and behaviors. Furthermore, they acknowledge their contemplation of more substantial spiritual questions brought on by their efforts to change.

First in this stage of personal transformation is the abuser's attempt to avoid relapse. The reformed abusers talk of the need to monitor themselves daily for abusive tendencies, much like an alcoholic may have to do. The clergy can provide the prodding encouragement and questioning that can help keep the abuser vigilant. Many churches' teachings on constancy, persistence, and faith may offer some appropriate lessons in this regard.

Second, the men report needing a new reference group for support. In the process of change, many of the men report discovering their feelings. These feelings enable the men to empathize with the feelings of others and treat their wives less like objects. But this emerging new man can find himself in a different kind of isolation. As one abuser commented in the course of a group meeting, "I can't talk about these sorts of things with the men where I work. They would all think I was crazy."

Along with their increased capacity for relationships, there must be potential new friends to relate to. Here the church community and fellowship come into play. Not only do they present men with the possibility of new or expanded friendships, but also with a body or people related in a spirit of mutuality and goodness that in itself can be a force for change.

Third, the clergy can help the man by supporting his consideration of the spiritual issues associated with purpose, identity, and happiness. Becoming a nonabusive person is, of course, more than a matter of just stopping the violence. It involves becoming an empathetic, caring, and even supportive person.

In general, reformed abusers tell us that they are wrestling with more spiritual issues in their lives. Some abusers will openly talk of "finding the Lord" or becoming a true believer. In a very practical sense, their turning to religion in this time of searching offers them some specific guidelines for changing or being saved. (The only caution here is that the abuser may bend some dogma to minimize his problem or avoid the demands of changing.)

Conclusion

In discussing the role of the clergy in respect to abusive families, it is clear that the religious leader can be a valuable asset in the change process. Throughout the three basic levels of change—denial, behavioral change, and personal transformation—pastoral counseling and education can enliven an abuser's questions, facilitate his search, and point him toward some meaningful answers. Biblical figures, for instance, can offer models of peaceful character. The message of so many faiths in itself can be a kind of therapy: We all, regardless of circumstance or background, can be transformed by a loving power and strength beyond our own.

References

Beck, A., J. Rush, B. Shaw, and G. Emery. 1980. *Cognitive therapy of depression.* New York: Guilford Press.

Bernard, J. L., and M. L. Bernard. 1984. The abusive male seeking treatment: Jekyll and Hyde. *Family Relations* 33:543–547.

Bogard, M. 1984. Family systems approaches to wife battering: A feminist critique. *American Journal of Orthopsychiatry* 54(4):558–568.

Bowker, L. 1983. *Beating wife beating.* Lexington, MA: Lexington Books.

Deschner, J. 1984. *The hitting habit.* New York: Free Press.

Edelson, J. 1984. Working with men who batter. *Social Work* 29:237–242.

Feazell, C. S., R. S. Mayers, and J. Deschner. 1984. Services for men who batter: Implications for programs and policies. *Family Relations* 33:217–223.

Gelles, R. 1974. *The violent home. Study of physical aggression between husbands and wives.* Beverly Hills, CA: Sage.

Gondolf, E. 1985a. *Men who batter: An integrated approach for stopping wife abuse.* Holmes Beach, FL: Learning Publications.

———. 1985b. Fighting for control: A clinical assessment of men who batter. *Social Casework* 65:48–54.

Gondolf, E., and D. Russell. 1987. *Man-to-man on wife abuse: A guide for abusive men.* Sarasota, FL: Human Services Press.

Gondolf, E., E. Fisher, and R. McFerron. 1987. The helpseeking behavior of battered women: A preliminary analysis of 6,000 shelter interviews. *Victimology.* 12:1.

Pirog-Good, M., and J. Stets-Kealey. 1985. Male batterers and battering prevention programs: A national survey. *Response* 8(3):8–12.

Roberts, A. 1984. Intervention with the abusive partner. In *Battered Women and Their Families,* ed. A. Roberts. New York: Springer.

Roy, M. 1982. Four thousand partners in violence: A trend analysis. In *The Abusive Partner,* ed. M. Roy. New York: Van Nostrand Reinhold.

Saunders, D. 1984. Helping husbands who batter. *Social Casework* 65:347–353.

Sonkin, D., and M. Durphy. 1981. *Learning to live without violence.* San Francisco: Volcano Press.

Taylor, J. 1984. Structured conjoint therapy for spouse abuse cases. *Social Casework* 64:11–18.

Walker, L. 1979. *The battered woman.* New York: Harper and Row.

Weidman, A. 1986. Family therapy with violent couples. *Social Casework* 66:212–218.

12

Building Self-Esteem: Overcoming Barriers to Recovery

Ginny NiCarthy

Battering is a pattern of control and coercion by means of physical and emotional abuse. Physical and emotional abuse negatively affects many women's sense of worth and their beliefs in their capacity to reorganize and control their lives. For many women this is a problem of short duration, but for others severe damage to self-esteem takes months or years to repair. There are many specific areas of self-esteem that you or the victim may see as important. This chapter will discuss relationships, negative self-talk, self-care, emotional control, and moral stature and describe how a formerly abused woman can be helped in each of these areas.

The Recovery of Self-Esteem

Research has presented no solid information about the situations or personalities that produce differential responses. The following are the most useful operating assumptions you can make about abused women's recovery of self-esteem:

1. The battered woman does not fall neatly into a certain psychological category or personality profile.

2. Her complex view of herself may not be immediately evident and may include many contradictions. For instance, she may work as a business executive from nine to five, yet be socially shy or afraid to dine alone in a restaurant.

3. She may see herself as generally competent, but emotionally or interpersonally out of control, or as a moral failure.

4. She may believe she is weak and impaired now, but see her "possible self" as successful and strong, or she may interpret her present inadequacies as evidence she will never achieve the standards she or others set for her "possible self."[1]

You can best discover the condition of the woman's self-esteem by sensitive listening. If she does not spontaneously provide information about her self-esteem, you can ask her what she likes and admires about herself now; how she contrasts that with the past and with her hopes, fears, and expectations for the future; how she thinks others see her; and how their standards compare with her own.

Effects of Physical and Emotional Abuse

Physical abuse gives a person a feeling of physical helplessness. Bruises and scars destroy her feeling of attractiveness. The knowledge that she continues to endure assault without leaving the partner may make her feel demeaned. Being assaulted by the person who claimed to love her most may have been especially humiliating, and may have contributed to her belief that no one else will ever love her or treat her with respect.

There are countless ways to emotionally abuse a partner, some of which are difficult to recognize and name. A woman may be prohibited from seeing or talking to other people, so that she is robbed of their appreciation of her valued qualities. Her partner may have found many ways to humiliate and degrade her, to enforce performance of menial tasks, to demonstrate power over her, and to insist that she focus all her attention away from herself and onto the threatening partner.

A major method of emotional abuse is to insult and verbally degrade, which over time causes the abused woman to doubt her competence and her judgment. An abusive partner may use many techniques to make the woman feel "crazy" or "invisible."[2] Emotional abuse may have been much more damaging to a woman's self-concept than physical abuse. Together they are powerful ways to control another person, and that control is the fundamental drive of the abusive person.

The Role of Relationships in Recovering Self-Esteem

As the formerly battered woman's spiritual advisor, you can play an important role in her recovery. *Recovery* is used to connote not a sickness, but a condition more analogous to that experienced by a war veteran. You may be the first person the woman has spoken to openly since she left the "battle zone," and her sense of worth may begin to revive through her interactions with you. She will begin to appreciate herself as she realizes that you are sharing a bit of her pain, anxiety, and sadness and that you can occasionally laugh with her even in the midst of her grief. Because laughter and tears are genuine, it will be hard for her to persuade herself that you are just doing a job.

If you keep a professional distance, avoiding an honest display of your feelings, you will contribute to the woman's sense of emotional isolation and the belief that no one can really care for her. So being emotionally open is important. If you are a man, you will need to exercise caution that she does not misunderstand your concern and feeling. Avoiding the formality of professional distance does not imply a lack of boundaries, and those should be made clear.

Rebuilding Relationships

Isolation is a major aspect of abuse for many women. Often, partners have forbidden them to see other people. A woman may also have been too ashamed of her bruises to socialize with others, or so intent on keeping her secret that she limited the depth of her relationships, even with her friends. She will benefit from making new acquaintances and contacting old friends, and you can be important in helping her get started.

Whatever the woman's lifestyle or orientation, once you have established a rapport and a sense of trust, you can encourage her to branch out to other people, step by step. If you can locate a community group, shelter, or safe home system that has groups or individual advocacy for battered women, as well as safe space, that may be the first place the woman is willing to go, and such a place is likely to be the most helpful. A group will help her understand her situation through the mirror of others who have had similar experiences. Other social contacts can be made through the relatively nonthreatening structure of classes, or with invitations to co-workers. These might begin with a carefully planned overture by her to share a cup of coffee with a classmate or co-worker.

Make it clear that you have faith that she can manage these contacts and can gradually learn to trust herself enough to know the extent to which she can trust others. At the same time let the woman know that you appreciate the impact of the abuse and her relative isolation during the abusive relationship—and that she has good reason to follow her own timetable, regardless of how it may appear to an outsider.

Abuser Control

If the woman behaves as if she is still involved with and restricted by the partner, you need to find out whether that is the situation or whether her fears may indicate she has not yet adapted to her new situation. It is important to make careful inquiries about how much contact she and the ex-partner still have as a result of custody arrangements, mutual work sites, or common family, friends, and entertainment spots. The abuser may be harassing her by telephone or in person. The harassment may be very subtle, yet she may have good reason to fear that she is in danger if the ex-partner sees her with friends or perceives her to be enjoying her expanded activities.

The abuser may control the woman by threats to withdraw child support or other monetary assistance, and she may continue to feel helpless and trapped. You can help her evaluate the reality of the current threat, weigh it against maintaining the relationship, and consider the likelihood of its diminishing as the ex-partner adapts to the new situation. It may take months or even years, during which the woman must be very self-protective, to determine whether the ex-partner will give up the harassment. Meanwhile, she must be certain she is not providing reinforcement in the form of unnecessary contact or emotional involvement.

In some instances, it will require a major move, or even a new identity, for the woman to free herself of the abusive person. While she is evaluating her options, you can play a crucial role in helping her realize that she is going through a process of gaining control, beginning with the way she respects herself, makes decisions, handles her feelings, and relates to you. It is not your job to assess the danger, but rather to help her evaluate it in a realistic manner. She is the one who will suffer the consequences—and it is she who must make the decision.

Trust—of others and herself—may be a major issue for the formerly battered woman, and for good reason. She placed her trust in someone who betrayed it, and she may now conclude (depending on who beat her) that all men, all white men, all charmers, or all lesbians, are not to be trusted. She might also fear that because her judgment was bad once, it can never be relied on again.

You can help her explore the reasons she chose her partner or allowed herself to be chosen and how she would make such a choice now. She can be encouraged to consider the qualities she will look for in friends, lovers, or acquaintances in order to maximize her safety.[3] You can help her see that she can slowly develop trust in herself by making tentative judgments, checking them out, and taking very small risks one at a time. You can reassure her that if she changes her feelings or her opinion of another person, she can shift the relationship from intimacy to a more casual basis. She *can* say "No"; she can be the one to end a relationship. You can help her view potential partners and friends as people whom she probably will not completely trust or distrust, but on whom she can rely in certain ways—ways that take time to discover and test. As she gains confidence, she will not need to place people in categories because she will be able to trust herself.

Changing Self-Talk

An abused woman may have absorbed her former partner's stated view of her and developed a habit of verbal self-abuse. After she has severed the relationship, she may still lash at herself with verbal insults, aloud or silently. You can heighten the woman's awareness of the derogatory remarks she makes about herself, and you can suggest that to speak in such an abusive way is colluding with the abusive partner, even after the relationship is ended. You can help the woman see that her statements about herself make a major contribution to her feelings of low self-esteem and fears about her future.

In an effort to reverse this negative self-talk, ask her to write a list each day of the self-criticisms she says aloud or silently, and talk with her about the dysfunction and indefensibility of broad criticisms such as "stupid" and "disgusting." Then ask her to substitute more factual, specific criticisms or a neutral comment. "I'm so stupid!" can become "I'm slower than I'd like to be at learning the word processor," and "I'm a horrible mother" can be changed to "I yelled at Mary twice today."[4]

Once the comments are specific, you can work with her on a specific plan. For instance, she can gradually speed the learning process or reduce the number of times she raises her voice when speaking to the children. Rather than becoming mired in the hopelessness to total failure, the woman is encouraged to recognize her specific shortcomings, put them in perspective, and work on slow but steady changes. An important role for you is to help her focus on the achievements she has made, choose reasonable goals, and appreciate each small change.

It is also important to be aware of social messages that may underlie feelings of low self-esteem. For instance, if the woman is part of an ethnic or racial minority, considers herself too old to try new activities, is physically disabled, belongs to a socially disdained religion, or is a lesbian, some of her self-criticisms may take the form of society's most demeaning slurs. If this occurs, you may want to discuss the idea of collusion again, and to find out if the partner has used those social stigmas to demean the woman. Even if the partner is also black, disabled, or a lesbian, he or she may still use the woman's identification with the same group to humiliate her. It will be useful to help her find others who have been battered and survived, who are part of the same group, or who share the same lifestyle or orientation.[5]

Along with messages of self-criticism, the woman may be beset by an inner monologue of helplessness and hopelessness statements: "I'm never going to change" or "It's too late for me to get an education." These ideas too can be modified by the woman's becoming aware of them, restating them in precise factual, believable statements, then beginning to test them. For instance, "I'm never going to change" might become "I don't know how much

I'll change now that I'm fifty-two, but maybe I can learn to be more assertive on the job." Then the program of practicing assertiveness can begin. Each time some small accomplishment is recognized, it builds esteem so that another can be tried.

Self-Care and Physical Activity

Self-care, exercise, and sports programs are all ways of saying to oneself "I am worth bothering with. I can take charge of my body." Most women who have been abused are far from ready to join a volleyball team, but they can be persuaded to take a walk a few times a week, even if just around the block. If even this is difficult to get started, you can get up from your chair and simply say "Let's walk around the neighborhood while we talk." When you return, ask the woman how she feels, compared with before she walked with you. She will probably be surprised that she feels better, even if she is a bit tired. This will be a good time to ask her to exercise on her own at specific times during the week. Ask her to name the day and the hour right there, rather than accepting a vague agreement to exercise "a few times."

Control of Feelings

During the abusive relationship the woman may have felt that her feelings were out of control, even though her fear, sadness, anger, or despair were appropriate reactions to her situation. Now that she is out of the relationship, she may feel ashamed that she is still out of control, when she thinks she should feel wonderful. Reassure the woman that her feelings are to be expected and that she is the one to decide whether to work at changing them and to decide when and how to express them. Knowing she can do so when she gets ready will give her a sense of control and bolster her esteem.

Fear

Fear may be a dominant feeling right after the woman separates from her partner, and sometimes it lasts for months or years. She may try to persuade herself she is exaggerating the danger, or she may take it as an indication she cannot endure the separation. Let her know it makes sense to be more afraid when she does not know her partner's whereabouts than when they lived together. At least then she had some knowledge of the partner's mood and intentions, and might have been able to prepare for the next assault.

It is important to help the woman recognize her fear as a potential protective device that must not be dismissed or denied. When she feels afraid in the house, she might double-check the locks on the doors and windows, see that the phone is working, and perhaps practice (with the receiver down) dialing 911 and saying "I'm at 622 Cedar Street and a man has just broken in." Or her fear may be a clue to purchase more effective locks or iron grates for the windows, or to make plans to move to a secret or safer residence.

Encourage the woman to remind herself of the precautions she has taken and that she has learned to protect and care for herself (and perhaps her children): "I've checked the locks, changed my telephone number, arranged for my neighbor to call the police if there are any strange noises. I'm taking care of myself. I'm using my fear to protect myself." This kind of message has a remarkable effect in reducing fear while validating the need for protection. The woman may also be encouraged to keep a daily log in which she notes the degree of her fear. If she finds that it is diminishing each day or week, she can hope that it will, in time, recede to a tolerable level.

Depression

The woman may be surprised, and even ashamed, to find that she is depressed, just at the time she has finally succeeded in rearranging her life. A letdown is commonly experienced after a whirlwind of moving, filing for divorce, changing the children's schools, finding a new job, or arranging to get public assistance, and perhaps going into and out of a shelter. You can let her know that she may experience a low period after the crisis, that she can weather it, and that you will be there to support her. If a woman does not allow for this period, she may believe her feeling of emptiness, depression, or hopelessness will always be with her. She might feel she has made a big mistake in separating and return to her former partner.

Stress

Discomfort in facing a stress-free existence does not mean the woman wants or likes stress; there are a number of possible reasons for it. It may indicate she is used to a certain level of stress or trauma and needs some time to get used to a new, relaxed pace. If she has not mourned the loss of her partner, she may be prolonging the crisis in order to deny the sadness. She may be embarrassed about feeling sad at the end of a relationship in which she has been brutalized, but she should remember that it is hard to give up the hope that the good times in the relationship might come again. That dream, which she must let go of, may be the most painful of her losses. During the relationship, there was always some shred of hope for change. When the partnership ends, the dream must die, and it is important for the woman to respect her feelings of sadness.

Sadness

If the woman fears her sadness will overwhelm her, she can choose a special time each day to indulge her feelings. She can play sentimental music or look through her photo album and cry. Then at the end of the time she has set— usually a half hour or an hour—she puts those feelings away until the next designated period. When she feels sad at other times, she reminds herself "I don't have to feel sad or cry now. I can do that at eight tonight." If she fears that once she lets herself cry she will never stop, this little gimmick helps her gain a sense of control. It works equally well for the woman who is over-whelmed by grief and "can't stop" crying, though her mourning times may need to be somewhat longer and more frequent.

Anger

As you learn about what has been done to the woman, you may be so angry yourself that any amount of rage seems justified. Justification does not, how-ever, necessarily indicate that the feeling is useful for the person who experi-ences it. A high degree of rage that persists long after the separation and interferes with a woman's desire to "get on with her life" may indicate that most of the feeling is displaced rage at herself for having remained too long with the abusive partner. When she feels better about herself and understands why she stayed, she will probably be able to mourn the loss of the relation-ship, and the rage will diminish.

If the woman becomes distressed about directing her anger at undeserv-ing targets or aware that the intensity of the feeling paralyzes her, she may decide it is important to gain control over the degree and expression of her anger. She can begin by keeping track each day of the instances that cause anger, rage, or irritation. With the help of a counselor she can discover the other, more vulnerable feelings that accompany those feelings. Helplessness, hurt, rejection, and inadequacy are common and are often harder to face than anger.[6]

Once the woman recognizes the vulnerable feelings the anger has masked, she can reduce them by accomplishing tasks, making connections with other people, and appreciating the changes she is going through. As she does that, she will have to cope temporarily with feelings more painful than the anger, but gradually the anger will recede and she will have gained con-trol.

The Sense of a Moral Self

Some women remain with battering partners because of religious commit-ments or because it gives them a sense of moral righteousness. They experi-ence a sense of pride—and even power—that they can endure, and that they are not being violent and abusive. Whether or not they have a deep religious commitment to remain married, whether or not they are even married, they may believe it is just and good to be loyal to their partners. After they leave, they may lose that moral sense of themselves; if that was a major source of self-esteem, they may experience depression and loss of hope.

You can help a woman in that condition maintain appreciation for the loyalty she demonstrated, if at the same time she develops an understanding that she owes loyalty and care to herself. It took a certain kind of moral strength to remain with the partner under threatening circumstances and it will take another kind of moral and psychological strength—which she has begun to demonstrate—to rebuild her life without the partner. If she has children, her duty to provide a safe environment for them should help her accept the righteousness of her decision.

Many women can benefit by examining their ethical and religious principles. They can evaluate the extent to which these principles are simply carry-overs from the teachings of childhood, whether they have been accepted as correct because the abuser insisted they were valid, or whether they have been thoughtfully considered from the perspective of a responsible adult.

A woman may also feel morally deficient because she has assumed that her church or the scriptures on which she depends frown on leaving a violent partner. She will need to find out how her church leaders interpret scripture and then decide whether she agrees with them. You can help the woman see herself as a deserving, moral person, one who has done her best to act on her highest principles under dire circumstances.

Conclusion

Somewhere in the formerly abused woman is a voice that says "Even though I have made mistakes, that is part of my humanity, and I am a valued and valuable human being. I am not the one who is wrong for being battered." You can help her nurture that voice. Your relationship is of great importance in helping the woman gain the confidence that she is a worthy and likable person. You can show her how to change her negative self-talk so she can reduce her feelings of helplessness, hopelessness, and self-criticism. You can encourage her to take small risks, step by step, and reassure her about moral decisions. Your concern and willingness to empathize, your refusal to blame her, and your counseling skills may make the difference between life and death.

Notes

1. See H. Markus and P. Nurius, September 1986, "Possible Selves," *American Psychologist* 41 (9):954–969.
2. See G. NiCarthy, 1986, "Emotional Abuse," in *Getting free: A handbook for women in abusive relationships,* 2nd Ed. (Seattle: Seal Press), 285–304.

3. "Questions to Ask Yourself About a New Man," in *Getting Free*, pp. 227–229.

4. See the self-criticism reduction exercises in *Getting Free*, pp. 118–123.

5. See Evelyn C. White, 1985, *Chain Chain Change: For Black Women Dealing with Physical and Emotional Abuse* (Seattle: Seal Press); Myrna M. Zymbrano, 1985, *Mejor Sola Que Mal Acompanada: Para La Mujer Golpeada/For the Latina in an Abusive Relationship* (Seattle: Seal Press; text in Spanish and English); and K. Lobel (ed.), 1985, *Naming the Violence: Speaking Out About lesbian battering*, Seattle: Seal Press.

When a shelter, group, or counselor designed to help women of specific ethnicity, sexual orientation, or belief system is not available, books can help women feel less alone.

6. See A. Ganley, 1981, *Court-Mandated Counseling for Men Who Batter: A three-day workshop for Mental Health Professionals* (Washington, D.C.: Center For Women Policy Studies) 80–86. Although intended for men who batter, women who want to understand and control anger will find the log described here useful.

13

Helping Battered Women through the Mourning Process

Constance Hoenk Shapiro
Susan Turner

R eligious leaders and counselors traditionally have been sources of solace and comfort to individuals and families experiencing losses in
their lives. In order to offer support to individuals coping with such
grief, the clergy has developed a wide repertoire of skills. In some circumstances, concrete services are needed, and the religious leader can provide
information and referral efforts. In other situations, counseling will be the
appropriate intervention to help the person in need deal with the loss of daily
functioning.

This chapter proposes an approach that moves beyond the traditional
provision of concrete services to address the powerful emotional ties that
keep many women from effecting a separation from their abusive partners.
Such an approach emphasizes the importance of helping the woman to articulate the losses that would be generated if she left her current relationship and,
once recognized, to work through the grief accompanying such losses.

Safety and Crisis Intervention

Initially, the concrete need for safety is what many concerned professionals
emphasize in their services to battered women, and crisis intervention and
separation has been the favored mode of treatment for accomplishing that
goal. Yet the victim's emotional needs are often central to her decision to stay
in a relationship that is abusive, degrading, and sometimes dangerous.

One of the clearest challenges clergy and secular counselors face when
advising battered women is the need to reconcile issues of the woman's physical safety with her wish for family cohesion. Battered women are often
caught in the dilemma of how hard to work at restoring a relationship with
an abusive partner, as evidenced by studies showing that over 70 percent of
women who leave their battering partners later return to them, and that over
half of those leave more than once. While the focus on safety is critical, this

chapter emphasizes the relationship issues and losses, which are also very powerful and painful for victims yet are often ignored.

Anticipating Losses

Central to helping a battered woman evaluate the relationship with an abusive partner is a recognition of the losses that the woman will face if she decides to separate from her partner. In the circumstances faced by a battered woman, some losses probably already have occurred, such as the loss of the idealized relationship. Other losses would be more apparent at the time of actual separation, such as role loss and loss of whatever security the relationship provided.

Loss of the idealized relationship occurs when the woman realizes that the relationship she has hoped for is not attainable with her current partner. Most women grow up with the expectation that they will marry as adults. The image of married women presented in the mass media and the culture (particularly in the religious community), the early peer pressures to become involved in a steady relationship, and the emphasis in social activities on couple participation all combine to encourage women to feel more valued as a partner than as an individual.

Initially, when a woman's partner is abusive, she is shocked and hurt. She does not anticipate that the abuse is going to continue. Later, when the woman comes to that realization, she must give up the dream that this relationship is going to be similar to what she pictures for herself. She loses hope for her ideal marriage.

In order for a woman to leave her partner permanently, she must overcome not only personal fears, the loss of status that marriage holds, and ambivalent feelings about her partner, but also the deeply ingrained attitudes that relationships should be held together at almost any cost, that the disintegration of a relationship is mostly the fault of the woman, and that a broken home is worse for children than a whole, though violent, one.

For a woman who has invested a great deal of time and energy in developing her role as a partner and in improving her performance in tasks associated with it, there is likely to be a feeling of emptiness and failure as she begins an independent existence. The loss of her role as lover, companion, and confidant, as well as whatever role the community saw her in as partner to the man, may cause an emotional void or feelings of emptiness. Depending on her religious upbringing and belief system, the loss may even affect her eternally.

When she considers ending the relationship, or soon after she leaves it, the battered woman also feels a loss of security. Even though she was being abused, she at least knew what she was up against. Once she leaves, she has to face the unknown. Additionally, abusive men are often highly jealous of relationships formed by their partners; the result is that many women are coerced into virtual interpersonal isolation.

For the woman who has had little opportunity to form and experience rewarding relationships, there may be tremendous apprehension at the prospect of meeting interpersonal needs outside the relationship with her former partner. Also, though her partner was abusive, he might have been loving and comforting at times. If he was her primary source of support, whether through coercion or caring, she will feel insecure in moving away from him or in forming new relationships.

The Mourning Process

Since society does not perceive that leaving an abusive situation involves losses, the battered woman may not identify her feelings as those associated with mourning. Nevertheless, such feelings often are felt deeply and, if not acknowledged and responded to appropriately, can be a factor in a woman's decision to return to her abusive partner. For this reason, a cleric must be ready to respond to the woman's emotional needs while at the same time assessing the woman's readiness for concrete services. This is a natural and much-needed opportunity, yet one that is often overlooked.

Working through losses is accomplished by the process of mourning, a process which proceeds with some predictable components. Elisabeth Kubler-Ross's (1969) framework is perhaps the most generic and will be used in this chapter to illustrate the range of emotional responses evoked as a battered woman comes to terms with her losses. The stages in this framework are not meant to be interpreted rigidly, either in terms of sequence or behaviors. Women will respond individually to their losses, depending upon past experiences, coping mechanisms, and the opportunity for anticipatory mourning prior to seeking intervention. However, this basic approach is an excellent one to use in working with these victims.

Denial

Denial can surface and recede for many years. During this stage the battered woman denies that the battering is occurring, or she denies that it is a problem. The former kind of denial is apparent when she is talking with others. The battered woman will make excuses for bruises and burns, perhaps saying that she is accident-prone, and will try to cover up marks with make-up and long-sleeved, high-necked clothing. Because most of the people around her have not seen her partner exhibiting abusive behavior, or do not want to acknowledge that someone they care for is abusive or being abused, it is possible for a battered woman to fool her acquaintances, often for years (see Chapter 1).

Ways to Assist Victims during the Denial Stage

Clergy will rarely be contacted during this stage, unless an abusive incident has just occurred and the woman has left her home. At this time it is very important for the religious leader to discuss with the woman what her initial expectations were for the relationship, and to reinforce the normality of these expectations and the abnormality of the current situation. Many support services for battered women have begun on the principle that no one deserves to be abused, and this concept should be discussed and supported with the woman.

If the woman is receptive, it is helpful to encourage her to assess the positives and the negatives of her relationship. These might be placed in the context of her initial hopes for what the relationship could offer. As the woman shares her feelings, the religious leader can assess the extent to which the woman may have begun to mourn the loss of the idealized relationship. Enabling the woman to speak of her disappointments may help her to move beyond denial to a more realistic assessment of her own needs in the relationship.

The religious leader must convey to the woman a feeling of understanding and support and indicate a willingness to be available in the future. It is also important to give the woman credit for seeking help and to encourage her to consider help-seeking as an indication of good judgment and strength under stressful circumstances. Though the woman may seem to ignore options that a religious leader suggests, such options often are remembered later on. It is important not to make the woman feel that she is doing the wrong thing if she returns to her battering partner. Clerics must remember that, statistically, this is to be expected; therefore, they should not feel a sense of failure if the woman does go back.

Anger

During this stage a battered woman is most likely to get in touch with a religious leader, either because she wants to change her situation or because she has just left her partner. Though the obvious target of anger will be the abusive partner, the battered woman may also feel anger toward parents who pushed her into a marriage or were not sufficiently supportive about her leaving; toward friends and associates who cannot understand why she is leaving her partner (the abuse is usually not public knowledge), or who never perceived that she was a victim of abuse and therefore never offered to help; toward his parents, who may blame her for being inadequate; and toward children who might resent being away from home and their father. In addition, there may be a certain amount of anger directed inward for having invested so much in the relationship and for not having left earlier.

The anger that is most likely to be discussed openly is anger towards the partner, and even that may be suppressed due to embarrassment, guilt, and partial denial. Anger that is suppressed may come out as a high level of energy directed toward change or as self-punishment. In the latter case the battered woman may become accident-prone or may develop a cold or illness that hangs on.

Helping the Angry Victim

The anger stage is usually the one most accepted by society, and as such it is reinforced heavily. However, as with any stage in the mourning process, it should not continue indefinitely. A woman may feel anger while still in the relationship, and this will tend to continue after she has left. The religious leader should encourage a battered woman to express her anger and reassure her that these feelings are rational. However, the religious leader might want to discourage the woman from severing relationships with family or friends based on the anger she presently feels toward them. Those people who have not fulfilled the hopes of the battered woman in the past may later be more supportive of the woman as they find out more about the abusive situation, or as they see the battered woman try to make definite changes in her life.

Anger against the battering partner is to be expected, but for two reasons acts of retribution are not desirable. First, a batterer will not necessarily stop the abuse when the woman leaves, so any malicious action that she takes against him may be answered with escalated violence. Second, these acts may be regretted in the future—to the extent that in her guilt the woman may return to the batterer.

If a battered woman is angry with herself, the religious leader should acknowledge this and be willing to talk about it. Some women, especially those who believe themselves to be at fault in the relationship, tend to direct their anger against themselves rather than at their partners. Clergy should be aware that this anger is self-destructive and can lead to depression.

One approach to refocus such anger is to help the woman become future oriented, instead of dwelling on the regrets of her past. This future orientation can stimulate discussion of new behaviors and directions the woman can undertake, as well as giving her a new sense of power and control over her life.

A battered woman is often at the most motivated stage when she feels anger. At this point she is likely to leave her partner and try to set up an independent living situation. She may want to get an Order of Protection, file for divorce, and get legal custody of any children. Though this is a healthy response to an unhealthy situation, the religious leader has the responsibility to discuss possible consequences with the woman, not to get caught up in the woman's energy and enthusiasm.

Bargaining

Bargaining is a measure of the ambivalence a battered woman feels at her decision to leave her partner. On the one hand, having discharged her anger, she may be more open to the positive feelings that her partner once was capable of generating. On the other hand, she may feel energized to take a chance, and her knowledge of the various options open to her may be both tantalizing and intimidating. Her response is likely to be vacillation between the wish to be secure and the wish to be free from the fear of abuse.

Since an abusive male's response to his partner's leaving is often abject dejection and profuse apology, the woman also is faced with pressure from him to return. Her response, bargaining for changes on both sides, may consist of a plan to return conditionally. The conditions for return usually include an end to the abuse and may include marital counseling, more autonomy for the woman, or working toward other improvements in the relationship.

Important Bargaining Considerations

Reality testing is an important response of the religious leader to the bargaining phase: How realistic is it to expect any or all of the changes? Has the partner ever shown the capacity to make such changes in the past? How long did those changes last? What will the woman's response be if she returns and the changes cannot be sustained? The woman can be reminded that the decision to return at any time is hers, but why now?

If the woman can identify that she is returning out of a sense of loneliness or being overwhelmed, the religious leader may be able to help her think of other ways of coping with these feelings. The woman should be helped to believe that any decision to return should be made from a source of strength rather than weakness. If the woman does decide to return to her partner, the religious leader should emphasize the continuing availability of services and should encourage periodic contact.

Grief

This emotion may not surface as a separate stage, but will usually appear on and off throughout the anger stage and then appear again when the anger is more fully resolved or after the losses have become concrete—that is, when the woman has left the abusive situation. Because of the social expectations to feel only anger and relief, grief is usually the most suppressed and misunderstood emotion. As such it will rarely be discussed directly, but a woman will often hint at it by saying how tired and defeated she feels. She might also experience physical pain, discomfort, or exhaustion. Another expression of grief may be evident when the woman discusses returning to the relationship and focuses on the good parts of that relationship. She may also seek to move precipitously into another romantic relationship rather than to acknowledge and work through the feelings of sadness she experiences.

Your Role in the Grieving Process

Clergy must serve a key role in helping the woman to recognize grief as a normal and expectable response to the losses she has sustained. It might be necessary for the religious leader to initiate a discussion of loss and accompanying grief because the battered woman may have internalized society's expectation that she feel relief at the separation, rather than sadness. Once again, though the woman may choose to bear her grief privately, the religious leader empowers her by increasing her range of options—in this case, her option of having various and seemingly incongruous feelings.

A sensitive counselor can help the victim to understand that depression, crying, inappropriate laughter, anxiety, agitation, and lethargy are expressions of the grief she is working through. For the woman who initially feels as if she is losing control rather than gaining it, this information may help her to make connections between her feelings and her progress in coming to terms with the losses she has sustained. A woman may experience a higher than usual incidence of illness or accidents during the grieving process. Such consequences might be especially pronounced in a woman who is trying to repress her grief or who has turned feelings of anger inward.

The religious leader must recognize that a battered woman is someone who probably has experienced prolonged periods of stress before seeking help. Medical professionals writing on the physiological impact of stress concur that it leaves one more vulnerable to illness (Moos, 1976; Pelletier, 1977). Therefore, clergy should be active during the grieving phase in helping the woman toward self-nurturing behaviors and toward finding interpersonal supports to offset the continuing effects of stress. Physiological symptoms should receive prompt medical attention.

Support groups of battered women are an important source of solace at this time, especially because the battered woman may be so caught up in emotional turmoil that she has little energy left to pursue plans for independent living. The woman may feel a compelling need to respond to her partner's entreaties to return and to believe his reassurances that he will never again abuse her. Other battered women can serve as a source of encouragement, concrete information, and hope at a time when life seems especially bleak.

In her desire to experience a respite from the painful feelings of grief, returning to her partner may seem like a desirable choice for the woman. At this point, without being judgmental, the religious leader will want to review with the woman the outcome of previous returns to her partner and to establish whether there are any new factors that cause the woman to expect a different outcome. This is also a time to remind the woman that in the loneliness of grief it is tempting to seek comfort in familiar relationships; the religious leader can help the woman recall constructive responses that she may have had to earlier grief experiences in her life and use these earlier experiences to help the woman appreciate that, though painful, grief does diminish in time.

If the woman holds firm to her decision to return to her partner, the religious leader should encourage the woman to keep in touch and should make clear that leaving the abusive situation is not a condition for maintaining contact, although it is an option to the woman if she chooses to pursue it.

Acceptance

This is generally the final stage in resolving the losses connected with leaving the abusive partner. The specific ways that this stage is expressed may be different, but leaving the battering relationship, beginning an independent living situation, and seeking means of becoming self-supporting are common moves. Acceptance has not necessarily occurred when the woman leaves the battering situation; indicators other than physical distance from the batterer are important for clergy to assess.

Acceptance is characterized by a firm feeling that the woman has made the right decision and is able to discuss her life by looking beyond the battering relationship. The woman can discuss her former situation with more distance, and without feeling the pain, guilt, and extreme anger that she once felt. This does not mean that she will no longer cry over her loss, but she will not experience those feelings as strongly.

The battered woman who has fully accepted her losses will start to feel more positive about herself and generally will feel in control of her situation. At this stage she will usually terminate the counseling relationship with the religious leader, due to a lack of need for these services and a desire to move beyond behaviors connected with the former relationship.

Completing the Mourning Process

Though the previous three stages often are not distinct or entirely sequential, acceptance can be seen as the final stage in the mourning process. The woman's coping mechanisms of denial, anger, bargaining, and grief no longer stand in the way of effecting a permanent separation from her abusive partner. Clergy can be helpful by providing technical assistance—helping the woman find a place to live, identifying child care options, letting her know about job assistance services, and perhaps explaining responsibilities such as checking accounts that may not have been within the woman's sphere of experience.

During this period the religious leader is not needed for support so much as during the previous two phases, but it is important not to feel that help given earlier in the relationship has been forgotten. Often a battered woman will want to start fresh by changing locations, reestablishing old friendships, and disengaging from support systems that may serve only as reminders of the battering situation. As the helping relationship nears its end, the religious leader should recount the progress made, help the woman appreciate her own role in the changes she has made, and make it clear that the religious leader will be available in the future—even if only to hear good news.

Conclusion

When people in crisis seek religious counseling, the tendency of many clerics is to offer concrete services that will promote and maximize self-sufficiency. However, provision of only concrete services to battered women may ignore the powerful emotional ties that hold them in destructive relationships. The feelings of loss and inadequacy that many woman experience at the prospect of living independently must be addressed before these women can be expected to utilize the concrete services essential to their independence and physical safety. Though women cannot be prevented from returning to abusive relationships, clerics can give them the option to leave by acknowledging the losses that they will endure and helping them to work through those losses.

References

Kubler-Ross, E. 1969. *On death and dying.* New York: Macmillan.

Moos, R. H. 1976. *Human Adaption.* Lexington, MA: Lexington Books, p. 12.

Pelletier, K. R. 1977. *Mind as healer, mind as slayer: A holistic approach to preventing stress disorder.* New York: Delta Books, pp. 71–73 and 109–112.

14
Culture and Ethnicity in Family Violence

In exploring the topic of cultural and ethnic sensitivity in working with abuse victims, the editors encountered a vast range of differences which demand the careful attention of both the religious and secular treatment community. Our limited space does not allow exploration of each religious denomination—not to mention the victim's personal interpretation and observance of their sect—nor does it permit adequate discussion of other minority issues. However, the importance of these differences and their therapeutic implications must be considered on an individual basis, and stereotyping must be rigorously avoided.

Overviews of three groups introduce some of these special considerations. Following these examples, Cassandra Mason and Rosie Bingham present a model and the tools needed to develop greater awareness of specific populations.

Needs of the Jewish Abuse Victim
Barbara Harris

Judaism and violence: the pairing is incongruous. Domestic tranquility *(Shalom Bayit)* has been a desired characteristic of the Jewish family for generations. It is a highly valued cultural trait and requires much teamwork, understanding, respect, forgiveness, and compromise. When abuse occurs and family breakdown occurs, the Jewish wife has great difficulty reaching out. She is trapped by the very myths that she has helped create. Because her role is one of bonding and divorce is unacceptable, the religiously observant Jewish woman cries in silence so no one will know of her shame and disgrace.

Meanwhile, the Jewish community that fosters these ideals believes Jewish homes are immune to such problems and does not have the knowledge or services to aid abuse victims. The religious community's basic reaction to domestic violence is denial: "It does not happen here." When I, as a shelter director, spoke to religious leaders of Reform, Conservative, and Orthodox Jews, I was told "not in my congregation; maybe the others, but not in my congregation." The most common reaction to wife abuse is the isolation of the woman from her support systems: family, friends, and religious community. Shame, guilt, threats, and a sense of failure have prevented the battered Jewish woman from reaching out to these resources. If help is sought, and it usually is not, it is often disguised by peripheral complaints: poor sleeping patterns, feelings of inadequacy, loss of appetite, inability to control her children, and a general feeling of depression. It may be several months before she feels confident enough to reveal the horrible secret she is carrying. The fear of being judged a failure and called the cause of the violence is great.

Jewish professionals working in the human service field may also isolate their Jewish clients. They believe in the myths surrounding courtship, marriage, and family life, and they have an idealized concept of the Jewish marriage. Yes, they may recognize reasons to seek help, but seldom do Jewish counselors consider violence as a contributing factor. Therefore, they may hesitate to ask the questions "Were you abused?" and "Did he beat you or the children?" They themselves are threatened by the existence of domestic violence. Family strength is an essential coping mechanism. Family problems are never to surface or be revealed to outsiders. Thus, Jewish professionals are reluctant to expose violence in the home or even to study it. They are torn between their professional commitment and their Jewishness. Greater education is necessary.

Abuse in interfaith relationships may create additional stressors because of strong cultural pressures against such marriages. Being Jewish and married in the Jewish community makes it difficult for the victim to reach out or to reach in.

Thus, the special needs of the Jewish woman have not been considered by the various agencies that deal with this population. They need to explore the cultural aspects of Judaism; the importance of the family and the parts various family members play must be studied. The impact of the stereotypical role of the Jewish wife and mother has to be examined, as well as that of the ideal Jewish husband and the Jewish professional.

Sensitivity training must be encouraged; in the religious seminary rabbis must be made aware of domestic violence and its impact on the family. They must learn not to be hesitant in asking women who come to them for help with marital problems if they have been abused. The woman who seeks solace in the rabbi's office needs belief, sympathy, and understanding.

Religiously observant Jewish women have other special needs that must be taken into consideration. Their lives heavily involve dietary laws and the schooling of their children. Many religious women have chosen to remain in abusive situations rather than leave because they lacked an appropriate shelter. Transition Center in New York City is the only city-funded shelter in the United States that offers kosher facilities upon request.

Religious education is another area in which the observant Jewish woman has special needs. When a woman leaves home with her children, she wants to be sure that their schooling has continuity. This may require special schools or yeshivas. Unless a community can offer this resource the woman will stay home—her children's religious education is important. A worker who has to plan for a Jewish woman must take into account where she falls in the Jewish religious spectrum; her beliefs could range anywhere from unaffiliated to ultra-orthodox. Dietary and religious practices, dress, and schooling must all be considered in formulating a feasible treatment plan.

Conclusion

Jewish women are not unlike other women who are abused. They hurt, bleed, and cry, but they also have special needs: the need to be understood by the community and professional, the need to overcome the myths surrounding Jewish marriages, and the need for people to understand them and their relationships within the Jewish world. They also have the concrete needs of dietary restrictions and special schooling for their children. As these needs are met, the abused Jewish woman will see a brighter future.

Native American Clients
Tillie Black Bear

Minorities as a whole have little control or power. This situation leads to patterns of helplessness and frustration—an ideal breeding ground for violence. Therefore, the Native American relies heavily on the values of the community and culture rather than Anglo rules and practices. The dominant values are concerned with the "here and now" and basic survival. Identity issues and communication differences are very critical in working with these clients.

Indian women in general are not tuned into themselves as women and do not perceive themselves as having any control. The Indian male's lack of a positive self-image results in a sense of normlessness and helplessness. On the Native American reservation there is a strong macho image which will be upheld by cultural standards regardless of Anglo dictates. Because the community is closed and resistant to outside influences, these values are likely to continue. Alcoholism is a strong contributing factor as well.

Counseling Indian women is impossible unless certain cultural distinctions are understood and observed. Because of their isolation most women are unaware of any resources and are not educated about abuse. For them it is a lifestyle from which there is no deliverance. If a Native American woman does seek counseling, she will not do so in the usual Anglo fashion. Anglo women are inclined to talk and express feelings whereas Indian women are more reserved.

Therefore, therapists are urged to develop a comfort with silence and approach clients initially in a nondirect way. It may take several meetings before the Native American client is willing to open up. Too much talk and a desire to rush treatment will often terminate the client's desire for contact. It takes time for trust to develop, and therapists need to be sensitive to this value rather than label the client as resistant.

Conclusion

Role conflict and communication difficulties slow down the war against family violence in the Native American family. Values are different from the values of the dominant society. For instance, the Indian woman will tolerate beatings but not infidelity. Because the community still gives cultural acceptance to abuse and offers few alternatives, the treatment community will see few Indian women. Therapists must develop a new style in approaching these victims and recognize that Indian and Anglo priorities are different.

Quaker Family Violence: Bringing Peace Home

Judith L. Brutz
Craig M. Allen

The 300-year history of the Religious Society of Friends has been a history of consistent advocacy for peace and nonviolence in the world. Unfortunately, recent findings have suggested that these pacifist values, surprisingly, do not ensure freedom from violence in Quaker families. This revelation among Friends in the United States and Canada is so startling that a growing movement has developed to focus on the problems and needs of these families and to find ways to respond that are healing and growth-producing.

Bringing Peace Home

An awareness has grown among Friends that many of their families are in trouble. Regardless of the strength of their particular theological beliefs or of the genuineness of their pacifist values, there has been an emerging, somewhat reluctant willingness to look at the realities of family life. Being a nonhierarchically organized religion has meant that efforts are independent and usually isolated from one group of Friends to another. However, because of intense interest across the various branches of Friends, individuals and groups are beginning to look toward more unified and unifying approaches.

Three main purposes of these new programs and approaches being offered are (1) to raise awareness, (2) to begin equipping members to respond to families in healing and growthful ways, and (3) to relate the religious faith and practice of the Quaker religion to daily family lives.

Initial engagements or writings have brought to the attention of audiences of Friends the existence of Quaker family violence. Frequently, some members in the audiences have problems accepting the information, but this basic information is the first step.

The second important area of exploration involves the barriers to receiving divine healing in the family. Particular problems are overextension in commitments and "chronic stoicism," or pretending all is well when it is not. These two dynamics help create a condition of denial that is toxic to spiritual, personal, and relational growth. From a desire to equip leadership for pastoral care, unwritten rules and attitudes that govern how religious leaders relate to families with problems are now being carefully identified and discussed. Some that are typically cited are these:

1. Do not interfere in family life.
2. Deal with someone's problem only if it affects the Meeting (congregation).
3. Do not act until someone asks for help.
4. Do not hurt anyone's feelings.
5. Avoid anger and conflict at all costs.

Finally, efforts at relating Quaker religious beliefs and practices to daily lives involve discussing the relevance of the Peace Testimony to family relations. A testimony in the Religious Society of Friends is an approved and corporate statement of belief about a particular subject; it is held up to the membership as a guide for conduct and is also a statement made to the world as a witness of faith.

In addition to the Peace Testimony, there are testimonies on education, equality, oath-taking, and using alcohol and drugs. Quite remarkably, there is not a testimony on family. Some groups of Friends feel that there needs to be a re-focus on the family.

Conclusion

Raising the awareness of family violence in the Friends' religion is opening new vistas to ministry and action. Not only are prevention and intervention programs developing, but exploration of theology is bringing a fresh approach to relating religion to daily family life. The implications for this movement go beyond the Religious Society of Friends to other religions. Openly dealing with violence and other family problems within a religion is likely to bring healing and spiritual growth for the whole religious body.

Developing a Sensitivity for Culture and Ethnicity in Family Violence
Cassandra Hoffman–Mason
Rosie P. Bingham

There is a dearth in the literature by, for, and about the various American peoples who do not ascribe to the European-American worldview in respect to their perception of counseling domestic issues about violence.

The negative and devalued status accorded to minorities is of utmost importance in this chapter. The authors have elected to use the concept and term *culturally/ethnically different*. The term therefore will refer to all oppressed peoples. Behaviors of these groups contrast with the European-American middle-class standard, but that contrast will not be considered negative here.

This chapter is intended to focus on those peoples in an effort to encourage and influence consideration by people-helpers. Clients' values are of the utmost importance when a professional is working with people from cultures different from his or her own. To ignore cultural differences is tantamount to coercing the client either to think as the people-helper does or to get no help.

Understanding the Client

Perhaps the most important skill that a people-helper needs to acquire and develop is sensitivity to the client's expression of the issues, concerns, and problems and to the client's wants, needs, and proposals for resolution. In context, people-helpers' priorities must necessarily be secondary to, and formed around, those of the client if counselors are to fulfill their responsibility.

Basic to working with clients are an acceptance of their perception of self as relevant and coherent in their own terms and an understanding of their individual worldviews. Without a clear understanding between counselor and client of their respective worldviews, the likelihood of progress is virtually nonexistent.

Therefore, the validation of cross-cultural differences is imperative. It seems appropriate to rethink the concept of the term *different*. Do you perceive difference as negative when counseling someone who is culturally or ethnically not the same as you? Some theorists have explored the topic of cross-cultural counseling and put forth their notions from the perspective of worldview.

Worldviews and Cultural Ethnic Sensitivity

Wade Nobles, in his article entitled "Extended Self, Rethink the So-Called Negro Self Concept," discusses the notion of worldviews. Sue (1981, p. 3) broadly defines a worldview as "how a person perceives his/her relationship to the world (nature, institutions, other people, things, etc.)." Nobles believes that one's worldview will dictate, or at least influence, the way one behaves. He describes two worldviews: one European, the other African. Figure 14–1 is his schemata of those two.

A counselor with a European-American worldview who works with a client possessing an African worldview will very likely have problems advising the client successfully. When the client perceives that abuse is occurring, the concern is about how her group, not herself, will be perceived. Though the client may want to end her pain, she is conscious of not wanting to cause harm to her group. She may feel that revealing her abuse will cast aspersions on other members of her culture/ethnic group. The insensitive counselor may believe that the client must throw all those beliefs out and concentrate on her own welfare. The therapeutic relationship may thus stagnate, and the client may end counseling before the situation is resolved. After this experience, the client may continue in the abusive relationship and be even more reluctant to pursue counseling in the future.

If, on the other hand, the counselor is sensitive to the client's value of collective responsibility, therapy could proceed quite differently. The religious leader or secular therapist could help the client use the community or a group of others with her same view to discover a reasonable solution to the problem. Such solutions might include group pressure so that the abuser is forced into the stance of acting as an individual rather than as part of the

European Worldview   African Worldview

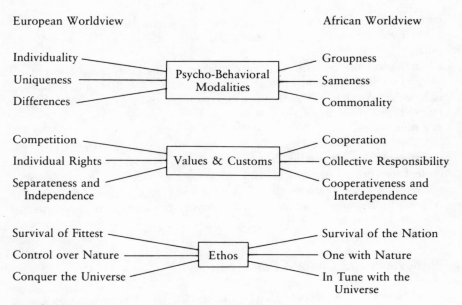

Figure 14–1. **African and European Worldviews**

Source: Wade Nobles, "Extended Self, Rethinking the So–called Negro Self Concept," *Journal of Black Psychology,* February, 1976.

group. Group pressure might also create cognitive dissonance for the abuser and group support for the client.

Sue's discussion (1981) on worldviews expands the notions presented by Nobles by presenting his ideas in terms broad enough to include a wide range of cultural and social orientations that manifest worldviews. Others (for example, Pedersen, Louner and Draguns, 1976) have described several world-views, including Asian, Native American, Black, and others. Sue even refers to the possibility that individuals with the same nationality and race but belonging to different economic classes may hold different worldviews. Therefore, his framework is particularly useful to clinicians and may be of further interest to the reader.

Self-Assessment

It is important for a counselor to perceive his or her own worldview. You could begin by looking at the worldviews that have already been described (Nobles, 1976; Pedersen, Louner and Draguns, 1976; Sue, 1981; Wilson-

Schaef, 1981). Does one describe your position more than another? What is different for you? What are your attitudes and behaviors?

When working with persons who are culturally/ethnically different from yourself, what is important to consider? Here are some questions to ask yourself: What are your preconceived notions and stereotypes? Do you have prejudices or are you making decisions based solely on your own experiences? Do you feel threatened by this person's difference? Do you think you understand enough about the client's cultural/ethnic perceptions to do an adequate job? Are you too biased or uncomfortable to be effective? Does this particular case pose issues that you think you cannot deal with or that you are unwilling to deal with? At the outset do you feel frustrated, philosophically at odds, or biased?

It is legitimate, professional, and responsible to decline to work with a client whom you think you cannot help or with whom you have basic disagreements. Indeed, it is more responsible to bow out early than to stay and possibly harm the client. Your final responsibility as a professional in these occasional situations is to help the client find someone who is better suited to her needs.

Others' Worldviews

After honestly answering the preceding questions, you will realize that there are many things about culturally/ethnically different groups that you do not know. When the culturally/ethnically different client comes to you for counseling, where do you begin? What information do you already have? And what do you need to know? How and where will you find out what you do not know? It is important to appreciate how complex the answers to these questions can be.

If you are a European/American, middle-class-oriented counselor working with a client who is not of that orientation, there will be a number of issues at hand affected by differing worldviews. Of course, in some ways this is true of all clients, because few clients and counselors have identical backgrounds. But in cases involving culturally/ethnically different clients, such issues become critical to treatment.

Therefore, it is often helpful to encourage a client to share her sense of self, especially since there are many people who ascribe to the European/American middle-class standard and worldview who do not initially appear to do so. Social, political, and economic pressures in our country have led many Americans to assimilate. Understanding the client's history of dealing with these pressures will encourage sensitivity about the client's worldview as well as your own.

What Can a People-Helper Do?

First, it is most important to listen carefully and solicit further clarification of issues or concepts you do not understand clearly. Second, accept the client's identification of issues in the context presented as valid. Emphasize the client's strengths and explore suggested options before addressing less positive factors. Ask clients specifically what expectations they have for treatment and what kind of help they expect from you.

It may be difficult for the client to articulate adequately what she wants. If so, the people-helper can employ different counseling skills to help the client identify more specifically. It is often helpful to have the client address what is not desired or liked in the relationship, then to help deduce from those expressions what is preferred. The client's extended family, neighborhood, community, and church group may offer support.

Where to Find Help

Parker, Valley, and Geary (1986) suggest some ways to facilitate understanding in addition to using listening skills and being sensitive to ethnic/cultural variations. Here are some experiences that can help.

1. *Read* histories (recent, remote, and current) authored by people of that particular group about whom you seek knowledge. Explore novels, autobiographies, plays, poems, and musical lyrics.
2. *Attend* or participate in a community event. Experience traditions, customs, and cultural/ethnic art forms.
3. *Visit* the community through personal liaisons with families to experience first-hand the lifestyles of the particular cultural/ethnic group about which you seek knowledge.
4. *Consult* with and solicit help from other professionals who have personal experience or knowledge about the cultural/ethnic group about which you seek knowledge.

In your quest for knowledge it is important to be open and flexible. There is always the potential for embarrassment, surprise, and even shock, as making progress and growth leaves us open to many kinds of experiences.

Conclusion

The increased mobility and migration of a variety of peoples to and within the United States creates a phenomenon that significantly affects individuals, families, and communities. The concomitant stresses of relocation, displacement, and cultural shock often exacerbate efforts to function effectively. The distancing from one's natal and extended family as well as one's usual geographical environment often provides a climate conducive to abusive, violent, and assaultive behavior. Isolation from one's usual environment under favorable conditions is difficult. Imagine the sense of insecurity, fear, and loneliness engendered in a family where there is abuse or violence. For the visibly identifiable culturally/ethnically different person who is frequently ostracized because of her or his physical characteristics, the problem is compounded. Our hope is to develop adequate cultural sensitivity and understanding.

References

Freire, P. 1970. *Pedagogy of the Oppressed.* New York: Seabury Press.

Nobles, W. 1976. *Extended Self: Rethinking the So-called Negro Self Concept.* Journal of Black Psychology. 2:15–24.

Parker, W. M., M. Valley, and C. A. Geary, 1986. *Acquiring Cultural Knowledge for Counselor Trainees: A Multi-faceted Approach.* Counselor Education and Supervision. 26(1):61–71.

Pedersen, P., W. Louner and J. Draguns. 1976. *Counseling Across Cultures.* Honolulu: University of Hawaii Press.

Sue, D. W. 1981. *Counseling the Culturally Different: Theory and Practice.* New York: Wiley.

Wilson-Schaef, A. 1981. *Women's Reality: An Emerging Female System in the White System.* Minneapolis: Winston Press.

15
Interviewing Children about Sensitive Topics

Marcia K. Morgan
Virginia M. Friedemann

E very abused child needs someone with whom to talk. Yet when a child
is in an unhealthy, abusive family environment, it is often difficult to
talk to that child about sensitive topics. Encouraging children to
avow their traumatic world can be challenging. This chapter will present
guidelines on how you can achieve this task and offer a vulnerable child an
alternative to abuse.

When we talk about *interviewing* a child about sensitive issues, it is important to define what is meant by this term. The role of the cleric in an
interview is to provide support to children who are experiencing problems.
The interview is the vehicle from which the cleric can determine what additional services are necessary for the child (for example, a report to police or
child protective service agency, or referral to a psychologist). We are not
encouraging clergy to take over the role of the social worker or police officer,
but we do hope that through appropriate interviewing techniques on everyone's part, the child will receive maximum help and support.

Problems in Interviewing Abuse Victims

Interviewing children who have been abused is not an easy task. If we recognize and anticipate the basic communication problems that may arise, we are
better able to assist the child who may be reluctant to talk. This reluctance
stems from four major factors: fear, limited vocabulary, embarrassment, and
short attention span.

Being Approachable and Accessible

Traditionally, a clergyperson has been thought of as someone in whom to
confide to obtain forgiveness or to help focus one's direction in life. A person
who confides in a minister is often an adult who knows of the clergy's services

and, during the interview, is able to articulate the problem. This is generally not the case with abused children. You must not only go out of your way to make your existence known to children, but you must show them that you are willing and able to talk about very sensitive, personal issues.

There are two preliminary steps necessary to set the foundation for your interviews. First, children in your congregation must know of your availability. You can make them aware by displaying posters that include your name, office location, telephone number, hours, and the types of things you are there to talk about, such as drugs, sex, and problems at home or school. These posters can be displayed in any area visible to kids, such as youth meeting areas or Sunday school rooms. You might consider making a poster pocket containing your business cards or cutting the bottom of the sign into one-inch pull-off strips with pertinent information on each strip. Try to attend youth activities from time to time. By doing so, you become a familiar face, and the opportunity to talk with kids and the probability of disclosure are increased. Make your availability to talk about sensitive issues known in other settings, such as from the pulpit or during children's story-telling sessions. Set up special youth programs specifically on sensitive topics; this might include inviting a guest speaker from a social service agency or police department to talk to kids about abuse prevention.

Even though you make yourself available, there is always a chance that a child might be reluctant to talk to you because you are a reminder of the abuser (due to your sex, age, hair color, race, or some other factor). Therefore, publicizing the availability of an alternative counselor, such as a spouse, co-clergy, or trained lay person, is also important.

The second preliminary step is that you must *prove* your approachability. Studies show that 85 percent of our communication is nonverbal. You may be saying the best things in the world to kids, but if you have a red face, are playing with a pencil, or are not making good eye contact, chances are abused children will not come talk to you. They probably think that revealing the abuse problem would only make you more uncomfortable. Therefore, practice talking out loud about abuse with a reliable friend or spouse or in front of a mirror. Also, practice responding to potentially embarrassing or difficult questions a child might ask ("What is rape?" "Is it OK if I touch my uncle's pee-pee?" "Does it mean I'm a bad person if I get spanked every night?"). This preparation will help make both you and the child at ease in the interview.

Make sure that in addition to exhibiting your ease in discussing sensitive topics, you show children your human side. Finger painting with the kindergarten, going to a pizza party, and playing softball or board games with children will let them see you as a real person.

A sensitive issue, such as the suspected emotional, physical, or sexual abuse of a child, could come to your attention in a variety of ways. Someone in the church—a family friend, the child's playmate, the Sunday school teacher—may accidentally or purposefully tell you about the suspected abuse. Even though you have set the foundation for children to come talk to you, there will still be others to whom you need to reach out.

In either situation, three preparatory steps are important in order to ensure a comfortable, effective interview. The first step is to gather adequate background information. Knowing something about the child and family may help you know what to ask and not ask. If the child has not sought you out, is there enough information to justify your seeking out the child? Second, selecting information to help facilitate discussion will make the interview go more smoothly. The more you know about the child, the more prepared you will be in selecting appropriate interviewing tools. Third, choosing an appropriate location will greatly affect whether or not your interview is successful. These three steps are outlined below.

Gathering Background Information

Gathering background information takes good interpersonal skills and a sensitivity to the concerns and insecurities of other people. If caution is not exercised at this stage, rumors can run rampant in a congregation. Nonetheless, doing your homework is important. You have only one opportunity to create an environment in which the child can talk freely and comfortably. The more facts you have about the child and the family's life, the greater the chances of achieving this goal. To establish rapport at the beginning of the interview, for example, knowledge of a child's interests and hobbies is a must.

Selecting Interview Tools

As you plan your interview time with the child, it is helpful to have a variety of items available. These should include blank paper, coloring books (not specific to abuse), crayons, modeling clay, a toy telephone, hand puppets, and drawings. Paper, coloring books, and clay help a young child dispense nervous energy. By engaging in familiar activities, a child will usually relax and talk more easily. Blank paper and crayons can also be useful if a child wants to draw or demonstrate something that has happened. Talking to an inanimate object, such as a toy telephone, can help a child open up and discuss a personal incident. This is especially true for a shy child who may have difficulty talking face-to-face with an adult. Likewise, talking through hand puppets and stuffed animals can be easier for the reluctant child who fears adult confrontation.

Although not to be used initially, anatomical dolls may help a child explain and describe incidents of sexual abuse (more on this later). However, anatomical dolls should not be used without first checking with the appropriate state agencies because some states would not accept this interview as valid in a court of law. Therefore the usage of dolls should generally be referred to professionals in the community who are familiar with the state laws, court and interviewing guidelines. (For more information about anatomical dolls, contact Migima Designs, Inc. 1243½ Oak Street, Eugene, OR 97401.)

Choosing a Location

An important decision to make before an interview is where it will be held. The location at which you initially contact a child will greatly influence the child's ability to talk openly with you. Although your office may provide privacy, it can be a scary place for a child. This is especially true if you sit behind your desk and put the child across from you. Try to find another quiet room or give the child your chair, bringing it around from behind your desk to make the setting more relaxed. Let your secretary know you need complete privacy, including no telephone interruptions.

If you must go to the family home to interview a child, try to follow these guidelines: (1) Schedule your contact for a time when you believe the suspected abuser is not at home. (2) Do not call before your arrival and explain the purpose of your visit. (3) Insist on privacy, which means a room with a door that can be closed. Explain that it is best not to have family members present at the interview since their presence often inhibits the child. (4) Do not use a bedroom, especially the child's, if you suspect sexual abuse. (5) If weather permits, sit outside on the grass, with the child facing away from the house.

Remember, your goal is to find a setting that is both safe and private where you and the child can talk without interruptions. Any interruption to which you attend gives the impression that it is more important than the child, usually resulting in the child's sharing little information because the child wants the interview to be the most important thing to you.

Establishing Rapport

When you first meet with the child, you must build rapport by establishing a level of trust and communication. If the child has been abused, doing so may be no easy task. Abused children often do not trust adults.

There are five phases to building rapport in an interview. First, respond to the child's questions and emotions with honesty, empathy, and concern. Second, be sure you respond in a calm, comfortable manner. Third, remind the child of your role as a clergy member who is there to help people with their problems. Fourth, reassure the child that he or she is not alone—that in fact, you talk to lots and lots of children about all sorts of things. Fifth, physically get down to the child's level. If the child wants to sit on the floor, you sit on the floor too.

Responding to the Child's Emotions

It is very likely that a child will display various emotions during an interview, especially when deciding whether or not to disclose information. It is very important in an interview to acknowledge the emotions you see. If a child cries, ask "Why are you crying?" If a child fidgets and seems nervous, ask "Are you comfortable? Why not?" Do not assume you know why a child is acting emotional. Likewise, you should not suggest specific feelings by asking questions such as "What are you afraid of? Are you scared? Embarrassed?" If you bring up these feelings, the child may sense they are to be expected. Do not suggest problems, but respond to the information the child offers to you. Many times a child will say something like "Bad things will happen if I tell." If so, ask the child what bad things, and at the same time, try to find out who might have suggested these things would happen. One by one, talk about the bad things the child has mentioned. Help the child understand that most of these things will not happen, but some might. No matter what happens, reassure the child that you will be there to help give support and guidance. Let the child know that everyone worries and, in fact, you have talked to other children with the same concerns. Explain that these children had some things change in their lives, but they are okay now.

This is a point in the interview where your special skills and expertise as a clergy member can be very helpful for a child. You can use scripture to reassure the child that it is appropriate to talk to you. Matthew 19:14 shows that Jesus always made time for children; as his representative in the church, you do also. Let the child know that, as the pastor, your job is to help shoulder burdens for your congregation and help solve problems: "Give your burdens to the Lord, He will carry them" (Psalms 55:22). Explain that as a child of God, the abused child is blameless in His sight: "You shall be blameless before the Lord your God" (Deuteronomy 18:13). Reiterate that you understand the abuse was something an adult did without the child's consent (even though the child may have "gone along"), so the child is not to blame for the adult's actions.

Many times a child will test you during the early part of an interview. This testing helps the child decide if you are a safe person with whom to talk and someone who can understand this information. To do this, a child may talk about a variety of things, but generally not abusive incidents. Above all, be patient and listen to everything a child discloses. Frequently, a child will offer related information, such as "My cousin Joe visited last week and he's mean." By pursuing any opening a child presents, you will be able to help problem areas surface.

Avoiding Leading Questions

Once you are involved in an interview, it is very important not to suggest anything from the information you may already have gathered. Even though you are not a part of the criminal justice system, asking leading questions may make it difficult for others to present a court case later. Leading questions are questions that present information not yet stated by the child, or include the answer in the question itself. Basically, any question that requires only a "yes" or "no" answer could be considered a leading question. Ask questions beginning with *what, where, when, how,* and *who:* for example, "What happened next?" "Where were you?" "When did that happen?" "How did you know that was called _____?" "Who was there?" It is hard to maintain this type of questioning throughout an interview, so practice with your family and staff and learn to monitor yourself. Avoid questions such as "I'd guess the next thing that happened was _____." Instead, ask simply "What was next?" or "What happened?" Instead of asking "Was it on your Dad's bowling night, your birthday?" inquire "Did anything special help you remember when this happened?"

If the child you interviewed ends up going to court, it is possible that defense attorneys might argue that such a young child can be easily persuaded or led in an interview. Children are told to obey adults, and unless your words are chosen carefully, the attorney might accuse you of putting words in the child's mouth. Valuable information obtained in your interview may therefore not be useful; the case might be dropped and the child left unprotected.

Heart of the Interview

Once you have established a level of rapport with a child, begin to ask questions gently about the child's family and home life. At this point, it may help to explain again your role as a caring friend to the family and child. Ask the child about relationships with everyone, including those the child lives with and others considered important. Ask the child to make a list of the most and least favorite things about the relationship with each of these people. You will be able to see the child's level of comfort with significant people during this exercise. It also gives the child an opportunity to see how you respond to positive and negative information.

Another way to introduce sensitive topics to the child is to share information from the person who first contacted you about the suspected abuse. Be careful not to use the word *abuse* or to suggest anything other than "I'm concerned about you." One important rule to remember is to maintain the child's right to privacy. This includes the child's right not to disclose the abuse and not to have information revealed indiscriminately. If a child chooses not to share information with you at this time, respect the child's decision. Let the child know of your continued concern and that you are available any time he or she decides to talk again.

To be sure you understand what the child told you, review some of the key points disclosed in the interview. Allow the child to correct you and clarify misinformation.

When you are talking to a child who you think is being abused, four important issues should be addressed in the interview: immediate reinforcement, long-term reinforcement, emotional/spiritual confusion, and confidentiality.

Immediate Reinforcement

Tell the child that you are glad he or she shared this information with you. You recognize that is is difficult sometimes to talk about personal things but also that it is so important to talk to someone about problems or concerns. Refer to "Share each other's troubles and problems, and so obey our Lord's command" (Galatians 6:2). Reassure the child that you believe what is being told. Be empathetic by expressing your sorrow that the child had to go through this confusing, unhappy, and hurtful experience.

Emotional/Spiritual Confusion

A child's guilt feelings and self-blame may be one of the most challenging psychological hurdles facing the clerical interviewer. Statistically, an abused child is victimized by an adult in an authority position who, more often than not, is related to the child. Traditionally, religious teachings have instructed children to love and obey their parents and respect their elders. If children are then betrayed by a grown-up and thus desire to go against abusive demands and stop the abusive incidents, they begin to question their own self-worth. They will have also gone against the teachings of the church by not obeying their parents. They may ask "Am I now a bad or sinful person?" The abuser has told them not to tell and they did anyway. Now the child who has disclosed feels not only disrespectful but dishonest as well.

Clarify for the child that the Bible teaches that no one should endure abuse and that telling you about it was the right thing. It is always necessary for the cleric to stress that the abuser is the one at fault and to blame. Do not express a dislike for the abuser as a person, since often the child still cares for him or her.

An abused child is often confused about love, values, and sexuality. Abusers may say "I'm doing this because I love you," "This is normal behavior in families who care about each other," or "I don't want you to have to learn about sex on the streets." All these manipulative statements must be addressed one by one, so that the child understands their intent. With very young children, you might explain that the abuser "broke a rule" (biblical and legal) and that the abuser is confused about love. "Your body belongs to you," you might say, "and you can control whom you touch and who touches you. You are a very special person whom God created and deserve only good, OK touches." Continually building a child's self-esteem is important to restoring the sense of control and self-worth that the abuser has taken away.

Spiritual encouragement can help a child and family through a difficult time by providing hope and helping to make sense out of trauma. That is not to say there is a simple, Christian solution to the hardship, pain, and devastation of abuse, but it can be a helpful catalyst to recovery. "God never abandons us. We get knocked down, but we get up again and keep going" (2 Corinthians 4:9).

Long-Term Reinforcement

Once a child has made a disclosure, you want to reassure the child that you will always be there if needed. You are not only the pastor but a supportive friend as well. Let the child know that it might not be a smooth road ahead, but you will always listen and believe. Read together "He will shield you with his wings! They will shelter you. His faithful promises are your armor. Now you don't need to be afraid of the dark anymore" (Psalms 91:4).

Confidentiality

How much confidentiality can you morally and legally guarantee to an abused child? All states have a mandatory reporting law for all suspected abuse.

Just before closing your interview with a child, explain that you will need to tell some people about the abuse (parents, child protective services). Negotiate with the child how much information about the abuse is to be shared with others at this time. To maintain the child's trust in you, you must let the child know exactly what you will say to others and who will need to know.

Parents need to know if their child has been abused. If a parent is the abuser, however, it may be better to allow child protective services or the police to go with you to talk to the abuser. Most abusers initially deny any responsibility. This is normal protective thinking. You can help the abuser recognize that to deny will further traumatize the child and could have a devastating effect on the family. Family members may become unsure about whom or what to believe. As a family's pastor, you can assure abusers that you will not abandon them even if the abuse did occur, and that you will provide support to everyone in the family in order to find the best resolution possible to the problem.

If neither parent is an abuser, tell them the information that you and the child agreed upon at the close of your interview with the child. Let them know that the child is hesitant right now to share details about the abuse because of concern over the parents' reaction. Ask them not to question the child, but to let the child bring up the topic when ready.

Generally, most other people in the congregation do not need to know anything about the abuse. If you are asked, let them know the Jones family is in need of support and prayer, but that you respect the confidentiality of all members of your congregation. If the family chooses to share information, be sure to let others know that the children should be treated as they always have been and that to treat them differently may add to their distress. It is this sensitivity to the family, to the children, and to the congregation that makes you such a valuable person in combatting abuse.

Interviewing Dos and Don'ts for Clergy

Pre-Interview Preparation

1. Let the congregation know of your availability to talk about sensitive issues.
2. Prove your approachability (verbally and nonverbally).
3. Gather background information on the child.
4. Select interview tools.
5. Choose the interview setting (minimal disruption, comfortable, free from parental pressure).
6. Do not videotape or record the interview.
7. Interview the child alone, if possible.
8. Do not interview children during their normal nap time.

The Interview

1. Introduction
   a. Introduce yourself and describe what you do.

b. Establish rapport by getting on the same level as the child, discussing hobbies, and so on.

c. Ask the child if she or he knows why you are there to talk. Give ample time for the child to disclose the abuse. If the child says nothing, say "Someone is concerned about you" or state generally what the child told the person who told you. Do not use words such as *abuse* or suggest a problem with a specific person.

d. Tell the child that you talk to a lot of kids and that no one is alone. Stress that "What you tell me won't surprise me; I am sure I have heard other kids talk about these same things."

2. Heart of the Interview

   a. Use the child's words and phrases: "You say he touched your bagina?"

   b. Create an opportunity to acknowledge that the child may be upset or afraid. Be reassuring: "I know you said this was difficult for you, but I am here to listen and to help you."

   c. When discussing the abuse, it is easiest for the child to talk about the first time it happened and work up to the present.

   d. Do not use leading questions; say "What happened next?" not "Did he touch your bottom next?" Leading questions generally elicit *yes* or *no* answers.

   e. Do not touch the child during the interview unless you are touched first. Then, if you ask the child's permission, the touching is appropriate.

   f. Generally underreact when the child is talking. A simple, caring "Uh-huh" accompanied by a nod is effective.

   g. Do not bribe the child to talk, with cookies or getting done early, for example.

   h. If you think the child is lying, do not be accusatory; say "Tell me about that again, only this time, tell me only the part that is true, OK?"

   i. Use active feedback or reflection—rephrase the child's statements.

3. Concluding the Interview

   a. Praise the child for talking to you. Reemphasize that the blame lies with the abuser and not with the child.

   b. Explain what the next step will be for the child. It is best not to discuss what might happen four months from now unless the child brings it up.

   c. End the interview by asking the child if there are any questions. Make sure the child feels the interview has been a positive experience.

   d. If the abuse is reported to the police or child protective services and it eventually goes to court, offer to accompany the child as a friend. A child needs a lot of support during this time.

Conclusion

Children who have experienced trauma may be hesitant to reveal or discuss their situations. They may be fearful of what could or will happen or even of being believed. Discussing sensitive issues with children requires sensitive people—a situation in which the clergy may play a crucial role. Eventually children in the congregation who are experiencing sensitive issues or situations will come to the attention of the clergy, and the clergy's being aware of the dos and don'ts of interviewing could make a child's traumatic experience less painful.

16
Counseling the Adult Survivor of Child Sexual Abuse: Concepts and Cautions for the Clergy

Barbara W. Snow
Geraldine G. Hanni

The crime of child sexual abuse is as old as the taboo against it. Society has only recently acknowledged the existence of a problem that generations of children have struggled to survive. Statistics tell us that their numbers are legion. Where are these victims now? Have the tragedies of their childhoods found resolution in adult life, or have they been left with a legacy of lifetime trauma? This chapter will address these questions and offer basic assumptions, counseling guidelines, and cautions in order to respond effectively to the issues and concerns of the adult survivor.

The Reality of Child Sexual Abuse

Dr. Robert Kelly (see Chapter 5) describes the frequency and extent of child sexual abuse. Therefore, the reader is well advised of the tragic proportions of this problem. Our concern is with the reality of abuse for those who are no longer children. This concern requires that common stereotypes of the sexual abuser be reexamined. There is general agreement that children are assaulted more often by people close to them than by deviant strangers who may lurk around school yards enticing children with candy. It is parents, siblings, extended family, step-relatives, neighbors, friends, and authority figures in the lives of children who are most often responsible for molestation. There are no physical characteristics, emotional responses, or lifestyle cues that signal "abuser." Offenders represent differences in age, sex, education, and socioeconomic status. Their actions may appear to be the exact opposite of deviancy, often reflecting model behavior.

Until you accept this information as more than mere fact, you cannot fully believe that the elderly grandparent, the successful father, the churchgoing mother, or dependable baby tender are perpetrators of child sexual abuse. They are always adept at denying their involvement.

The Denial of Abuse

The only individual for whom denial is as important as it is for the offender is the victim. Denial helps block out unpleasant memories, including feelings of helplessness, anger, betrayal, and possible sexual arousal. Incomplete memory, with a failure to recall significant portions of childhood, and frightening flashbacks of early life events are typical reactions in the denial system.

The suggestions that fantasy may also be at the root of an abuse history is inconsistent with the denial process. It also blatantly ignores theories of child development and sexuality and rejects the individual's pain and trauma as invalid and unimportant.

Virtually all cases of child molestation involve the element of secrecy. Forced silence creates additional trauma for the child. Disclosure of the abuse is conditioned in the child's mind to be associated with fear, disbelief, shame, and possible retaliation. Denial assists in managing emotions and circumstances for which there is no other resolution. The denial which served as an early survival technique often continues to operate into adulthood. It can prevent the individual from identifying the source of current life problems and seeking help to solve them.

Empirical studies confirm that sexual abuse is a serious, long-term mental health problem consistently associated with the following (Browne and Finkelhor, 1986).

1. Depression
2. Self-destruction
3. Anxiety
4. Feelings of isolation and stigma
5. Sexual dysfunction
6. Failure to trust
7. Substance abuse
8. Poor self-esteem
9. Tendency toward revictimization

These symptoms are not inevitable, but they are frequent and show the potential impact of abuse.

Although such problems may serve as witness to the reality of an abuse history, adult survivors may unwittingly deny any meaning or connection to the past such symptoms may have. The individual may mask evidence by presenting it as more general or socially acceptable problems such as those related to marriage, employment, depression, or stress. Adult survivors often report being in counseling for years yet never disclosing their abuse.

Responsibility for the Abuse

Sexual abuse of a child is solely and squarely the responsibility of the adult. Whatever the rationalizations or excuses, the bottom line is that there is no true choice for the child. Lack of life experience and an inability to understand the meaning of sexual activity combine to make an informed decision impossible. The child is enticed by an adult who has greater sexual experience and who is in a position of greater power, influence, and trust. A child may cooperate in the activity, but as Dr. Suzanne Sgroi has stated, "cooperation is not consent" (1984). If there is inappropriate sexual behavior on the part of the child, it is the responsibility of the parent or adult to correct it, not exploit it. This is as true for adolescents as for young children.

Dr. Nicholas Groth has offered an example from his practice as co-director of The Sex Offender Program at the Connecticut Correction Institution in 1984 of an offender who described being approached sexually by his young child as he slept on the couch. The child reportedly slid her hand down inside his pants and fondled his genitals, which led to other, more intimate activity. Dr. Groth responded to this account by stating, "The only difficulty I have with your story is that if she had reached in and touched your wallet, would you have taught her to steal?"

Offenders often fantasize about the child's mutual interest and involvement in the sexual behavior and convey such a message repeatedly to the child. The perception of the child as seductive is a rationalization used to justify the abusive behavior. Spouses and siblings may find it difficult to accept that the offender was capable of engaging in such deviance on initiative alone, so they support these efforts and excuses.

The message of complicity, whether conveyed overtly or not, is a central issue for the adult survivor. Guilt and shame become overwhelming emotions. This myth of the seductive child clouds the reality of the past and haunts future efforts to find relief and resolution.

The adult survivor often finds it easier to accept that the abuse was a result of her own wrong behavior than to believe that a trusted loved one betrayed her. Minimizing what happened—"It was only fondling" or "It only happened a few times"—and rationalizing why it occurred—"It happened to him as a child" or "She never meant to hurt me"—are excuses often used by adult survivors who feel responsibility for the abuse. As Dr. Eliana Gill has concluded, "The crucial aspect of the abuse is not what occurred, but what impact it had on you, how you explained it to yourself and others, and how it has affected your life" (1983).

Adults who reexamine their childhood abuse experiences often question why they did not stop the molestation. The assumption is that their failure to do so implies endorsement of what happened. They fail to realize that they are analyzing their childhood actions from the perspective they now have as adults. As mature individuals, they possess greater authority, power, and intelligence. More choices are now available to them.

In addition to responsibility for the sexual abuse itself, the adult survivor often struggles with misperceptions (others' and her own) of her responsibility for the consequences that followed the discovery: "If she'd only put up with it a little longer, then she could have been out of the house and Dad wouldn't be in jail," or "Why tell now? It's been over for years and it will only hurt Mom." There is no convenient time to disclose sexual abuse. Whenever it is revealed, pain, turmoil, and changes follow. Consequences such as financial stress, separation, and loss are responsibilities of the offender, who as an adult made choices that produced those results.

Counseling Guidelines

After you realize that the adult who has sought you out for counseling may be a victim of sexual abuse, the question arises: How can I best help her? Your ability to let her know that you believe her, that she was not responsible for what happened to her as a child, and that she is acceptable to God will open the door to further trust. A safe place in which to ventilate innermost thoughts and feelings is a top priority. Your challenge will be to reassure worth, to prove that there are men and women who can be trusted, and to skillfully encourage ventilation of feelings.

Here are ten suggestions for working with adult victims.

1. Ask her to bring a picture of either herself or another child who is the age she was when the sexual abuse began. As both of you look at the picture, discuss the age, interests, and development of this child. Lead into the idea that children have natural curiosity about their bodies but that explicit sexual activity is learned. The child is under the control of adults who can either lead her for good purposes or exploit her.

2. Suggest that she keep a journal to record all of her thoughts and feelings. She can decide whether or not to share it with you as her spiritual advisor. The act of writing will offer her a method of expressing her feelings other than talking. It will be more effective if the writing is directed to the sexual abuse issues.

3. Writing an *un*delivered letter to either the offender or to the nonoffending parent is another powerful way to deal with her feelings of anger or sadness. Be prepared to spend some time with her to process this letter, as it will bring up feelings that will be traumatizing to her if not handled carefully.

4. Encourage the use of positive affirmations to build self-esteem. Have the victim write a series of statements such as "I am a good and capable person. I deserve to be happy. I can make goals and achieve them." These

are to be repeated aloud morning and evening as she looks into a mirror. It is important that the victim compose them herself and say them aloud, not mentally.

5. Bibliotherapy is the use of reading materials for therapeutic purposes. There are several first-hand accounts available in paperback. Read them first since some material may be offensive. In addition, we suggest the following publications written by professional counselors.

Incest, Years After: Putting the Pain to Rest by Mary Ann Donaldson.
The Village Family Service Center
1721 South University Drive
Fargo, North Dakota 58130

Outgrowing the Pain by Eliana Gill, Ph.D.
Launch Press
P.O. Box 40174
San Francisco, California 94140

Why Me? by Lynn B. Daugherty
Mother Courage Press
Racine, Wisconsin

6. Giving permission to be angry can be a comfort to the victim. Brainstorming to discover nondestructive ways to express anger can be helpful to her. Hitting pillows, breaking pencils, smashing old dishes, physical exercise, and using inflatable bats are a few ideas. In addition to ventilation, an understanding of the dynamics of her specific abuse situation can lead to significant relief of anger.

7. Discuss her spiritual concerns openly. She cares about her position with God and her church, or she would not be there. Use every avenue to give her assurances of her acceptability to God and her place in His plan. Critical issues include repentance, forgiveness, chastity, anger toward God, and honoring parents.

8. Work with the victim to discover her strengths. She often feels that she does not have any. Her sense is that she is as powerless as she was as a child. Assist her to move from passive acceptance of herself as a victim to being aware that she now has options not available to her earlier in life.

What skills has she developed that enabled her to survive?

What does she need from life to make her happy?

How would giving to others enrich her own life?

9. Help her evaluate the advantages and risks of disclosure of the abuse at this time of her life if it has not already been accomplished. She must understand that confronting the offender or other family members presents

the possibility of both help and hindrance. There is no definite answer as to whether or not this should be done. Ask her to visualize herself with any of them and imagine his or her response. Will they

be angry?

seem sad?

say that it never happened?

beg for forgiveness?

ask for pity?

blame her for what happened?

Most important, what will be her response to each of these possibilities? Only then will she be able to decide whether confrontation would be beneficial. Often it is helpful to approach the issue if the offender or mother is available to her. However, there is always the risk that they will continue to place the responsibility for the abuse on her. This could be destructive to her attempts to leave the victim role behind.

10. Professional group therapy is often a valuable experience for the adult survivor. It helps decrease her sense of isolation, that feeling of being the only one *it* happened to. As she listens to the experiences of others, she begins to discern the family patterns that encouraged incest. She can express her rage and grief over both her loss of innocence and her lack of a normal childhood. She can be angry at others for neither protecting nor believing her. She can see the methods the offender used to gain cooperation and silence. She can practice social skills which help her everyday life. Others can show her ways to gain control of her life and to move away from being a victim over and over again.

Cautions

1. Provide support and nurturance without appearing to be seductive.

2. Demonstrate a willingness to hear detail about the abuse, but avoid appearing voyeuristic.

3. Take care that you do not allow the adult survivor to develop an unhealthy dependency on you as her spiritual leader.

4. Be aware of the effect your gender may have on your relationship.

5. Avoid making her feel that she is overly special or different. She already

senses that she is marked by her experience, so she will be sensitive to anything that gives the impression that she is unusual or tainted.

6. Realize that her response to what happened is more important than the degree of sexual activity or the length of time it went on.

7. Understand that the early betrayal of trust may produce a barrier in your pastoral relationship—she may be unwilling to fully trust anyone perceived as an authority.

8. Recognize that forgiveness is not simply an act but a process that can be completed after working through the issues and their accompanying feelings. Do not try to rush this process by questioning her pace or suggesting forgiveness as the first step.

9. Do not assist in denying the reality of her childhood experience. It may not feel real now, but that does not mean that it did not actually occur.

10. Recognize that many of the problems presented by adult survivors may be very serious and require the intervention of specialists trained in this area. Deep-seated problems such as eating disorders, multiple personality, substance abuse, severe relationship problems, sexual dysfunction, suicide ideation, self-mutilation, fears of abusing children, and overwhelming depression are signals that demand professional treatment. Guide her to a professional therapist who will treat her value system with respect.

Conclusion

Child sexual abuse is not a determinate sentence to a lifetime of problems and pain. It, however, may leave survivors who as adults struggle to understand and put to rest the trauma of their childhoods.

There is nothing simple about undoing years of abuse and its consequences. However, supporting the survivor and contributing to her progress as she leaves her victim role behind constitute an exhilarating experience.

References

Browne, A., and D. Finkelhor. 1986. Impact of child sexual abuse: A review of the research. *Psychological Bulletin* 99(1):66–77.

Burgess, A., A. N. Groth, L. L. Holmstro and S. M. Sgroi. 1978. *Sexual Assault of Children and Adolescents.* Lexington, Mass.: Lexington Books, D.C. Heath and Co.

Gill, E. 1983. *Outgrowing the Pain.* San Francisco: Launch Press.

17
A Pastoral Response

James M. Alsdurf
Phyllis Alsdurf

Much criticism has been directed toward the church as an institution for endorsing a system which many charge is the spawning ground for wife abuse. The clergy has been cited by victims, researchers, and feminist writers for contributing to the victimization of women in a variety of ways. The claim is frequently made that as church leaders, men have used patriarchy to discriminate against women by advancing theological perspectives on women's roles, marriage, and family life which result in the victimization of women. Pastors have been indicted for perpetuating the mistreatment of women through the advancement of patriarchy as God's designated order for the world. This chapter reports long overdue research designed to evaluate the experiences of religious leaders and describe their perceptions of the problem of wife abuse. A list of practical guidelines is provided to assist concerned pastors in their complex dual role of spiritual leader and safety provider.

The Clergy and Wife Abuse

Sociologists William Stacey and Anson Shupe summarize the experiences of battered women who talked with a religious leader about their dilemma: "A number of women were quite bitter about their futile attempts to get clergy to help." Highly invested in retaining family order, these clerics were likely to "recall the admonitions of Saint Paul on controlling women and use them to justify telling the woman she must stay in the abusive home," said Stacey and Shupe (1983). Similarly, psychologist Lenore Walker reported that some victims were either denied help by the clergy or sent home after a crisis period in order to "preserve the family." Such advice was usually accompanied by instruction from their religious leader to pray for the batterer's soul and hope that he would become a better person (Walker, 1979).

The result of this focus upon keeping the family together and emphasizing wifely submission, researchers claim, is that women only feel more trapped after conversation and counsel with a pastor (Langley and Levy, 1977). Victims also assert that pastors do not understand their plight. Investigation proves that the clergy's response to the problem of wife abuse has been inadequate (Stacey and Shupe, 1983).

A Pastoral Response

Many of the charges about the church's response to abused women have been based solely upon the reports of victims (Martin, 1976). The lack of data gathered directly from pastors to support or refute this view precipitated our investigation into the role of clergy in responding to the problem of wife abuse. A two-page questionnaire was sent to 5,700 pastors from Protestant churches throughout the United States and Canada. It was designed to evaluate the pastor's experience with and awareness of the problem of wife abuse, especially in regard to theological presuppositions in the areas of marriage, divorce, and marital roles. (The sample was 99 percent male and 1 percent female.)

Pastors from conservative Protestant denominations accounted for the majority of respondents, with a total of thirty-four denominations being represented. Ages ranged from twenty to over sixty, with a median age of thirty-five. Forty-seven percent of the respondents were seminary trained, while the others had graduated from Bible college or graduate school. The greatest number of responding pastors lived in the Midwest (32 percent) and West (32 percent), followed by the East (20 percent) and South (13 percent). The size of the pastors' church staff ranged from one to twenty-three, and the ethnic composition of churches was predominately Caucasian (80 percent). The population of the pastors' communities was less than 50,000 for half of the respondents, and exceeded one million for 10 percent of the pastors. The number of years in the pastorate varied substantially, with 14 percent having been in the pastorate for three years or less, and 50 percent for over ten years.

Since fewer than 10 percent of the questionnaires were returned, generalizations made from this survey are tentative and limited to pastors who did respond. Nonetheless, we venture that the information drawn from these pastors may well reflect the experience and opinions of a much larger percentage of Protestant pastors. What the response rate might indicate, unfortunately, is the pastors' lack of interest in and even denial of the problem of wife abuse.

Interestingly enough, the National Association of Evangelicals (NAE), an organization of pastors from 44 conservative Protestant denominations, surveyed its members on family concerns in 1984. The response rate to that organizationally endorsed study was almost identical to ours.

Eighty-four percent of the pastors in our study said that they had confronted wife abuse in their ministry and had counseled a woman who had been physically abused by her husband. The majority of these pastors had counseled such a victim during the six months prior to completing the questionnaire, indicating that wife abuse is a problem with which pastors are currently dealing.

Women, Marriage, and the Sanctity of Personhood

As a group, pastors did indeed seem to hold patriarchally informed attitudes toward women. Their comments revealed them to be concerned about battered women and yet torn by the theological perspectives that appear to conflict with this concern. Certain sociotheological presuppositions emerged which seem central to the clergy's response to wife abuse regarding three important issues: women, marriage, and the sanctity of personhood.

On Women

A pastor's perspective on women was assessed from the response to items that pertained to a woman's role within marriage and the indication of trust in her report of violence. Those pastors who discounted a woman's report of violence and affirmed the belief that a wife should occupy a submissive role in marriage linked her failure to be submissive to her husband's violence (implying that her lack of submission somehow caused his violence).

A third of the pastors questioned the reliability of an abused woman's report when it comes to the issue of who is responsible for the violence. While 28 percent believed that the unwillingness of wives to be submissive to their husbands accounted for much of the marital violence, an even greater percentage (35 percent) said that wives overestimate the husband's responsibility for violence within a marriage. Twenty-six percent felt that a wife should submit to her husband and trust that God would honor her action by either stopping the abuse of giving her the strength to endure it.

Overall, about a quarter of the pastors specifically endorsed items which affirmed the belief that the lack of submissiveness by wives accounts for the violence. When the pattern of responses was analyzed, a connection was found between those pastors who discounted women's reports of violence and those who called for a woman to submit to her husband and endure the violence as her spiritual responsibility. Pastors calling for "submission to husband and spiritual endurance" were also opposed to advising a victim to protect herself by obtaining legal or medical aid.

On Marriage

A pastor's perspective on marriage was the second key factor seen as influencing his response to the problem of wife abuse. Most pastors in our study were more willing to accept a marriage in which some violence was present even though it is "not God's perfect will" than they were to advise a separation that might end in divorce. Seventy-one percent would not advise a battered woman to either leave or separate immediately because of abuse, and 92 percent would never tell her to divorce her abuser. This suggests more of a commitment to the concept of marriage than to the woman's physical safety, and a view that minimizes the impact and destruction of violence.

On Sanctity of Personhood

A third issue concerning the response of pastors to victims of wife abuse is a moral one: the sanctity of personhood. One-third of our sample endorsed items that called for the wife to remain in the home until the abuse became "severe," and nearly half (45 percent) expressed concern that the husband's violence not be overemphasized and used as "a justification" for breaking the marriage commitment. Such a stance fails to take seriously a woman's safety and *right* not to be assaulted and reveals the difficulty that many clerics have in balancing their commitment to the sanctity of personhood with their commitment to marriage.

Numerous pastors, however, were aware of this moral dilemma. One pastor charged that "the church must dispel the rumor of woman's nonequality with men," while another contended that "treating women as second-class citizens has the effect of de-humanizing them—which allows a husband to mistreat his wife because she is not his equal." A third stated, "we must act now to identify this as a problem and offer love, support, and protection to women, regardless of the cost."

The Pastor as a Counselor

The study results also suggest that these pastors do not perceive themselves as experiencing difficulty in counseling battered women and regard themselves as competent to perform the task. This finding is of particular concern, given the fact that other professionals working with battered women often cite the emotional demands, frequent legal complications, and complex psychological and relational issues as a significant consideration in working with victims and victimizers (Hilberman and Munson, 1977–78). The majority of the pastors in our study reported that they were not personally uncomfortable with the topic or frustrated by the lack of information available to them on the issue. Nor did they find the emotional demands of victims or their own lack of training in counseling creating problems for them in their work with victims.

Once again, the NAE's Task Force on the Family reached similar conclusions. It characterized the pastor as a lonely person "in matters of competence and security in assisting family development. Almost half of those surveyed have never or only once attended any sort of workshop or program of assist-ance related to skills in dealing with family matters." And, the report stated, though pastors may appear to be lonely, they present themselves to be a "rather secure and even self-confident set of human beings" who "judge their own level of competence to help other people with family concerns as being relatively high" (National Association of Evangelicals, 1985, p. 4).

Since the accounts the pastors in our study gave about how they have interacted with battered women conflict with the negative reports of many victims about pastoral advice they have received, the results of our study could be interpreted as reflecting the *need* by pastors to provide socially ac-ceptable answers and to perceive themselves as compassionate and helpful, rather than reflecting what pastors actually *do* and the counsel they give when dealing with abused women.

Pastors who, in order to maintain a marriage, minimize the violence a victim reports to them and disregard her immediate need for safety have mis-taken the purpose and substance of marriage in much the same way that the Pharisees mistook the intent of the Sabbath ("The Sabbath was made for man, not man for the Sabbath," Mark 2:27). They created a law which alien-ated, rather than redeemed, its adherents. Violence by a husband toward his wife is always an offense to the integrity of human life because ultimately it destroys both the marriage and the victim. The pastor who has not recog-nized this truth has not yet seriously examined either the cycle of violence or the message of scripture in response to such violence.

Guidelines for Pastors

While deficiencies in the clergy's response to the problem of wife abuse are undeniable, the same could have been said (until very recently) about most professionals. The pastor's role in responding to situations of wife abuse is perhaps more difficult than that of other service providers, because the pastor is called upon to uphold the values and beliefs of the church and to respond practically to the needs of victims. To handle such tension, the pastor must confront the theologically sensitive issues of sex roles, marriage and divorce, the history of the church's treatment of women, the sanctity of personhood, and the practical realities of his own limitations as a counselor.

No one who deals with the issue of wife abuse has a potentially more difficult role than the pastor. He is expected to be both priest and prac-titioner, and this dual role can indeed be burdensome. Thus, a question that other professionals in the field need to be asking themselves is "How can I help the pastor?"

Because the pastor is in many situations the first or most frequently con-tacted institutional resource, the influence that the pastor can have in helping people in abusive marriages is significant (Bowker, 1982; Pagelow, 1982). In light of that fact, we submit the following suggestions.

Admit the fact that wife abuse exists in your church. Many pastors hold patriarchal worldviews which they believe to be divinely ordained, and because of this commitment find it more difficult to hear or effectively respond to the problems of battered women than to other situations of oppression. By not acknowledging the problem, a pastor only perpetuates it and discourages the victim from pursuing help.

Recognize that wife abuse is a sanctity-of-life issue. To be *for* life means to actively crusade against wife abuse and the social structures which foster it. Pastors can open the door for an abused woman to approach them by making announcements from the pulpit about area shelters or support groups for abusers and victims. They can introduce and discuss the problem in Sunday school classes, invite a local spokesperson to speak at a church forum on the topic, or preach a sermon on the topic.

Examine your own attitudes toward women and your views on women's roles in the marital relationship. The issues of sex roles, marriage, and divorce are central to a discussion of wife abuse. Pastors need to be aware of their attitudes in these areas because those attitudes will seriously affect the counsel given. Before accepting the challenge of working with an abused woman, pastors should have a clear understanding of the circumstances under which they would permit or support divorce. This is not to suggest that divorce is the only option in situations of abuse, but in some cases the sanctity of a woman's life will call for the termination of her marriage.

Work in conjunction with other trained professionals when counseling battered women. Few pastors have acquired the necessary counseling skills, or have the time available to respond to all the complexities of an abuse situation. Unfortunately, many pastors are unwilling to refer victims to appropriate resources, a fact which further complicates their involvement with victims. An abused woman should be directed to appropriate legal counsel for information regarding her physical protection, be introduced to local programs for victims, and be encouraged to confide in a friend who can struggle with the issues of faith that abuse raises.

Pastors need to read their Bibles with a new alertness to the problem of wife abuse. Much in scripture very specifically addresses the issue of violence, and it is the responsibility of the clergy to preach and teach such passages in relation to this problem. In many cases the research that has considered the relationship between wife abuse and Christian faith has presented theological understanding of Christian faith and church history that are biased and contain unorthodox or even simplistic theological assertions. (For instance, to identify the Apostle Paul as a misogynist on the basis of a few biblical passages taken out of context is misleading and reflects a lack of thorough scholarship in the interpretation of scripture.) A separation must be made between what pastors do or feel about wife abuse and what in scripture and Christian tradition actually speaks to that issue.

Conclusion

To respond effectively to wife abuse, the clergy must examine certain theological and biblical realities and integrate these into the moral context of pastoral care. This cannot be done unless a pastor first approaches the theological task with a desire to read scripture in light of the experiences of battered women.

References

Bowker, L. H. 1982. Battered women and the clergy: An evaluation. *Journal of Pastoral Care* 36(4):226–234.

Davidson, T. 1978. *Conjugal crime.* New York: Hawthorne.

Hilberman, E., and K. Munson. 1977–78. Sixty battered women. *Victimology* 2:460–470.

Langley, R., and R. Levy. 1977. *Wife beating: The silent crisis.* New York: E. P. Dutton.

Martin, D. 1976. *Battered wives.* San Francisco: Glide Publications.

National Association of Evangelicals. Deerfield, Illinois. May 1, 1985. *Report of the Survey of Family Development Concerns of Pastors Task Force on the Family.*

Pagelow, M. 1982. *Woman Battering.* Beverly Hills: Sage.

Stacey, W. A., and A. Shupe. 1983. *The family secret.* Boston: Beacon Press, pp. 106–107.

Walker, L. 1979. *The battered woman.* New York: Harper & Row, p. 164.

18

Stand By Me: The Role of the Clergy and Congregation in Assisting the Family Once It Is Involved in the Legal and Treatment Process

David W. Delaplane

The assistance that can and should be given by the clergy and religious community to the victims of both child abuse and family violence can be of inestimable value. Nowhere is this more significant than when a religious leader or congregation attempts to support a family, victim, or offender through the complexities of the legal system and treatment process.

Since my primary work has been in child abuse (both physical and sexual), this chapter will emphasize that area. However, it will be readily seen that many of the ministries to those involved in child abuse can apply as well to the battered or sexually abused spouse or partner. Comments on the role of the religious community in assisting those caught up in domestic violence will be offered at the conclusion of this chapter.

When a report of child abuse is finally made, whether by a religious leader or another, there is often a feeling of relief. The reporting individual might be tempted to say, "Well, I have met my responsibility. It wasn't easy, but now, at least it's up to law enforcement and the Child Protective Services." However, it is vitally important for clergy to be aware that reporting is not the end of the responsibility of a caring professional or community. And, certainly, the leaders and congregations of our churches, temples, or synagogues are, or should be, among the most caring professionals and community members in our society.

This chapter intends to cover the "What next?" phase of the child abuse intervention and treatment process. When involved religious or lay leaders help a family through the often confusing and frustrating process of "the system," they may make the difference as to the success or failure of that process. The clergy and religious community can do many things that would be of vital assistance to the victim, family, and the offender. The caring stance of every religion should mandate the undertaking of these activities. In this chapter, as each step of the legal and treatment process is covered, suggestions will be offered for appropriate and helpful clerical and congregational involvement.

To anyone not involved with it daily, the legal process in child abuse cases can be confusing and complex. In order for the religious leader and congregation to be of maximum assistance to the victims (who also include the nonoffending parent and siblings if any) and the offender, it is necessary for them to have at least a general understanding of what happens. The religious leader, to be of greatest assistance, should counsel the involved parties and even attend as many of the hearings as possible with them. This obligation, particularly if the victim, offender, or both are members of the congregation, is as important as hospital visitation. "I was sick and you visited me; I was in prison and you came to me" (Matthew 25:36).

Initial Intervention

The investigation may be of an emergency (crisis) nature by either law enforcement or the Child Protective Services (CPS) of the Department of Welfare (Social Services) or both. This type of investigation could result in the immediate arrest "on probability" of the alleged offender or the taking of the child into protective custody. The investigation may also be on a nonemergency basis, meaning that more time is taken by the Child Protective Services' court intake personnel and that a decision is made whether or not to file a petition to make the child a ward of the court.

In either case, in regard to the abused child, such petitions must be filed in Juvenile Court. This is a civil action. If the child is judged to be a ward of the court, foster placement may result.

The religious leader may be called in by the nonoffending parent, the direct victim if this person is old enough to make such a call (for example, a sexually molested teenager) or even by the offender at this stage. It is important to be totally objective when this occurs. It may be that one of the parties involved is more active in the congregation than the other. And it must be stated here that there are as many perpetrators who are active members of religious congregations as those who are not. To put it more bluntly, the molester or heavy-handed abusive father may well be a deacon, an elder, a trustee, or even another member of the clergy. The immediate question might be, "How could this good person do such a thing?" Already, with such a question being even in the mental suspicion stage, the dynamics are perhaps being set up to doubt the victim, particularly when the victim is not as loyal a member of the congregation or is a child.

Much attention has been paid and research devoted to the question of whether a child can be a credible witness. The conclusion held by most who work in the field is still that, before all the chaos and trauma of the process come down upon them, very young children tell the truth. Many times these children will use words that they would not even know if they had not been molested. True, the language will be childlike. The child may say something like "He put his pee-pee in my mouth and yucky stuff came out." There is no valid reason to doubt such statements by children.

Denial is the perpetrator's first line of defense. A lot is at stake, so the denial may be strong and eloquent. Clergy should withhold judgment. Law enforcement, Child Protective Services, and the courts deal with these matters every day. (The county in which I reside, with a population approaching one million, receives between 1,000 and 1,500 reports of child abuse every month. Many are dismissed, but unfortunately a high percentage are proven valid. This county is not exceptional when compared with national statistics.) Remain neutral and helpful, but let the process decide. It is established for that purpose. You have a different role.

The victims will need great support at this time. Often the issue comes down to either/or: Either the perpetrator is required to leave home, or the child taken into protective custody. Even though a child may have been abused in the home, most parents are still extremely reluctant to see either the child or the other parent removed for the child's protection. The security instinct is very strong in the former, as is the parental instinct in the latter.

In this crisis clergy must always take the position that the highest priority is the protection of the innocent and vulnerable child. This is a mandate of all religious faiths, and most certainly of the Judeo-Christian ethic. Often there must be a separation of the perpetrator from the victim for the immediate protection of the child until it is determined by the courts, upon the recommendation of court-mandated therapists, that reunification is possible (unfortunately, in many cases it never is). Clerics are oriented to preserving the family. This is also a biblical mandate. But neither the Christian nor the Jewish faith asks us to preserve a sick family. Certain precautions are taken to remove or quarantine individuals with highly contagious, potentially fatal diseases. Such precautions are seen as the only right thing to do for the protection of the well. This situation is similar. Although painful, the separation can also be helpful. Extreme measures of facing up can bring about ultimate healing in some cases.

There are significant cases where Child Protective Services do not feel that legal steps are justified, particularly if the family will submit to the services of the Family Maintenance Unit of the CPS (in counties that have one). Of course, clergy should encourage this process and participate in it as part of its pastoral duties.

The Courts

The legal process involves many further steps. They are the arrest, either by warrant or, in crisis situations, for probable cause; arraignment before Municipal or County Court; and if the defendant pleads not guilty, the preliminary hearing to determine if there is enough evidence to go to trial.

Most preliminary hearings result in a holding order, since a low standard of proof is required (not proof "beyond a reasonable doubt"). The defendant is then sent to Superior (District) Court. In this higher court there is another arraignment, wherein counts may be increased or decreased. Following this are pretrial conferences to determine how to proceed. Within sixty days (in California) there is a hearing before Superior (District) Court and final disposition.

Parallel to this process are the Juvenile Court hearings which, as already stated, determine whether the child should become a ward of the court. For the child's protection this determination is usually faster than the criminal action because the defendant is often out on bond or recognizance. (Note: If a pastor breaks privilege of confidentiality and testifies, the testimony can be received in this civil action, but not in the criminal action in Superior District Court.)

Up to this point there are many ways that clergy and responsible congregational members may be of assistance. If the defendant is required to live separately from the family, there is an added financial burden as well as other problems of daily living. A caring congregation should seek ways to give practical financial, housing, transportation, and child care assistance where needed. Perhaps the most important assistance is to give nonjudgmental emotional support in this most difficult time. Again, it should be emphasized that assistance should be rendered to all parties. The court has the responsibility of determining innocence or guilt. If it becomes obvious to the religious leader that the courts or any other part of the legal or child protective system are not performing well, then he or she may need to take on another nonfamily role, that of advocating.

There is a great need throughout the nation for foster homes. Most counties offer minimal, barely adequate reimbursement to the foster parent for the child's needs. Some congregations have formed organizations to assist those in their midst who have volunteered to take children—both for short periods from the county receiving homes, where the children are being held pending disposition, and for the longer period of permanent foster placement. These volunteers have provided diapers, cribs, transportation to the doctor or to hearings, respite care, and many other services for the foster parents. An excellent model of such a program is that of Child S.H.A.R.E., % Westwood Presbyterian Church, 10822 Wilshire Blvd., Los Angeles, CA

90024. Needless to say, the recruiting of foster parents is also a very helpful activity that congregations can undertake.

Clergy can be of great assistance by merely being present with all parties involved during this maze of hearings, consultations, and evaluations. As a pastor, I have on occasion found myself sitting in the courtroom with both the nonoffending partner and the defendant. I have assisted with filling out forms, locating proper offices, and recommending therapists. I have been the sounding board for all the expressions of pain, anger, and anxiety that this severe problem produces. I have prayed with and for both the victims and the perpetrators. The prayers are not that the offender will "get off," but rather that strength will be given through the process, that justice will prevail, and that therapy will be healing.

In our state the child victim is entitled to have an adult support person with him or her in court. Often parents are not the best suited for this purpose because their nonverbal language may influence a jury. A caring religious leader or qualified volunteer from a congregation who is close to the child and who has the child's confidence may perform this important service.

Disposition: Probation or Prison

The Court Division of the Probation Department obtains back-up information on the family. In our state a psychiatric evaluation is required before the judge can grant probation. Clergy may be called upon by the probation officer at this point to give information on the family. Factual information on church, temple, or synagogue membership is appropriate. Judgments should rarely, if ever, be made. Certainly the pastor should not question the defendant's guilt because he or she was a pillar of the congregation. There should not be an attitude tilt toward being guilty because the defendant may have had other church-related problems such as lack of attendance and personality conflicts. At times the religious leader may be put under some pressure by the Defense Attorney to be a character witness for the defendant. At other times the clergy may be called upon by the District Attorney to testify in court about such matters as conditions in the home. Truth, uncolored by personal bias, is an imperative.

Clerics are advised to gain some information about the addictive and pathological nature of abuse, and to constantly remind themselves that, although an individual may be exemplary in many areas of life, he can have deep-seated difficulties in others. These must be faced, opened up, and treated in order that real healing and reunification may occur.

If there is a conviction or an admission of guilt, the final disposition of the court is either probation (invariably with counseling being a requirement) or prison. In most cases, with the possible exception of fixated pedophiles, the former is preferable because physical abusers and molesters are not usually helped in prison, but they are released to abuse and molest again.

Therapy

It is important that the religious leader encourage the defendant to cooperate in therapy. A good Defense Attorney will often suggest that the defendant enter therapy voluntarily before it is court-ordered. And, in many jurisdictions, if there is an immediate admission of guilt, the District Attorney has a right to divert the defendant to therapy before even filing. The clergy can play a strong role in encouraging such admissions and seeking to break through any fear-motivated defenses. This is delicate because one cannot assume guilt, even if it is strongly suspected. But appeals can be made: "If you are guilty, it will be so much better for you in the process to admit it." Clerics cannot promise therapy as a result, but they can certainly advise that such an admission will greatly increase the chances for such.

It is important that any therapy undertaken voluntarily be with credentialed therapists who have a track record of successful treatment and who can satisfy the court qualifications. Many strong sexual molestation therapy programs can take three or more years before the therapists are satisfied that family reunification (if desired) is possible. With some resistant clients reunification is never indicated. Clergy can, again, be helpful here by encouraging openness and cooperation in the therapy process.

Therapy programs and the courts generally arrange supervised visitation between the perpetrator and the child victim. Some programs offer this supervision themselves. Some do not. I have been asked as a minister if I or someone responsible in our congregation could perform this vital service.

The tension between spiritual counseling and psychological treatment enters into all of this. Many times clerics are suspicious that secular therapists will undermine the tenets of their faith. Secular therapists fear the clergy will let the offender off too easily with a prayer or a profession of conversion by the client, and not realize the extent of the illness. Most faiths accept the position that true conversion resulting in a major change is accompanied by a willingness to go anywhere and do anything necessary to get help for addictive problems. No faith assumes that conversion immediately clears up all problems. Faith cannot substitute for treatment.

Clergy should not hesitate to communicate positively with the therapist concerning values and tenets of faith, and vice versa. There is great value in both the spiritual and the psychological dimensions of healing. Great potential danger can arise if a professional in either one of these helping disciplines feels a need to undermine the work of the other. By giving the proper attention to the matter, religious leaders can locate qualified therapists who will understand the values of their faith. Likewise, therapists will find that, even though there are clerics who tend to discredit psychological treatment, there are many others who accept the value of such treatment and who can be of great assistance by adding the extra dimension of faith.

Clergy and Congregational Attitudes

Recently a pastor of one of the churches in the ministerial association of which I am a member related an experience involving child sexual molestation in his church in Minnesota. It occurred when he was a young, inexperienced minister.

This very kind and sensitive man stated frankly that both he and his church totally mishandled the case. First, the leadership tried to cover up the incident so as not to disturb the congregation. It is certainly true that such matters should be handled discreetly and in confidence, but when it is known that the problem exists (and such problems do have a way of becoming known), it is not helpful to deny that it has occurred in the church. A frank admission, with encouragement by the pastor that the congregation continue to love and support those involved, is certainly preferable.

In this case, however, there was probably good reason for the leadership to be concerned about the congregation's knowing. When the members did learn of it, they took very damaging stances. Half of them said that the girl seduced the perpetrator. The other half said the perpetrator should be castrated! Of course, neither approach made any sense. The importance of rendering firm, but nonjudgmental, assistance cannot be overemphasized. Clergy should not shirk taking the steps that must be taken to protect the victim, but during all the procedures outlined in this chapter, many of which are painful, all parties should be the recipients of care and concern. The outcome in the therapeutic and redemptive process will be affected.

Comments Concerning Family Violence

Clergy should always be alert to the signs of abuse. It is a very common malady in our society, and one can safely say that no congregation is without the high potential of having this problem among its members. Dark glasses, heavy makeup to cover bruises, concern about possibly having to make a move or train for a job, a demeanor of fear: any one or a combination of these can be indicators. Many times an abused woman is embarrassed to open up the issue to her pastor or congregation. The pastor should not hesitate to inquire.

Often a woman does not leave an abusive partner because she has no place to go or means of support or child care. The religious community should be a "city of refuge." The fleeing victim should not be coerced by use of the Bible or any other means to go back to an abusive husband. Physically abusive behavior can be equated with alcohol, drug, or sexual addiction, and should be addressed accordingly. Yes, if possible, the abuser should be helped in obtaining therapy, but the first response should be to ensure the safety of the victims, whether a partner or children or both.

Congregations can be a great resource for "safe homes." Local women's shelters exist in many communities, but most of these are totally inadequate to fill the needs for temporary housing of abused partners and children. For this reason, many of them offer training for volunteers who wish to offer their homes on a temporary basis for such a purpose.

Concerning the legal aspect of this problem, there is increasing evidence that the stronger the law against spouse abuse, the better the possibility for cessation of this unacceptable behavior. Statistics show that when a man is arrested for beating his partner, he is less likely to repeat and more likely to seek help. This action is more effective than the victim's obtaining a restraining order, although this is important as well.

Assisting the offender through the hearing process, visiting him in jail, and encouraging him in therapy whether or not he is placed on probation are all important ministries, and can be of great assistance to the abused partner as well. There are support groups and therapy programs for abusers. The battered women's shelter or the Department of Social Services can put the religious leader in touch with them.

A Final Word

The people of God are a major, largely untapped resource in assisting the abused and the abuser. The unspoken cry of the abuser is "Please help me!"; of the abused, "Stand by me!" May God enable us all to respond in wisdom.

19

A Model Program for Training Religious Leaders to Work with Abuse

James Friedrich

Training religious leaders is a most ambitious task even for educators who are well known within particular religious communities. For trainers in domestic violence programs outside the religious community who would like to offer something to religious leaders, the task may seem even more ominous. "What kinds of concerns will they raise?" and "How can we handle religious perspectives that may be at odds with our views?" are some of the questions that may well arise.

Our own work in training religious leaders, both clergy and laity (church or synagogue members), has offered some insight into perils that can be avoided. We have conducted multiple training sessions in congregational settings and at large ecumenical gatherings of leaders in one-day events. This work has been done in a large metropolitan area (San Jose and suburbs) using several local resource people with specialized skills. While this blessing may not be readily available to you, it may offer some guidelines for quality training. Increasingly, however, there are resource people in communities of all sizes who can add the depth and conviction of personal experience to make for good training.

A Brief Background

We first became involved in training because of the continual appeal from colleagues in battered women's programs and child abuse and elderly abuse services to get the religious community more involved in understanding and confronting the problem. To be sure, some leaders may always resist the idea of training, holding onto a denial of the problem ("I don't think abuse is a problem in this congregation!") or building other defenses. Still others are looking for tools with which to do a better job of managing other ecclesiastical problems they face. However, more and more clerics are getting advanced counseling training to supplement the little they had in seminary.

More of them are learning the value of using referrals and not feeling they must deal with problems all by themselves. If religious leaders can be approached and offered something that will cater to *their* needs, enhance *their* ministries, relieve some of *their* worries, then their commitment to training may well follow. An existing training program should not assume that what it currently offers will meet these needs, and the following model is therefore being offered as a guide.

Principles for Structuring Good Training Events for Religious Leaders

Build a foundation for growth. It is only natural to focus your effort on what you want to cover in your training event, and make it a comprehensive experience. But what training needs will remain after you are through teaching? If staff members of agencies involved with domestic violence are present at your training, how can you foster their continuing interaction with the religious leaders in attendance? If issues are raised about the need for more services to abuse victims in your community, what roles can religious leaders play in the movement to get more services? Can participants at your training session be recruited to play a more significant part in reaching others?

Be sensitive to the denomination(s) you are working with. If you represent an agency or organization that is not well known to the religious leaders you plan to train, establishing a relationship with them is an important prerequisite to training. Many denominations are quite parochial in their scope of relationships, and even if the social service world knows all about you, the clergy may not. There may be a particular pastor, for example, who is known as the expert or consultant on domestic violence issues in his or her denomination. Getting that person's endorsement and support could be crucial to your success.

We have found that it is best to involve a mixture of church and synagogue representatives early in our planning activity. These people will know the most about how their groups function, who carries influence, and what training they really need. They can help identify the best training times, find affordable facilities, and do the best job of publicity.

These people can also help you evaluate an important concern: How religious should your training be? How much time will you need to devote to developing a biblical or religious basis for abuse work? In some groups, the use of key passages such as Psalms 22 or 55 may be sufficient to show the sensitivity of the scriptures to suffering. In other groups, however, a much more significant attempt will be made to develop a theology of abuse or a religious perspective on abuse ministries.

Identify pastoral issues related to abuse. Most religious leaders have had some experience in dealing with abuse. What are the most common experiences or dilemmas they have faced? Did they confront a child abuse situation and wrestle with reporting responsibilities? Have they felt caught in the middle of a relationship where there is spousal abuse? How do they define their roles when they perceive abuse may be occurring—as advocates for the victim, protectors of the family unit, or confessors who may hear confession but may not be involved as a counselor?

Religious leaders may well benefit in a training event if they struggle directly with the question, "What is pastoral care in cases of abuse?" The discussion can show differences between more traditional pastoral counseling and the need for more confrontation in abuse situations. The question may also help pastors see the limits of their role and the need to form secular partnerships in the community.

Planning the Training Program

The model we used is shown in Table 19–1, which reflects some concerns, that require further comment.

Establish Clear Goals and Objectives

Generally, our training was intended to sensitize and educate about abuse issues, identify service roles, and build skills in prevention, intervention, and treatment. All are important, and any one of them may be the sole goal of a particular event. Training that is not clearly focused and limited in its scope can easily lead to frustration. Also, abuse is an emotionally draining issue with many dimensions. Training must help the participant to manage the adjustment to it, not be more undone by it.

Objectives must be measurable in some way, and while our outline does not reflect quantifiable outcomes, our final evaluations, completed by participants, helped us measure success. Extensive questionnaires that examine attitudes and knowledge about abuse can be used as a pre- and posttest to reflect changes in these areas. Also, the level of participant satisfaction is an important consideration, particularly in formulating future presentations.

Methods of Presentation

Clergy and other religious leaders will be sensitive to how the speakers communicate, how open community resource people are to genuine dialogue with religious leaders, and how clearly the written materials reflect their theological perspectives. In other words, use speakers who are good speakers, not

Table 19–1
Introductory Training for Religious Leaders

Goals: To provide an opportunity for participants to

1) learn more about counseling victims and perpetrators of family violence
2) become more familiar with local resources for victims and perpetrators of family violence
3) begin a process of community interaction to stop the violence increasingly common in homes throughout this area.

Objectives	*Methods/Activities*
To sensitize participants to the pathos of abuse as a motivation for learning	Media presentations, testimonies of victims, special speakers
To present a definition of abuse that reflects the scope of the problem, i.e., physical, sexual, and psychological abuse and the destruction of property and pets	Charts, transparencies, or speaker. Use examples, local statistics, local news events, or other illustrations
To identify prominent perspectives on the pastoral role in some common abuse situations	Well-respected local religious figure, expert, or panel of speakers of different denominations or faiths
To provide introductory training on counseling with victims of abuse (may be focused on child abuse, both physical and sexual, spousal abuse, or elder abuse)	Lecture by identified trainer(s) or small group session with local people as trainers or facilitators. Written materials for each participant
To provide introductory training on counseling with perpetrators of abuse	Same as previous methods
To introduce participants to the local resource people and agencies that may serve as good sources for referral and consultation	Panel of speakers discussing particular areas of expertise or responsibility. Opportunity for whole group dialogue or questions
To emphasize the role of the religious community in abuse prevention activities	Speakers, handouts describing resources for marriage and family enrichment and other prevention programs
To facilitate interaction among the participants with the aim of strategizing for future involvements in abuse issues	Large or small group discussion of local needs and developing responses. Solicit commitments for future events and/or activity.

just knowledgeable. Instruct resource people to be good listeners, especially if they are not involved in a religious community. Get reactions to the written materials you plan to use. Do they speak to leaders in language they are familiar with?

A good mixture of educational activities also helps bring life to the event. Note how the outline makes use of media, lectures, small and large groups, handouts, and so forth. Evaluate to find what has worked best and what needs improvement.

The Planning Committee

It will require a group of dedicated planners to put together a successful event. Involve the best combination of religious leaders and community experts on your planning committee and be sure to ask for their input as you work through each phase of your plan. Getting their opinions ensures their support.

Some tasks of the planning committee will involve the following:

Establishing an initial budget

Collecting good resource materials appropriate to goals

Identifying good accommodations, in the best case a neutral site that will encourage maximum participation

Developing plans for a publicity campaign

Some Special Considerations

Special responsibilities also may arise during the training. It is not unusual for some percentage of participants in your event(s) to attend because they have been victims of abuse themselves. Religious leaders may identify their interest in the subject as professional, but in reality it is personal. Consequently, thought must be given to how these needs might be met.

We have found it helpful to express the concern early in the training:

Some of you are here because you have experienced or are experiencing abuse. We hope that this training will give you a better handle on how to deal with your concerns. We want to be as much help to you as we possibly can and would be happy to make available to you a private place where you can speak with a designated counselor. Also, we would be happy to help you identify other contacts which might be of personal help.

Conducting the Training

With all the preparatory work behind you, conducting your training event still offers a number of challenges. To eliminate the unexpected from your event, you must make it clear that you could not possibly think of everything and that the energetic involvement and participation of those attending is therefore vital. A good way to begin the workshop is to initiate a good participatory activity at the outset of training.

Here are some common ways of inviting participation.

1. Invite participants to share the reasons they have come and what they would like to get out of the event.
2. Ask all of the participants to respond to at least one of several questions. Questions such as "What was your congregation's reaction when you

Table 19–2
Checklist for Managing Training Sessions

___Room temperature comfortable
___Comfortable chairs provided and arranged to invite participation
___Directions provided to restrooms
___Process explained for getting messages
___Adequate break time planned
___Good public address system if needed
___Space for small group discussion free of distractions from other groups
___Good meals and comfortable dining arrangements
___Adequate time for informal conversation, networking
___Packets provided for information arranged in organized fashion
___Registration process easy and smooth
___Trainers and support staff give clear assignments
___Media equipment, newsprint, etc. in place and working
___Parking adequate
___Space provided for displays, brochures, etc.

said you would be attending a conference on family violence?" and "What one word would you use to describe your role if you learned of child abuse (or spousal or elder abuse) in your congregation?" are appropriate.

3. In smaller groups especially, you might invite participants to share some of their own experiences and relate those experiences to how the training will help address the kinds of problems they experienced.

During the course of the event, you want to continue to invite comments and questions. If your agenda is flexible, it may be good to give the group options of spending more time on particular training aspects or going to the next topic.

If your training group includes leaders of various religious groups, you may well encounter perspectives that conflict with your own views or those of other participants. How you handle this kind of conflict will depend on what your training interests are. You may want to confront those views to which you take exception and simply make it clear that "we don't agree on this matter." If you see yourself primarily as a facilitator of the group, then you may want to encourage the group to talk through their views and not say much yourself. In groups with mixtures of religious leaders and abuse workers, you should be sensitive to polarization. The checklist in Table 19–2 identifies some other basic considerations for effective conference management.

It is always helpful to monitor your event while it is in progress so as to make appropriate mid-course corrections. Of course, follow-up meetings will also be necessary to wrap up details and plan ahead. It is good to have prepared a thorough summary of participants' evaluations for the planners to review.

Conclusion

Training religious leaders is indeed a most ambitious task but one not lacking in rewards. The time spent in careful preparation plays an important part in the event's success. This model may help you prepare and succeed. (Note: For selected training resources, a Resource Directory is included at the end of the book.)

20

Reporting Child Abuse: An Ethical Mandate for Ministry

Marie M. Fortune

T he epidemic problem of child abuse in the United States (physical, sexual, and emotional) presents persons in ministry with a challenge and an opportunity. When child abuse is disclosed, the religious leader can intervene with sensitivity and compassion to bring an end to this suffering, which has most likely been chronic. Yet intervention by a minister is not necessarily forthcoming because of hesitancy, confusion, lack of information, and ambivalence. Situations of child abuse are complex, and a minister may well try a private solution and avoid using other community resources, usually to the detriment of the child and the family.

An Ethical Mandate

The ethical mandate for Christian ministry in response to the abused child is rooted in Jesus' gospel teachings. In Matthew, Jesus points to the child as the one who is the greatest in the kingdom:

> Whoever receives one such child in my name receives me; but whoever causes one of these little ones who believe in me to stumble, it would be better for him to have a great millstone fastened round his neck and to be drowned in the depth of the sea (Matt. 18:5–6, RSV).

Jesus is consistent in his assertion of the specialness and value of children in a cultural context that regarded children as property of their father. He also points clearly to the responsibility of those around children to care for them. This teaching must have been consistent with Jesus' understanding of the Hebrew custom of hospitality, in which the orphan, widow, and sojourner were identified as being the responsibility of the entire community, which was to provide for their needs and protect them. What is at stake here is these persons' vulnerability, which is a consequence of their life circumstance. Children are by definition vulnerable and in need of care and protection by adults. When this care and protection are not provided by adults, and when those whose responsibility it is to protect are in fact the source of pain and abuse for the child, then someone else must act to provide for the child. Such is the situation faced by a religious leader to whom it is disclosed that a child may be abused.

The other ethical principle that applies here is that of "justice-making" in response to harm done by one person to another. Christian scripture here is very specific: "Take heed to yourselves if your brother sins, rebuke him, and if he repents, forgive him" (Luke 17:3, RSV). The one who harms another must be confronted so that he might seek repentance. Both Hebrew and Christian scriptures are clear that repentance has to do with change: "get yourselves a new heart and a new spirit! . . . so turn and live" (Ezekiel 18:31–32, RSV). The Greek word used for repentance is *metanoia,* "to have another mind." In this context of repentance, accountability, and justice, forgiveness and reconciliation may be possible. These should be the primary concerns of the religious leader.

Final Goals

As with all forms of family violence, child abuse requires an immediate response and a recognition of a larger context. The goals of any effective response should follow this order:

1. Protect the child from further abuse.
2. Stop the abuser's violence.
3. Heal the victim's brokenness and, if possible, restore the family relationships; if not possible, mourn the loss of that relationship.

Taking these steps in order provides the best possible opportunity for eventual restoration of the family. Until the first two goals are successfully accomplished, the third is unachievable. It is certainly possible to have the victim and offender living in the same place and giving the appearance of being an intact family, but unless the victim is safe and the offender has taken steps to stop the abuse, there is no restoration and no intact family.

In situations of child abuse, these goals can best be accomplished by the early reporting of suspected child abuse to legal authorities. Every state in the United States provides a mechanism at the state level for reporting, investigating, and assessing situations where children may be at risk. They also have the professional resources with which to assist victims, abusers, and other family members in addressing the three goals of intervention.

Reporting: Reasons to Report

1. *Facts about child abuse:*

Offenders will reoffend unless they get specialized treatment.

Offenders against children minimize, lie, and deny their abusive behavior.

Offenders rarely follow through on their good intentions or genuine remorse without help from the outside.

Treatment of offenders is most effective when it is ordered and monitored by the courts.

The pattern of the abuse must be broken in order to get help to the victim and offender.

Quick forgiveness of the offender is likely to be "cheap grace" and is unlikely to lead to repentance and change. These factors emphasize the need to use an external, authoritative, specialized resource in order to bring change for the family.

2. *Access to specialized resources for treatment:* Unless the ministers are specially trained to provide treatment for victims and abusers of family violence, they alone are not an adequate resource to the family. The pastor's role is critical throughout, but the most important first step is reporting.

3. *Access to a means to protect a child and require accountability from an offender:* The child protective service or law enforcement offices in a community are the only bodies authorized to investigate allegations of abuse, provide physical protection for a child, and restrain the behavior of an adult who is abusive.

4. *Deprivatizing the situation:* Involving the services of a community agency requires that the silence which has supported this chronic situation be broken. It is not simply a private, family matter; it is a community concern. The consequences can no longer be avoided. Again, this offers the best chance to provide help to a hurting family.

5. *Setting a norm:* Involvement of the wider community clearly communicates to all involved that the physical, sexual, or emotional abuse or neglect of a child is intolerable because children are important and it is our collective responsibility to protect them.

6. *Mandatory:* In every state, persons in helping professions are mandated to report the suspicion of child abuse to the authorities. In some states, the religious leader is exempt from this requirement. In every state, any citi-

zen *may* report suspected child abuse and not be liable for an unfounded report if the report is made in good faith. With or without a legal mandate, clergy should consider the weight of an ethical mandate to report.

Why Ministers May Hesitate

The ambivalence many ministers feel about reporting child abuse comes at the point when other considerations supersede the fundamental goal of protecting the child. Such things as protecting family privacy or the status of the adults in the family, fears of breaking up the family, or perceptions of the social service providers as punitive or insensitive to the religious beliefs of the family make it difficult for a religious leader to refer or report. Yet once ministers receive a disclosure, they have the authority and responsibility to protect children who cannot protect themselves.

Reporting: How-Tos

Sometimes the hesitancy to report comes from a lack of understanding of what will happen once a report is made. Every state has a statewide agency responsible for child protection.[1] Generally, a report is made to indicate there is suspicion that a child is being harmed. The religious leader need not have specific evidence and need not attempt to gather evidence or detailed information from the person who discloses. If it sounds as if abuse may have occurred and the child is still at risk, then the child protection agency should be notified. It will investigate the situation and assess the risk to the child. In some communities, it will encourage the alleged abuser to temporarily leave the home. Frequently, when there is no other available option, it will remove the child temporarily from the home. If there is evidence of abuse, it will take the case to the prosecutor, who will then decide whether to file charges. Whether charges are filed or not, the child protection agency will offer counseling to the child victim and nonoffending family members. If the abuser is convicted, the court may mandate counseling as an alternative to prison time. Adults seldom serve time for child abuse convictions.

Problems and Suggestions

Another cause for hesitation in the religious leader is the fear that reporting will be perceived by abusers as turning them in and thus will damage, perhaps irrevocably, the pastoral relationship. Two factors mitigate against this fear. First, it is seldom the abuser who discloses; it is most likely the child/teenage victim or the nonoffending family member who calls for help. Second, the way in which the report is made significantly shapes the perception of the person who has disclosed.

For example, if a religious leader conveys any ambivalence to someone at the first hint of abuse by saying "Don't tell me any more or I will have to report this," the context is set for a punitive and secretive situation. The minister is also withholding possible assistance from the person who is seeking help. Further, it is not helpful for the minister to listen to a disclosure, never indicating that a report must be made, then wait until the person leaves to call and report anonymously. This may relieve the conscience, but does not help create a context in which the religious leader can continue to minister as a part of wider intervention.

Instead, it is helpful when hearing a disclosure to indicate that additional help will be needed in order to aid the victim, save the family, help the abuser, and so forth, and that the best resource to begin with is the child protection service. Suggest that the person who has disclosed call the agency with you present, and offer to be with them when the social service provider comes to talk with them. Help the person disclosing to understand that the child protection worker can provide much more in addition to what you can do and reassure the discloser that you will not desert him or her. Then seek to work *with* the child protective service worker to provide for the needs of the members of the family seeking help.

What to Expect With Disclosure/Reporting

Offenders will frequently be the last people you would expect to sexually molest a child. They may well be highly regarded, upstanding citizens who are active in the congregation. Do not allow your impression of these people in public settings to prevent you from entertaining the possibility that they may have molested a child.

Initially, the offender will usually deny all responsibility and will seek to discredit the victim's story by attacking its credibility: "She lies about everything, but this is the most ridiculous one she's told yet." It is always tempting to believe the adult's denial because our society has never taken children's words very seriously.

Very rarely do victims falsely report an offense. If they have summoned the courage to tell someone about their situation, they almost always have been harmed by someone. Victims may also quickly recant their story because they feel extreme pressure from family members and maybe even the offender to do so. Their recantation does not mean the abuse did not occur or that this person is now safe. Nonoffending family members (usually mothers) initially may not believe their child, but instead feel pressure to support the offender against the child. The mother may also be a victim of spouse abuse.

When a report is made to the legal authorities, chaos usually erupts. The whole family is in crisis. It may take several weeks for this very complex situation to be sorted out. The results of disclosure and reporting may not be a final resolution to the incestuous abuse situation in a family, but some attention to this matter is better than none.

Special Considerations

Confessions and Confidentiality

Many people in pastoral roles perceive a contradiction between their obligation to preserve confidentiality of communication with a congregant and their obligation to report the suspicion of child abuse. They see this contradiction as a conflict of ethical demands. Part of the perceived conflict arises from the interpretation of confidentiality and its purpose, particularly as it rests within the responsibility of the religious professional. The context for an analysis of these ethical demands is the understanding of confidentiality that comes to the religious professional from multiple sources.

The purpose of confidentiality has been to provide a safe place for a congregant or client to share concerns, questions, or burdens without fear of disclosure. It provides a context of respect and trust, within which help can hopefully be provided for an individual. It has meant that some people have come forward seeking help who might not otherwise have done so out of fear of punishment or embarrassment. Confidentiality has traditionally been the ethical responsibility of the professional within a professional relationship and is generally assumed to be operative even if a specific request has not been made by the congregant or client.

For the minister, unlike the secular helping professional, confidentiality rests in the context of spiritual issues and expectations. In Christian denominations, the expectations of confidentiality lie most specifically within the experience of confession. The responsibility of the pastor or priest ranges from a strict understanding to a more flexible one—from the letter to the spirit of the law. For example, for Anglican and Roman Catholic priests, the confessional occasion with a penitent person is sacramental; whatever information is revealed is held in confidence by the seal of confession, with no exceptions.[2] The United Methodist *Book of Discipline* does not view confession as sacramental but states, "Ministers . . . are charged to maintain all confidences inviolate, including confessional confidences."[3] The Lutheran Church in America protects the confidence of the parishioner and allows for the discretion of the pastor: "no minister . . . shall divulge any confidential disclosure given to him in the course of his care of souls or otherwise in his professional capacity, except with the express permission of the person who has confided in him or in order to prevent a crime."[4] Even within Christian denominations, there is a range of interpretations of the expectations of confidentiality which are not necessarily limited to the confessional occasion.

What are Confidentiality and Secrecy?

It may be useful in this discussion to make a distinction between confidentiality and secrecy. Secrecy is the absolute promise never under any circumstance to share any information that comes to a member of the clergy; this is the essence of sacramental confession. But a commitment to secrecy may also support maintaining the secret of child abuse, which likely means that the abuse will continue. Confidentiality means to hold information in trust and to share it with others only in the interest of the person involved, with their permission, in order to seek consultation with another professional. Information may also be shared without violating confidentiality in order to protect others from harm. Confidentiality is intended as a means to help an individual get help for a problem and prevent further harm to herself or others. Confidentiality is not intended to protect abusers from being held accountable for their actions or to keep them from getting the help they need. Shielding them from the consequence of their behavior will likely further endanger their victims and will deny them the repentance they need.

In addition, confidentiality is not intended to protect professionals; it is for those whom they serve. It should not be used as a shield to protect incompetent or negligent colleagues, or to protect them from professional obligations. Thus, confidentiality may be invoked for all the wrong reasons and not truly in the interest of a particular congregant or of society. This was never the intent of this special provision of pastoral communication.

Disclosure within Different Faiths

When a disclosure is made by an offender in a confessional setting, the religious leader has the opportunity to respond within the parameters of a particular faith's tradition while keeping in mind the overriding priority of protecting the child victim. For example, a Roman Catholic priest can hear the confession of a child abuser, prescribe penance to report himself to the child protection service, and withhold absolution until the penance is accomplished. Confession to a priest does not carry with it the priest's obligation to absolve in the absence of penitent acts. Confession opens the opportunity for the penitent persons to repent and to make right the harm they have done to others. Likewise, for a Protestant in a nonsacramental confessional situation, directives may be given and actions prescribed which include the abuser reporting himself to child protection services. If it is clear that the penitent will not follow the directive of the religious leader and self-report, then some Protestant ministers have the option and the obligation to report directly. The vulnerability of the child and the significant likelihood that the abuse will continue supersede an obligation to maintain in confidence the confession of the penitent.

Cooperation: Working with Secular Service Providers

In addition to a long-standing breach between religious and secular professionals concerned with mental health issues, some substantive concerns have often prevented ministers from working effectively with social service providers or therapists. All these concerns come to the fore when the issue of reporting child abuse is raised: separation of church and state, involvement of the criminal justice system, disregard for a family's religious beliefs, and breaking up families. While the state should not interfere with the practice of ministry, it does have the lawful responsibility of protecting children from harm. The church should see this as a common agenda and work with those designated to carry out this mandate. Even with its multitude of shortcomings (not the least of which are sexism and racism), the criminal justice system can provide a mechanism to enforce accountability for offenders and should not be avoided to protect offenders from embarrassment or the serious consequences of their abuse. A family's religious beliefs deserve respect. But any effort by family members to use religious beliefs to justify abuse of a child or deflect intervention intended to stop abuse should be challenged by both religious and secular professionals. Finally, outside intervention to protect a child does not break up the family. The abuse which preceded the intervention broke up the family and endangered its members. Temporary separation of family members may well be the only possible means of healing and restoration, and should be used when appropriate.

Cooperation between religious and secular professionals expands the resources available to a family experiencing abuse. The special skills each can bring are much needed by family members. Religious leaders can concentrate on their pastoral responsibilities in concert with the social service provider, who can guide the intervention and treatment.

Conclusion

Situations of suspected child abuse are seldom simple and straightforward. Religious leaders should be guided by a commitment to the overriding priority of protection of children and by a clear sense of the limits of their own resources. The mechanism of reporting child abuse and the resources that follow from it are invaluable tools for the minister. Clarity of purpose will direct an ethical mandate to use every available means to stop the abuse of a child.

Notes

1. Religious leaders should familiarize themselves with the child protective services office in their community. Some child protection programs do only investigation of possible abuse; others do both investigation and treatment. Ask about the specifics of the agency staff's approach to reports and the possible options available to them. Approach them as a professional ally and resource. Invite them to a discussion with local ministerial groups.

2. See Seward Reese, 1963, "Confidential Communications to Clergy," *Ohio State Law Journal,* 24:55.

3. *The Book of Discipline of the United Methodist Church,* 1980 (Hasville, TN: United Methodist Publishing House), 220, paragraph 440.4.

4. *The Minutes of the United Lutheran Church in America,* the 22nd Biennial Convention, 1960, as quoted in Reese, *op. cit.,* p. 69.

21
Developing a Religious and Secular Partnership

Judith A. Kowalski

As a religious leader who is in a counseling position, you may be uneasy about tackling the subject of domestic abuse. If you have not had formal training or personal experience with abuse, you may fear saying the wrong thing and making matters worse. This chapter covers steps any religious counselor can take to become informed, assured, and equipped with some referral and informational partnerships.

Self-Preparation by Leader

Before publicly encouraging people to disclose domestic abuse situations, you should do necessary self-preparation. In the interest of saving time and energy, some of this preparation can be done for you by associates. Other preparation, however, is personal and you must do it yourself.

Self-Examination

This is preliminary and personal. No one but you can look into your own heart and no amount of information can replace this introspection, since it is your attitude and belief system that may determine whether a life is saved or sacrificed. It is your attitude that will determine whether you take a person seriously or dismiss some timidly offered hint as "nothing." Here are some suggestions.

1. *First and foremost, confess you do not know everything about family abuse, especially if you have not had experience.* Carefully examine your own life to see whether you have suppressed the memory of abuse as a child or whether you may be treating your own family in an abusive manner. In

any case, your personal experience will not be the same as someone else's. Therefore, take the initial role of concerned listener and *LISTEN*.

2. *Adopt an attitude of sympathy toward, and interest in, abusive family situations.* It is easy to withdraw from encounters with abuse victims, and even easier to back off from confronting an abuser. However, LOVE will compel you to lean forward with attentiveness and concern if you give yourself to it.

3. *Examine your own biases, preconceptions, and theology relating to family abuse.* Do you *really* think abuse is as widespread as people say? Are you convinced there is no other way to discipline children than spanking? Is the Bible the source of the saying, "Spare the rod and spoil the child"? Such beliefs need to be looked at, not because anyone is trying to make a liberal or humanist out of you, but because you cannot proceed with any intentional program against abuse unless you know exactly where you stand, and why. Only then can you develop your own personal plan that is authentic and merciful.

4. *Be willing to learn and to change your outlook.* Knowing where you stand and why is a beginning, and an important one. However, unless growth and grace mean nothing, you can hardly close off the possibility of change. Allow that change to happen. Be open to being transformed.

5. *Be prepared for a shock.* The stories you will hear from your people are not pretty. They will involve some of your most respectable members and some of your most generous contributors. You may be faced with the choice of either believing an unemployed woman who says she is beaten regularly, or accusing her husband, a well-known business executive who contributes $1,000.00 a month to your treasury. It will require some difficult wrestling with your own conscience. You may need to reorder your priorities, in order to ensure that the suffering of women and children *must end,* even if it is at *your* expense, when your congregational income and your own vocational security suffers.

6. *Spend some time with God.* Pray. Meditate. Listen. It might seem strange that a topic like domestic abuse can bring you closer to God or enhance your spirituality. It can. In your role as helper to victims of violence, you are acting in God's stead as a giver of life, mercy, love, and peace. It is an honor and a responsibility that will not go unrewarded.

Self-Education

Not everyone can attend training sessions, continuing-education, or other formal classes about family violence, nor are there enough opportunities available. Much of the information about this topic needs to be sought out and learned on your own. Such research can be done by others and brought to you at your convenience but you will need to initiate and coordinate the task.

1. A place to begin is in your own congregation or constituency. Beginning here will serve several purposes. It will bring you information, and it will also start building service networks and identifying needs. Begin by distributing a professionally composed questionnaire, asking people to anonymously reveal their experience with family abuse. Consult with professional abuse counselors and advocates regarding this questionnaire before distributing anything to the public. In addition to that survey, invite professional abuse counselors and advocates, nurses, medical doctors, social workers, police, abuse-trained lawyers, and women's shelter workers *in your congregation* to identify themselves by name. Once you have an idea of the needs and the resources under your very roof, you can better organize your self-education and congregational program.

2. Communicate with your denominational headquarters about programs or information they may have on domestic abuse. Ask them to begin a study and strategy for your denomination if they have not done so already. If necessary, submit a convention resolution requesting such a resource.

3. Read newspapers, news magazines, books, articles, and other churches' resources on family abuse. More and more material is being written on the many forms of abuse. Most of these articles and books are clear and concise, and you will not need much of your time to survey them. Set aside some time each day or week to keep up on this reading. The lives and health of others depend on it.

4. Find out what the laws are in your state and local area regarding mandatory reporting of child abuse, clerical confidentiality, legal protection for victims, restraining orders, mandates to police for pressing charges, and prosecution of perpetrators. Determine whether those laws are enforced.

5. Draw up a list of people, offices, telephone numbers, and addresses of entities that legally must be notified in the cases of child abuse, battery, harassment, criminal assault, rape, incest, and other crimes against family members. Learn the time limits within which such reporting must be completed and whether it must be in writing, by telephone, or both. Especially know the phone numbers of your state child protection agency, family abuse hotlines, hospital emergency rooms, and local police department.

6. Consult with people outside the congregation regarding the topic of family abuse, with the intent of developing referral services. See people from your denominational social service agencies, welfare agencies, AFDC (Aid to Families with Dependent Children), shelters, food shelves, community agen-

cies that give vouchers for food and gas, police departments, and hospital emergency rooms. Develop a relationship with people from some of these agencies, for the purpose of referring victims to them in an emergency and for ongoing counseling, treatment, or services. See Table 21–1 for a checklist and information guide to help you organize this referral material.

Preparing Your Congregation for Combatting Family Abuse

Now that you have prepared yourself for dealing with abusive situations (although nothing can really prepare you for the danger, the violence, and the shock of seeing the dark side of your people until you experience it), you are ready to bring the concern to your congregation.

1. Prepare your staff for ministry with the abused and abusers by sharing pertinent information about family abuse and emergency intervention strategies. If your staff has helped you collect the information, they know at least part of the story already. Make sure all staff members are fully informed. Remember that women who have been victims of sexual abuse may not trust any man. If you are male, but have staff members who are women, let them serve as contact people for members who prefer to consult first with another woman.

2. In consultation with your committee of congregational professionals and your church council or governing body, devise and announce a policy regarding family abuse. List all the behaviors that are abusive. Note those that are clearly illegal in your state, those that are physically dangerous, those that are psychologically dangerous, those that are demeaning, those that are sexually abusive, and those that are destructive to relationships or self-esteem. Declare the intent of your congregational leaders to end such behavior patterns and encourage healthy lifestyles.

3. Announce through sermons or homilies, bulletins, newsletters, and bulletin boards that you are available to help in family abuse situations. Express your sympathy for all members who are caught up in the problem, and offer your concern and assistance. Members who are living through this situation often need to hear your invitation before they will approach you for consultation. Too often, church members are afraid they will be judged or condemned, even though they are the victims. The church has an unfortunate reputation of being unsympathetic toward family abuse victims, so you will need to overcome that negative reputation as well as the personal guilt and shame felt by victims.

4. Be prepared to hear disclosures of abuse from some of the most active members in your parish. Being respected and well liked does not eliminate

Table 21–1
Checklist and Information: Family Abuse Prevention

[Fill in telephone information for your local area, and keep this list handy.]

POLICE _____   SHERIFF _____

EMERGENCY Police/Fire/Medical HOTLINE _____

Ambulance _____

Hospital Emergency Rooms

Battered Women's Shelters

Emergency Food Pantries

Emergency Child Care

Emergency Elder Care

Emergency Care for Mentally and Physically
Disabled

Emergency Transportation

Abuse-Trained Lawyers

Abuse-Trained Doctors

Nurses

Child Protection Agencies

Social Service Agencies

Welfare Agencies/AFDC

Community Voucher Systems

Battered Women's Support Groups

Men's Support Groups

Teen's Support Groups

Missing Children's Network

Respite Care for Caregivers

Prayer Chain or Prayer Partners Groups

Other Referral Services

the possibility of abusive personal behavior, especially behind closed doors. Some members may even deliberately abuse their children because they believe the Lord demands that kind of discipline. Other members may not know of any other way to behave in stressful situations.

5. Offer opportunities to discuss the topic of family abuse in a non-threatening setting. Arrange informal discussions using, for example, the American Lutheran Church statement *Families and Violence: The Church's Role.* (Contact national headquarters in Chicago, Illinois for copies.) Invite speakers to come to your church school, confirmation class, high-school class, and adult education sessions. Get a number of speakers who will each discuss a different aspect of family abuse. There are many facets to this problem: child sexual abuse, woman battering, marital rape, psychological harassment, spouse abuse, child physical abuse, child abduction, elder abuse, torturing and killing of pets, and more. In order to communicate the seriousness and complexity of the problem, more than one session must be dedicated to it.

6. Publish a list of authorities and counselors whom members can approach outside your congregation. Many more people would seek help if they were assured their identities would not become known among their friends and religious associates.

Enabling the Congregation to Become Actively Antiabuse

Educating your congregation to the situations surrounding family abuse is a step in the right direction. It is a lot of work, but it needs to be done. Stopping the abuse in family situations is also necessary work. There is no substitute for it. Unless the church steps in now to end abuse, victims may choose to leave the church as well as their abusing family members. The church needs to be a friend, not a threat, to people who suffer. It is not helpful to victims to be ignored by the church, and it is not helpful to the church to be seen as an institution that condones or even causes abuse.

While those remedial and emergency measures are being taken, however, preventive action also is necessary. Unless we turn the trend around, the circle of abuse will perpetuate itself, and the next generation will be worse than the one we have now.

1. First, state clearly that abuse will not be tolerated in your congregation. State clearly that you are ready to help people in abusive situations—both victims and victimizers. If your denomination does not have a formal position paper or resolution on the topic, develop your own within the con-

gregation. Publish it for all to see. Formally adopt it at a congregational meeting.

2. Include antiabuse discussions in premarital counseling sessions and high-school education opportunities. Many couples do not wait until marriage to harm one another. Abuse can begin during the courting stage and is an ominous portent of worse abuse to come. Many teenage couples, even those not intending to get married, are physically and sexually abusive. Sometimes young couples do not stop to realize that such behavior is abusive and harmful. They grew up in homes where violent methods of control were used, and they know no other pattern of behavior. Perhaps they have seen it on television, in the movies, or in pornographic magazines and think it is the adult way to behave. These erroneous perceptions need to be corrected as soon as possible.

3. Include antiabuse vows in the marriage ceremony. Rather than wait to see whether one spouse will abuse the other, it would be a better preventive measure to alert people at the beginning that certain behavior is wrong. Ask them to vow not to do violence to one another or to their children. That way, an abused spouse will not feel guilty for seeking help, nor will she blame herself for the violence. She has already been assured by her spouse's vow that violence will not be used. If it is, he has betrayed his own word.

4. Include antiabuse vows in the baptismal ceremony. Child abuse, some committed against very young victims, is rampant in our society. Parents may think little of it, or they may think no one will know how they treat their children in privacy. Some are unaware that simply shaking a child can cause a fatal brain concussion. Others do not have a clear notion of the difference between discipline and dangerous abuse. Conversations with child sexual abusers reveal some strange ethical standards. Some men will say they can do anything they like with their own children, but would not touch someone else's child. Others say sex with their child is wrong, but any other children are fair game. As a church, we need to state clearly our ethical teachings about right and wrong, as basic as that might seem. Asking the parents to take a public vow that they will not physically or sexually abuse their children will make them stop and think about their actions. It will also remind everyone that God is a witness to the relationship between child and parent.

5. Place specified amounts of congregational money in antiabuse organizations. There is nothing like money to express where one's commitment lies. Congregational members will see that the church is serious about antiabuse if the church generously funds abuse prevention programs, battered women shelters, hotlines, and emergency care facilities.

6. Begin immediately to develop a program of education on the topics of loving family relationships and abuse prevention. Take nothing for granted. If the church does not clearly teach its members how to behave in

a loving manner, where will they learn? In the streets, on television, from magazines, from the marketplace, and on the battlefield. What will they learn there? Perhaps that "might makes right," that "sex sells," and that "everybody does it."

We, as a church, have a responsibility before God to offer hope and love to people. We cannot, at the same time, ignore the violence in our midst.

22
Saving the Family: When Is Covenant Broken?

Mitzi N. Eilts

For those of us in the church, there are critical questions presented by the reality of domestic violence. Is maintaining the family unit more sacred than the well-being and safety of the individuals within it? Is there any spiritual reason for suffering or abuse to be endured which is perpetrated by one member of the family against another? Who is responsible for breaking up the family—the one who leaves home and partner or parent to escape the abuse *or* the one who is being abusive?

To find some answers to these questions requires that we reexamine what constitutes family in our faith traditions. What is the nature of the covenant around which we build family? What are the principles of covenant as established by God on which we pattern our covenants with each other? Is there any evidence or precedent in scripture or our faith traditions for the breaking of covenant? What are they? Is the only kind of family "to be saved" the nuclear family with father *and* mother and children? In this chapter these questions are examined so that the religious community and service providers might consider what a danger it is to apply a save-the-family ethic without equal consideration of other spiritual ethics and values.

Covenant Making

Covenant making is older than the Judeo-Christian tradition; there is evidence of this in the language used in the Old Testament that comes from treaty-making language of the nations and tribes occupying the territory into which the Israelites moved.[1] Covenant making is the establishment of an agreement between two parties defining the relationship (responsibilities and obligations) between them. It may be an agreement between equals (mutual, parity) or a unilateral agreement (suzerainty) in which one party must accept the conditions presented by the other due to favors owed or difference in power.

It is generally understood and accepted in the Jewish and Christian traditions that covenants with God are initiated by God. There is nevertheless some recognition of mutuality in God's covenant making with us in that God takes on promises and responsibilities to uphold as well as naming obligations to be upheld by those to whom the covenant is offered. (In other words, covenants are good for us *and* good for God.) A common thread in all of God's covenants is a promise of deliverance and well-being, liberation from suffering, persecution, or oppression (either already bestowed, to come, or to be continued), and in exchange God seeks loyalty and commitment—commitment of heart reflected in behavior.

Consider the covenants established with Noah (Genesis 9:1 out of chaos a promise never again to destroy the earth); with Abraham and Sarah (Genesis 17:1 out of barrenness the promise of generations to carry on); with Moses (out of bondage a promise of a home). Covenants made with the God of the Hebrew Scriptures and the Christian Testament have as their most basic element the offer of liberation from bondage or affliction—the offer of new life, life as God intended it to be for us.[2]

> For I the Lord love justice, I hate robbery and wrong; I will faithfully give them their recompense, and I will make an everlasting covenant with them (Isaiah 61:8).

> I call heaven and earth to witness against you this day, that I have set before you life and death, blessing and curse; therefore choose life, that you and your descendants may live (Deuteronomy 30:19).

> I came that they may have life and have it more abundantly (John 10:10).

We should remember that as the people of God we are in a constant process of renewing and reestablishing the covenant between God and ourselves. It is common to speak and act as though God's covenant with us is a settled event. Yet the covenant with Moses was offered anew to the Hebrew people through Joshua as they entered the promised land. The original covenant with Moses was a revision of the ones made with Noah and Abraham and Sarah, then renewed with Jacob. The Davidic covenant was seen as new, yet it was related to the one made with Abraham and Sarah. Jeremiah and the New Testament authors represented the covenant as being reestablished in new ways. Renewal of covenant has been seen as necessary and has been practiced as new generations have emerged with different conditions in their lives, so that all covenants are relevant to the present circumstances.[3]

> Behold, the days are coming, says the Lord, when I will make a new covenant with the house of Israel and the house of Judah, not like the covenant which I made with their fathers when I took them by the hand to bring them

out of the land of Egypt, my covenant which they broke . . . But this is the covenant which I will make with the house of Israel after those days, says the Lord: I will put my law within them and I will write it upon their hearts; and I will be their God, and they shall be my people (Jeremiah 31:31–33).

Blessed be the Lord God of Israel, for God has visited and redeemed his people, and has raised up a horn of salvation for us in the house of his servant David . . . that we should be saved from our enemies, and from the hand of all who hate us; to perform the mercy promised to our ancestors, and to remember his holy covenant, the oath which God swore to our father Abraham, to grant that we, being delivered from the hand of our enemies might serve God without fear (Luke 1:68–69, 71–73).

Consequences of Covenant Breaking

Additionally, there is history of covenants being broken between God and God's people. The language of God's covenants acknowledges this possibility by the use of blessings and curses.

[BLESSINGS] If you walk in my statutes and observe my commandments and do them, then I will give you your rains in their season and the land shall yield its increase, and the trees of the field shall yield their fruit. . . . And I will give you peace in the land, and you shall lie down and none shall make you afraid; . . . And I will have regard for you and make you fruitful and multiply you, and will confirm my covenant with you. . . . And I will walk among you and will be your God and you shall be my people.

[CURSES] But if you will not hearken to me, and will not do all these commandments, if you spurn my statutes, and if your soul abhors my ordinances, so that you will not do all my commandments, but break my covenant; I will do this to you: I will appoint over you sudden terror, consumption, and fever that waste the eyes and cause life to pine away . . . and I will break the pride of your power (Leviticus 26; see also Psalms 78 and Deuteronomy 29).

These verses illustrate that there are consequences for the breaking of covenant—not so much wrath or vengeance, but the consequences of living life without God. For once we have broken the covenant(s) we make with God, we are in essence living in a world devoid of God and God's ways. Though it has become clear over time that God has an unending ability and desire to forgive our unfaithfulness or breaking of covenant, it has also remained true that there are consequences when we desert the ways of God. Change and amends (repentance) are necessary to restore covenant relationships.

And when all these things come upon you, the blessing and the curse, which I have set before you, and you call them to mind among all the nations where the Lord your God has driven you, and return to the Lord your God, you and your children, and obey his voice in all that I command you this day, with all your heart and all your soul; then the Lord your God will restore your fortunes and have compassion upon you, and will gather you again from all the peoples where the Lord your God has scattered you (Deuteronomy 30:1–3).

Who Decides When a Covenant Is Broken?

When a covenant is broken, who names that fact? Is it the covenant breaker, the one who has ignored, forgotten, transgressed the promises made? Or is it the one who is still living by the promises, the one who is attempting to keep covenant? Again and again, throughout the scriptures, it is God or one called by God (prophets such as Jeremiah, Isaiah, and John the Baptist) who calls attention to the fact that the covenant has been broken. It is God who says "if you want to be in a relationship with me you must change your ways—return to the promises you made with me." God, the one who has been faithful, is the one who says the covenant is broken; the covenant no longer stands. It is the one who is faithful to the covenant who calls attention to the fact it has been broken, and *that* makes common sense, does it not?

Covenant Making in Human Relationships

The idea of covenant between God and human beings was quickly picked up and applied to human relationships in the scriptures. In the book of Genesis we find Abraham making covenant with Abimelech, and then Jacob and Laban using the idea and language of covenant with each other. Their oaths of loyalty and promises of peace are bound in the language of covenant.

Similarly, as people of faith, we have continued to apply the model of covenant with God to our human relationships. A prime example of this is our understanding of marriage as a form of covenant—making and keeping promises with God as an essential witness. Historically, marriage has sometimes been understood as a mutual covenant between two equal parties, and other times as a covenant of protection/caretaking by one person in exchange for nurturing/obedience by the other. (Notice the parallel to the model of treaties—mutual/parity and suzerainty.) Evidence supports the mutual marriage covenant as the one that most closely resembles and fulfills the purpose of God in covenant making. It is the mutual/parity form of relationship which establishes a way of relating and a setting for the promotion of health and well-being (physical, emotional, and spiritual), a setting within which life as God intended it to be for us might be nurtured and sustained.

Rev. Joy Bussert in her book *Battered Women: From a Theology of Suf-*

fering to a Theology of Empowerment examines some theological premises that have been instrumental in making the marriage covenant one of suzerainty. Her thesis is that ideas such as mind-body dualism (debasing the very nature of femaleness) or that men have a right and a spiritual duty to chastise women, have distorted the nature of relationships between women and men, setting the stage for domestic violence to occur.[4] Friar Cherubino in the Rules of Marriage adhered to in the city of Sienna in the middle to late fifteenth century, for example, expressed a rationale used today by some abusers.

> When you see your wife commit an offense, don't rush at her with insults and violent blows; rather first correct the wrong lovingly . . . but if your wife is of a servile disposition and has a crude shifty spirit, so that pleasant words have no affect, scold her sharply, bully and terrify her. And if this still doesn't work . . . take up a stick and beat her soundly . . . for it is better to punish the body and correct the soul than to damage the soul and spare the body. . . . You should beat her . . . only when she commits a serious wrong; for example, if she blasphemes God or a saint, if she mutters the devil's name, if she likes being at the window and lends ready ear to dishonest men, or if she has taken to bad habits or bad company, or commits some other wrong that is a mortal sin. Then readily beat her, not in rage but out of charity and concern for her soul, so that the beating will resound to your merit and good.[5]

Any covenant of marriage based on the protector/provider and obeyer/nurturer model lends itself too easily to the idea that a man ought to, even has a duty to, keep his woman in line, for his sake and hers.[6] In contrast, a marriage covenant based on mutual respect and responsibility expects both parties to work on and uphold their promises to love, cherish, and obey—the command of God, not of each other.

Rev. Marie Fortune has outlined the elements necessary to a marriage covenant based on mutuality; these elements make possible the fulfillment of God's intentions for us in the relationship and are parallel to those in the covenant between God and God's people.

1. It is made in the full knowledge of the relationship.
2. It involves a mutual giving of self to the other.
3. It is assumed to be lasting.
4. It values mutuality, respect, and equality between persons.[7]

Such a marriage does not leave room for abuse. If and when abuse does occur, it is clear that promises and vows have been broken and the covenant (trust) has been breached.

When physical violence or emotional abuse occurs within a marriage relationship, the very intent of the covenant is being broken. When abuse is occurring, marriage becomes a setting of bondage and affliction rather than a setting for God's ways of compassion, justice, and love to be practiced and lived out.

Yet a woman victimized in an abusive domestic relationship feels serious ethical/spiritual dilemmas about the marriage covenant. She has made promises that are still important and meaningful to her. One of those is that the relationship will be a lasting one. To stay in the relationship means to suffer further abuse, but to leave (temporarily or permanently) makes her feel as if she is breaking her promise. Many women thus stay and suffer the abuse, precisely because they take their commitment seriously. Seldom does it occur to the victim of the abuse (at least in the beginning)—or to friends, family, or the church—that the covenant has already been broken by the behavior of her partner.

Saving the Family

There is a big problem with the concept of saving the family (keeping covenant or the appearance of covenant) when it is applied indiscriminately to families in which domestic abuse/violence is present. The problem is that meaningless suffering and sometimes even death are very real consequences. The victim holds on for many reasons, one of which is usually hope—hope that what the marriage is supposed to be might be restored. It is common for the victim to persist in the hope that her patience will last longer than his abuse. Often this attitude is reinforced by church teachings on long suffering which may apply in settings where one is *choosing* to make a stand on behalf of God's ideals in this world, but which do not apply when the suffering is perpetrated by another who has promised to live according to God's ways with her.

In abusive families, hope and patience without safety for the victims and intervention for the abuser are dangerous because unless he takes responsibility for his actions and seeks help, the cycle of abuse will continue and worsen. Any chance that the covenant relationship might be restored requires both confession (taking responsibility for wrongdoing) and serious repentance on the part of the abuser, achieved by consistent participation in an abuser's program.

Victims often remain long past the danger point for some other emotional and religious reasons as well. Guilt is a common reason. The world around us reinforces the notion that the marriage relationship is primarily the responsibility of the woman. In many Jewish and Christian traditions women are told that marriage is the domain in which they are to live out their service to God. Therefore, if something is going wrong it must be their fault.

Most battered women have been told by at least one person that she must have done something to deserve such treatment. Most women hear that message from many sources, including their religious leaders and communities. Too seldom is the belief voiced that covenant is a two-way street, a partnership with responsibilities and obligations for both people involved. Too seldom is the one who is really breaking covenant, the abuser, being called to account for creating a home environment that is so oppressive that his partner needs to seek safety and peace elsewhere.

Victim/survivors often stay on in an abusive relationship for years because of the idea that marriage is permanent. For some women separation or divorce from their partner will also mean separation from their religious community. The first decision is tough in itself; feelings of failure are strong. For those women for whom separation or divorce from the partner also means the censure of or expulsion from their faith community, the decision is excruciatingly painful. The victim who seeks safety, or eventually decides to seek separation or divorce, *is* acknowledging that the covenant which she had established with another no longer exists, *but she is not the one breaking the covenant.* In fact, she is taking steps toward the basic purpose of the marriage covenant: to provide a home where the ways of life intended by God might be practiced: the ways of justice, peace, and mutual caretaking.

While marriage is a covenant that is *meant* to be lasting, there is nothing in scripture that can be construed to justify a lifetime of meaningless suffering, and there is substantial evidence calling for covenants with God to be ended when their purpose has been forgotten, ignored, or transgressed. Should it not be the same with covenants between people? When the marriage covenant is treated as more sacred than the way of living that it is intended to provide, are we not then abusing the very purpose of the covenant?

Conclusion

The intent of family, or marriage, covenants is to provide a place where justice, mercy, and love are lived out in keeping with God's covenantal ways. But when the family environment deviates from this intention due to the presence of abuse or violence, then the saving grace is to release the victim from the obligation. In families afflicted by domestic abuse, the only way to save the family is to allow the victim the opportunity to rededicate herself to life abundant in an environment free of the abuse.

The definition of who makes up a family is different with different cultures, circumstances, and generations. It is time we began focusing on what is really important—and that is the promise that for each of us God wishes life in all its abundance. Saving the family means ending the violence that is destroying it.

Notes

1. For more detail on treaty language and form see George E. Mendenhall, "Covenant Form in Israelite Tradition," in E. F. Campbell, Jr. and D. N. Freedman, eds., 1970, *The Biblical Archaeologist Reader,* 3rd ed., Garden City, New York: Doubleday.

2. All scripture quotations are from the Revised Standard Version.

3. For further examples and discussion of covenant renewal see G. F. Mendenhall, 1962, "Covenant Forms in Israelite Tradition," p. 38, in Gerhard von Rad, ed., *Old Testament Theology,* Vol. 1 (New York: Harper & Row).

4. For more in-depth discussion of these issues see Joy M. K. Bussert, 1986, *Battered Women: From a Theology of Suffering to an Ethic of Empowerment* (New York: Division for Mission in Northern America/Lutheran Church in America).

5. Cherubino da sienna, *Regole della Vita Matrimoniale,* cited in Bussert, pp. 13–14, from O'Faolain and Martines, *Not in God's Image,* p. 177.

6. See Bussert, *Battered Women,* chapters 1 and 4 for further discussion.

7. Rev. Marie M. Fortune, 1980, "A Commentary on Religious Issues in Family Violence," Seattle: Center for Prevention of Sexual and Domestic Violence Newsletter. Marie Fortune's writings and workshops have made immeasurable impact on my thinking as expressed in this chapter.

23
Forgiveness: The Last Step

Marie M. Fortune

Forgiveness is a pastoral resource available to those who have been victimized by others' actions; it is a means of restoration to wholeness. It should be viewed from the experience of the victim and understood as only one aspect of the healing process.

Because of the obligation to forgive which is taught in Christian formation, persons who are the victims of family violence often feel that they must forgive their offender immediately. This obligation is communicated through pastors, family, and friends. For the victim, however, there is beyond the obligation a desire to forgive that is related to the hope that forgiveness will bring healing and resolution to the pain of the experience.

To Forgive and Forget

For many victims or survivors of family violence, the longing or obligation to forgive is superseded by the subjective sense of not feeling forgiving. The guidance they are receiving from family members, friends, their pastor, and their church points in the direction of "forgive and forget." Even though they may speak the words of forgiveness, they cannot forget; they know very well that popular piety and platitudes are not enough; they know that nothing has changed for them.

Forgiveness is the last step in a process of healing from the brokenness of family violence. Prior steps are necessary in order for a victim of violence and abuse to be *freed to forgive*. In Luke's gospel, Jesus describes part of the process very concretely:

> Take heed to yourselves; if your brother sins, rebuke him, and if he repents, forgive him; and if he sins against you seven times in the day, and turns to you seven times, and says, "I repent," you must forgive him. (Luke 17:3–4, RSV)

The scripture clearly points to the need for preliminaries to be accomplished before forgiveness is considered. These prerequisites are best described as elements of justice. Once justice has been accomplished, even in a limited way, forgiveness becomes a viable opportunity. Prior to justice, forgiveness is an empty exercise.

From the offender's perspective, forgiveness is often viewed as an immediate way to be relieved of guilt for wrongful actions. An offender may approach a pastor seeking forgiveness or may ask the victim to forgive. Usually these requests are accompanied by genuine remorse and promises of changed behavior: "I'm sorry, honey; I'll never hit you again." Or the offender may bargain with the victim: "If you forgive me and take me back, then I'll go into treatment." But forgiveness by the victim or by the church is inappropriate and premature in these situations. Forgiveness before justice is 'cheap grace' and cannot contribute to authentic healing and restoration to wholeness for the victim or for the offender. It cuts the healing process short and may well perpetuate the cycle of abuse. It also undercuts the redemption of abusers by preventing them from being accountable for their abusive behavior.

Justice as Precondition

Making justice begins with acknowledgement that harm has been done to one person by another. In Luke's gospel, this is referred to as "rebuking," or confronting, the offender. Pastorally, the offender's act of confession is the beginning of acknowledgment. To be confronted (whether by family member, pastor, or district attorney) is to be called to accountability for unjust acts. To confess is to acknowledge responsibility for harm done.

Second, repentance is needed. Remorse may be easily forthcoming, but repentance is harder; repentance is derived from *metanoia,* or fundamental change. The prophet Ezekiel called for repentance:

> Repent and turn from all your transgressions . . . and get yourselves a new heart and a new spirit! . . . so turn, and live! (Ezekiel 18:30–32, RSV)

But change from a pattern of abuse in the family is not accomplished through good intentions; it requires time, hard work, and therapy. Involvement in a treatment process may be the most useful penance that could be prescribed for an abuser.

Another aspect of "justice-making" is restitution. It is the responsibility of the abuser to provide materially for the restoration of those harmed. Thus, paying expenses such as medical treatment, housing, and therapy that a victim incurs as a result of the abuse is a very concrete and symbolic act of justice. Some adult incest survivors have sought and won restitution from their offenders in civil court. Restitution acknowledges the real cost to the victim and represents an effort to make right what was broken.

Each step is dependent on the willingness of the offender to participate in the healing process, but often the offender is unwilling or unavailable.

Providing Elements for Justice and Forgiveness

Justice, forgiveness, and healing for the victim cannot be dependent on the offender. These steps then become the responsibility of the wider community. The church, the legal system, and family and friends can also make justice for victims. It is the task of helping professionals to provide the elements necessary for justice. These include the following:

1. *Truth-telling/acknowledgment of the harm done to the victim.* In expressing this acknowledgment to the victim, belief and outrage are fully communicated.

2. *Deprivatization/breaking the silence.* Dealing with the offense openly breaks down the secrecy that has sustained the abuse for so long. The silence only protects offenders from the consequences of their acts; it does not protect the victim or future victims. (But care should be taken to respect the privacy of the victims and their choices as to public discussion of the experience.)

3. *Deminimization/hearing the whole story.* Many people tend to minimize the seriousness of family violence. It is one way of dealing with the horror of its truth. Deminimizing—being willing to hear and believe the experiences of victims—is a means of standing with the victim.

4. *Protection of the vulnerable.* Regardless of what action is taken by the courts or by the offender, the responsibility remains to protect any others who might be at risk.

Thus, when an incest offender is not remorseful or repentant, the survivor needs justice from other sources. Victims need to have their experience acknowledged by others within some wider context, and they need to know that others will help keep the children away from the offender. If a victim chooses to bring a civil suit for damages, the choice should be supported and not discouraged.

When a batterer is not remorseful or repentant, the victim needs support for her decision to leave that relationship and try to make it on her own. If she chooses to file criminal charges, she needs support, not someone trying to talk her out of this action. She needs safe shelter rather than someone trying to get her to return to the abuser.

What Is Forgiveness?

For the victim, forgiveness is letting go of the immediacy of the trauma, the memory of which continues to terrorize the victim and limit possibilities. The memory is the lens through which the world is viewed. Forgiving involves putting that lens aside but keeping it close at hand. It is the choice to no longer allow the memory of the abuse to continue to abuse. But this step of healing must be carried out according to the victim's timetable. For the incest survivor who is now thirty to forty years old, but is just now remembering the incestuous abuse, the traumatic events may be long past but the memory fresh and painful. Healing will take time.

Forgiveness is not forgetting. Victims never forget experiences of abuse in families. Consciously or unconsciously, the memory remains. Trying to forget is a waste of valuable energy. Putting the memory into perspective so that it no longer dominates one's life is more useful.

Forgiving does not necessarily mean automatically trusting or returning to the offender. Trust that has been so savagely broken can be regained only over time, if at all. The return to a relationship is entirely dependent on trust: Can the survivor genuinely trust this person not to abuse her again? The choice to forgive should not be tied to these decisions.

Pastoral Encounters and Treatment Suggestions

From a pastoral perspective, the temptation to skew the justice and forgiveness processes is great because the road to healing and restoration is long and arduous. But shortcuts never serve the victim, the offender, or the wider community.

The first pastoral encounter with a situation of family violence may well be with the offender who is arrested or who comes to the pastor expressing remorse and asking for forgiveness. One incest offender approached his pastor and told him that he had been molesting his daughter for two years: Could God forgive him and could the pastor forgive him? The pastor assured him that God forgives those who repent of their sin, and then he offered to pray with him. He also said that as soon as they were finished praying, he (the pastor) wanted the father to call the Child Protection Service and report himself. The man was surprised; but he did as he was instructed. Then the pastor explained to the man that he would eventually be placed in a treatment program for incest offenders and the pastor wanted him to attend that program once a week. He also wanted to see him once a week for Bible study and prayer and he wanted him in church every Sunday.

The pastor could easily have said a prayer over this man and sent him home. The offender would have felt absolved of any responsibility and, although genuinely desiring at that moment not to repeat the offense, would be highly likely to do so. Instead, the minister used the authority of his pastoral office to give guidance and direction to the offender, which he knew would be in the offender's best interest in the long run. (Reporting any suspicion of any form of child abuse is required by most helping professionals in every state. In some states, clergy are exempt from this requirement; see Chapter 20 of this book.)

Conversion

Another fairly common circumstance a pastor will encounter is the offender's religious conversion. This is particularly common when arrest has already taken place. A pastor would be well advised to approach this situation with caution.

An experience of religious conversion may well be genuine, but should not then be used as a reason to avoid the consequences of the offense: "Judge, I've found Jesus Christ; I'm a new man and I promise you this will never happen again." If it is a genuine experience, this conversion becomes an invaluable resource to the offender who faces incarceration and possibly months of treatment. The pastor's task is to help guide and direct this religious resource in order to support the offender's process of repentance. If it is not a genuine experience, the pastor is virtually the only person who has the authority to call the offender's bluff. It is the pastor's responsibility not to allow the offender to manipulate and distort the process in order to avoid negative consequences.

Mediation

Another temptation for the pastor is the resource of mediation. Mediation is the process now widely available (often through church channels) for conflict resolution. It is sometimes recommended as a resource to families dealing with violence and abuse. Mediation is not an appropriate resource with which to address a situation of violence for the following three reasons.

1. Mediation seeks to resolve a conflict between two parties as a way of stopping the abuse. Since the abuse is not the result of a conflict or disagreement, but is a chronic pattern of abusive behavior by the offender, mediation is not appropriate.

2. Mediation is used primarily as an alternative to the criminal justice

system. Avoidance of the criminal justice system is usually unwise in addressing family violence. There may be some legitimate reasons why a victim or offender would seek to avoid this system, such as the unequal treatment often given to people of racial or social difference. But it is more likely to be white, middle-class families that seek to avoid this system. It is important that the criminal justice system be used if at all possible, because it unequivocally communicates that the offender is held accountable for the abuse and it has the best chance of directing the offender to treatment.

3. Mediation presupposes that two equal parties come to the table to resolve a conflict. Victims of abuse in families can never come to that situation and feel safe from, much less equal to, their abuser.

Mediation may be a valuable resource to call upon *after* the violence and abuse have stopped and family members need to resolve division of property, custody, and other such problems. But it should not be used as an intervention to stop the violence.

Conclusion

For the Christian, it is finally the power of the Holy Spirit that enables the healing process to take place. This spiritual power gives the victim the strength to forgive, to let go. It gives the victimizer the strength to repent, to change. It gives the church the strength to help both persons in the justice-making process. But the power of the Holy Spirit is released only when justice is made manifest for the victim and offender. Whenever there is an attempt to cut the process short and jump to premature reconciliation, the possibility of authentic healing is lost.

A group of incest offenders in a treatment program made a powerful plea: "Don't forgive so easily." All were Christians and had gone to their pastors as soon as they were arrested, asking to be forgiven. Each had been prayed over, forgiven, and sent home. They said that this pastoral response had been the least helpful to them because it enabled them to continue to avoid accountability for their offenses. Withholding forgiveness and absolution from an offender until certain conditions have been met may be the best way to facilitate a permanent change. Waiting patiently with victims until they are ready to forgive may be the most charitable and compassionate act the church can offer. In these ways, we take seriously the power of forgiveness to bring people to healing.

24
Wife Abuse and Scripture

Phyllis Alsdurf
James M. Alsdurf

"I would never in my wildest nightmares have dreamed that my husband would ever abuse me, but he did," a woman wrote to us. "My husband is a Christian, but his rage at things is unreal. I took our two-month-old son and fled after the fourth time he struck me, but I had received counsel that it was my duty to stay and suffer for Jesus' sake."

Suffering for Jesus' sake: Is that what Scripture has to say to the victim of abuse? Can the minister offer more than platitudes about submitting and trusting God to the battered women who seek pastoral counsel? Often, battered women are among those who accept the authority of Scripture in their lives, and they come to their pastors struggling to reconcile the Bible's seemingly harsh words on submission and the sanctity of marriage with the reality of their abuse. Many times abusers also appear to adhere to these rationalizations of violence in their marriage and home. This chapter explores the position of the Scriptures in respect to spouse abuse.

Suffering and Scripture

The connection that many battered women make between their ability to suffer violence from their husbands and their Christian commitment reflects what is widely and erroneously taught within evangelical churches about submission of women in marriage. It is a perspective that makes women more susceptible to violence and also heightens the likelihood that battered women will remain in abusive relationships long after they should.

For those who accept Scripture as authoritative, a legitimate understanding of what the Bible says in regard to abuse can come only when Scripture is considered in its entirety, when its broader themes are the backdrop against which isolated texts are interpreted. An appreciation for the principles, laws, and methods of interpretation is a necessary part of this task. One basic hermeneutical principle is that the parts of Scripture be interpreted in relation to one another. To take verses out of their context is to distort and violate the inspired truth of God.

Susan Brooks Thistlethwaite, a theology professor at Boston University, contends that "women with a violent spouse have believed that the Bible actually says what they have been taught it says—that women are inferior in status before husband and God and deserving of a life of pain." While women may accept this viewpoint through many episodes of violence, she says, eventually *some* women come to an awareness that the violence against them is wrong.

> But no sooner do women in violent relationships begin to develop an ideological suspicion that their subordination is wrong, than they are told that resistance to this injustice is unbiblical and unchristian. They are told that Christian women are meek and that to claim rights for themselves is the sin of pride. Some women at this point cease to struggle further. Some continue to struggle but abandon the church. . . . Some in fact do come to a new hermeneutic and begin to apply it to the Scriptures with the incredible discovery not only that the Bible does not support battering of wives, but that the Scriptures are more on the side of such women than they had ever dared hope (Thistlethwaite, 1981).

Submission and the Battered Woman

At the heart of the view that the battered wife must "suffer for Jesus' sake" is often the belief that the woman must submit to her husband in all things, a heresy that runs counter to Jesus' attitude toward women. When a woman cries out to Jesus, "Blessed is the mother who gave you birth and nursed you" (Luke 11:27), He replies "Blessed rather are those who hear the word of God and obey it." He thus explodes the confines of traditional Jewish roles for women and clearly demonstrates that He sees women as disciples on equal footing with men, not as sexual stereotypes. In sharp contrast to the culture of His day, Jesus taught women as well as men, using both males and females in his parabolic illustrations. He first announced his Messiahship to a woman and first appeared as the resurrected Christ to women.

It is Jesus himself, points out New Testament theologian S. Scott Bartchy (1984), who calls us to examine the ways we use the power we have and "any satisfaction we may feel with one-sided submission." Bartchy cites Mark 10:42–43 as an example of how Jesus confronted the presuppositions of male power and dominance:

> You know that those who are recognized as rulers of the Gentiles lord it over them; and their great men exercise authority over them. But it is not

so among you, but whoever wishes to become great among you shall be your servant; and whoever wishes to be first among you shall be slave of all.

Although Paul is often labeled a misogynist by his detractors (usually based upon a cursory look at one or two problematic passages), a more comprehensive examination of his writings reveals that the principle of mutual submission also undergirds his views on Christian marriage. In Colossians 3:18–19 he writes, "Wives, adapt yourselves to your husbands, that your marriage may be a Christian unity. Husbands, be sure to give your wives much love and sympathy; don't let bitterness or resentment spoil your marriage" (Phillips Translation).

From his examination of 1 Corinthians 7:4–5, Bartchy (1981) concludes that Paul understood marriage between Christians as "a matter of full mutuality. . . . The term *homois*, translated 'likewise,' is the strongest word available in Greek to express the meaning, 'in the very same way.' With these words Paul rejects the chain of command in the patriarchal households that were so typical of the Mediterranean area in the first century." But, Bartchy notes, too many men have used Ephesians 5:23 ("the husband is the head of the wife as Christ is the head of the church") as permission to discount other texts that call for mutuality in decision making and the principle of submission.

The Law of Love

It is not a one-sided, hierarchial view of submission that emanates from Scripture. Rather, the principle of mutual submission (Ephesians 5:21; 1 Corinthians 7:3–4 and 11:11–12; Galatians 3:28) is the model for relationships between husbands and wives, ensuring that the qualities of mutual respect, protection, and kindness characterize marriage. It is a "way of living," says author Pat Gundry (1980), that is both God-honoring and person-honoring. Such a biblical view of relationships, if actually endorsed by pastors, could provide a strongly needed support system for battered women and a basis for holding men accountable for their behavior.

To stress wifely submission in a vacuum devoid of husbandly love can result in a disregard for a woman's report of violence and place the woman and her children in great physical danger. Ultimately, it can perpetuate the cycle of violence. For to endorse submission one-dimensionally is to reject the whole counsel of Scripture. What it means practically is that the sanctity of the woman's personhood is ignored and the view of wife as property is perpetuated.

As Richard Foster rightly discerns, if anywhere, "the sting of the teaching [on submission] falls upon the dominant partner" (Foster, 1978, p. 104). To recognize the call to submission is not to ignore the "law of love as taught by Jesus" (p. 105), Foster states, and when submission offends this law it is no longer legitimate, biblical submission. Submission, therefore, "reaches the end of its tether when it becomes destructive." An inordinate emphasis upon the principle of wifely submission can cloud the fact that wife abuse represents a profound disregard for the law of love.

The risk of not submitting to the law of love, says Foster, is that the words of Jesus and Paul are turned into a new legalism: "If a woman comes in telling of marital rape and every conceivable inhumanity, she is simply and grandly told that unless there is adultery or desertion she has no 'biblical' basis for divorce" (p. 144). Such a mentality, Foster declares, subtly reinforces the view that men are to remain dominant.

Fidelity and Person-Keeping

Ongoing violence by a husband toward his wife is an offense to the integrity of human life. Ultimately, the violence may destroy both the marriage and the victim. The Epistle to the Hebrews says that marriage should be "held in honor among all, and let the marriage bed be undefiled; for God will judge the immoral and adulterous" (13:4). If we understand fidelity to imply much more than sexual faithfulness and to encompass the honoring of one's partner in a life-giving way, marital violence becomes a manifestation of infidelity.

Lewis Smedes (1983), professor of ethics at Fuller Theological Seminary in Pasadena, California, offers an important perspective: "Fidelity is a dynamic, positive posture that needs renewing and recreating constantly. It is not achieved simply by staying out of other people's beds." Instead, fidelity is a "person-keeping" commitment in which each partner in the marriage works at the "other's happiness, healing, wholeness and freedom." Under such a standard anything that violates a marriage would be considered adultery. Violation of the marriage by any means is basically what the seventh commandment addresses, Smedes asserts.

Far too many battered women have been told by their pastors that in response to their submission God will either stop the violence or, as an equally acceptable solution, give them the endurance to live with it. Thus, the expectation is that a wife should submit to her husband regardless of whether the abuse continues, since her responsibility is first and foremost to be submissive; her safety and right not to be violated are secondary to that spiritual responsibility. To endorse such a view of submission is to distort the biblical intent of submission and to pervert God's intention for the marriage relationship.

Marriage and Divorce

When you talk about divorce to a Christian woman who is the victim of physical abuse, she may cite Malachi 2:16—"'I hate divorce,' says the Lord God of Israel"—as a major reason that she is staying in her marriage. Many victims have heard sermons preached against divorce on the basis of that verse or have been counseled to submit to their abuser because "God hates divorce." And almost without exception, those very women are shocked when they find out what the last half of that verse proclaims: "'and I hate a man's covering himself [or "his wife" says a footnote in the New International Version] with violence as well as with his garment,' says the Lord Almighty."

"Why haven't I heard anyone preaching about that?" asked one amazed woman who attended a workshop in which we pointed out this passage. She is by no means alone.

The violence that an abusive husband perpetuates against his wife is a betrayal of his oath to love, honor, and commit himself to her. This truth is clearly revealed in that same Malachi passage, when God clarifies just why tearful prayers and offerings will go unheeded: "The Lord is acting as the witness between you and the wife of your youth, because you have broken faith with her, though she is your partner, the wife of your marriage covenant." That break in faith and in the marriage is the outgrowth of the abusive husband's actions.

A husband's violence toward his wife always offends the covenant and partnership that is under the rule of God's love, and may in some situations indicate that the couple no longer has what scripturally can be identified as a marriage. We agree with theologian Karl Barth in his assertion that when the integrity of human life is not sustained within a marriage, then

> the word of God may contain a "No" and powerfully and authoritatively express the final condemnation of a marriage, so that one is forced to conclude that the marriage itself no longer is undergirded . . . by the divine command. In this case, dissolution by divorce is a recognition of the fact that God has already brought the marriage under the judgment of nonexistence. (Anderson and Guernsey, 1984, pp. 138–139)

Clearly God's intent from creation was for people to experience companionship, not divorce. But there will always exist the tension between God's intent and people's choices. And when a marriage is being suffocated by the destructive presence of violence, threat, and intimidation, the "law of love (agape) dictates that there should be divorce." (Foster, 1985, p. 145). Jesus' words on marriage and divorce have been abstracted into a new "law of marriage and divorce," notes theologian Ray Anderson, and the unfortunate result is that pastors use this as their framework for making decisions about how they will minister to battered wives. In such marriages the perpetuation of abuse is far more damaging and sinful than is the danger of divorce. And the burden should not be placed upon the victim to justify her actions, but upon the abuser to confess his sin and demonstrate that destructive patterns have changed.

A New View of Women

The Old Testament resounds with the theme of God's identification with and care for the oppressed—the fatherless, the widow, the stranger (Proverbs 3:31–32 and 6:16–18, Psalms 82:2–4). And Christ's coming was the fulfillment of that central message. He was the one anointed "to preach good news to the poor . . . to proclaim freedom for the prisoners and recovery of sight for the blind, to release the oppressed" (Luke 4:18–19, New International Version). If Jesus is Good News to anyone, it is to those who are oppressed.

No wonder women in particular welcomed the Good News which Jesus proclaimed. He announced the Kingdom of God as a festive, glorious banquet to which all persons are invited, including the maimed, the poor, the sinners, the ritually unclean—all the outcasts of society. No doubt these fringe categories were composed of a majority of women (Storrie, 1984).

Even a cursory look at church history provides ample evidence that the church has failed women. Rather than proclaiming their equal standing as heirs in Christ, it has perpetuated their victimization through the misapplication of Scripture. By its failure to stand courageously against a patriarchy that has oppressed women, the church has fallen prey to the same process by which Scripture was used to defend slavery. Though God never supported slavery, it was not until social upheavals made slavery impractical that most Christians stopped using Scripture to defend that oppressive institution of which they were a part.

If we know that a hierarchial view encourages abuse and that submission to abuse reinforces it, should we not then seek to examine what Scripture is saying in its entirety about male/female relationships? The church must no longer lend its support, tacit or otherwise, to hierarchy and patriarchy. It must support Christ's emancipation proclamation to women.

References

Anderson, R. S., and Guernsey, D. B. 1984. *On being family.* Pasadena, CA: Fuller Theological Seminary.

Bartchy, S. S. 1984. Power, submission, and sexual identity among the early Christians. In Roberta Hestenes (compiler) *Women and Men in Ministry*. Pasadena, CA: Fuller Theological Seminary, pp. 103, 105–106.

Foster, R. 1985. *Money, sex & power*. San Francisco: Harper & Row.

Foster, R. 1978. *The celebration of discipline*. New York: Harper & Row.

Gundry, P. 1980. *Heirs today*. Grand Rapids: Zondervan, p. 94.

Smedes, L. 1983. *Mere morality*. Grand Rapids: Eerdmans Publishing Company, p. 163.

Storrie, K. 1984. New yeast in the dough: Jesus transforms authority. *Daughters of Sarah* 10 (1):10.

Thistlethwaite, S. 1981. Battered women and the Bible: From subjection to liberation. *Christianity and Crisis*, November 16, p. 311.

25

Religious Victims and Their Religious Leaders: Services Delivered to One Thousand Battered Women by the Clergy

Lee H. Bowker

How often do battered women seek out members of the clergy for help? What kinds of help do they receive? How effective are services given by the clergy to battered women in helping them end the violence in their lives? Most studies of battered women ignore these questions entirely, and others give only the most cursory treatment to the subject.[1] This chapter will describe studies of spouse abuse victims and discuss their experiences with the clergy and other helping professionals.

The Milwaukee Study

Bowker has reported an in-depth interview study of 146 battered wives from southeastern Wisconsin in *The Journal of Pastoral Care*.[2] Of these women, fifty-nine (40 percent) sought help from the clergy after 132 separate incidents of wife abuse. These contacts generally led to an extended series of helping sessions with a member of the clergy. The average request for help resulted in eleven separate counseling sessions or other instances of help, extending over a period of four months.

A "helping behaviors scale" developed by Gottlieb[3] was used to analyze the nature of the help given by the clergy to the battered wives. The most common helping behaviors delivered by the Milwaukee clergy were these:

1. Focused talking (26 percent of all incidents).
2. Command or direction about problem solving (22 percent).
3. Material aid or other direct service (11 percent).
4. Making suggestions about problem solving (5 percent).
5. Ensuring that the wife obeyed their directives (5 percent).
6. Directly intervening in the environment to diminish stress (4 percent).

The *Woman's Day* Study

While the Milwaukee study provided in-depth information about interaction between battered women and the clergy, this information was of limited application because of the small sample and its restricted geographical distribution. It was therefore decided to seek a much larger sample with a national distribution.

Methodology

An article drawing heavily on the findings of the Milwaukee study appeared in the March 9, 1982 issue of *Woman's Day* magazine.[4] Women reading the article were invited to join in the research effort by writing to Dr. Bowker for a six-page questionnaire on which they could summarize their experiences with domestic violence and the estimated effectiveness of a wide range of help sources. These included personal strategies, informal help sources (such as friends and family), and formal help sources (from clergy and psychotherapists on one end of the scale, to lawyers and the police on the other).

The first 854 questionnaires returned were added to data from the 146 Milwaukee interviews to constitute an internally consistent data base of 1,000 battered women from all sections of the United States. The return rate for these questionnaires was 85 percent. As an added bonus, many of the women added lengthy written accounts of their experiences. These letters add a much-needed human element to the abstract statistics derived from the computerized data base.

Like other volunteer samples of crime victims, the *Woman's Day* sample cannot be regarded as technically representative of all battered women in the nation for the purpose of statistical inference. Instead, it is the testimony of 1,000 women who became experts on wife battering through their own suffering. This researcher's task is (1) to be a good secretary in summarizing the information the women have provided, (2) to develop from these data generalizations about what works in ending the violence, and (3) to offer recommendations to helping professionals about the needs of battered women.

The Place of Religion in Violent Families

Most of the battered women and their husbands were part of the mainstream of American religious bodies. Religious affiliations held by the battered wives were as follows: 49 percent Protestant, 31 percent Catholic, 15 percent other religions, and 5 percent none. Affiliations for the husbands were 39 percent

Protestant, 29 percent Catholic, 12 percent other religions, and 20 percent none.

Official religious affiliation does not, however, tell much about the importance of religion in the homes studied. Religiosity (frequency of church attendance) is a more useful index of the importance of religion in the lives of these husbands and wives. Forty-eight percent of the husbands never attended church services; 30 percent attended less than once a month, 11 percent one to three times a month, and only 10 percent went to church every week.[5] The wives tended to exhibit greater religious involvement than their husbands. Only 23 percent never attended church services; 28 percent attended less than once a month, 24 percent one to three times a month, and 26 percent weekly.

Religious preference did not differ between the violent and nonviolent families, nor did it vary according to the backgrounds of the husbands and wives, the nature and extent of the wife beating, or (for the three-quarters of the women who ended the violence in their lives at least one year prior to their participation in the study) the personal strategies and the nonreligious help sources the women found most effective in stopping their husband's physical abusiveness.

In the Milwaukee study, religious preference did appear to affect the effectiveness of help offered by the clergy to the battered women, but the *Woman's Day* results contradict the Milwaukee findings. While Protestant clergy was more effective than Catholic clergy in Milwaukee, just the reverse was true in the *Woman's Day* study. The most helpful clergy was from religions other than Protestantism or Catholicism (41 percent very or somewhat effective), followed by Catholic clergy (40 percent very or somewhat effective), and Protestant clergy (30 percent very or somewhat effective).

Religiosity of both husband and wife played a much more important role than religious preference in the *Woman's Day* study. Husbands who scored a relatively high score in religiosity were less likely to drink alcoholic beverages before assaulting their wives or to use weapons in these assaults. They also tended to have better jobs and to show less evidence of involvement in a male subculture of violence. Wives who were relatively high in religiosity also tended to have better-than-average jobs if they worked outside the home. Families in which one or both spouses were frequent church attenders had more children and were more likely to own their homes than the other violent families in the study.

Use and Effectiveness of the Clergy

One-third of the battered women received help from the clergy, which indicates the important role that the clergy have an opportunity to play in reducing wife beating. Police, lawyers, physicians or nurses, and social service counseling agencies were used more often than was the clergy, while women's groups, battered women's shelters, and district attorneys were less likely to be used by the battered women.

The clergy was most likely to be used by wives who were high in religiosity, had more children than average, were beaten frequently, and were better educated than the other women in the study. The husbands of women who received help from the clergy also were above average in education and religiosity. A multiple regressions analysis of these factors shows that the wife's religiosity was by far the most important factor in receiving help from the clergy, followed by husband's religiosity, the number of times the wife was forced to seek shelter away from home because of the batterings, and a lower probability of alcohol involvement in the batterings.

As a group, the clergy rated lower on effectiveness than most other formal help sources. Thirty-four percent of the battered women who received help from the clergy rated them as very or somewhat effective. Formal help sources receiving a higher effectiveness rating were district attorneys (38 percent), the police (39 percent), social service or counseling agencies (47 percent), lawyers (50 percent), battered women's shelters (56 percent), and women's groups (60 percent). Only physicians and nuses (31 percent) were rated below the clergy in effectiveness. One out of every ten of the battered wives reported that their husbands also received help from the clergy. This figure does not necessarily reflect badly on the clergy, for most husbands failed to seek any help at all in altering their battering behavior. In just twenty-two families did the battered women feel that the clergy was more effective than any other help source used by their husbands. When asked to give advice to women still being battered, only thirty-five women mentioned praying, contacting the clergy, reading the Bible, or any other religious theme.

Members of the clergy were not equally effective with all the women who sought their help. They tended to be most effective with families in which both husband and wife were frequent church attenders, the wife's marital satisfaction apart from the battering was relatively high, and both frequency and severity of the violence was lower than average for the families studied. Finally, the clergy tended to be particularly effective with families exhibiting low geographical mobility. This suggests that the longer a family was part of the community, the more likely were clerics to be effective in reaching out to end the wife beating.

Although the battered women wrote extensive letters about their experience, they rarely mentioned the clergy. A few quotes presented below fairly represent what these women had to say about their involvement with the clergy:

> When I left my husband years ago, I met with great opposition about my decision to divorce him . . . from church leaders.

After I made the initial step towards divorce, I depended greatly on my family, friends, minister, lawyer, local mental health counselors, and the local police to help me stick to my decision.

A clergyman suggested that maybe I wasn't pleasing my husband in bed; and that was why he beat me.

The feeling I got from our church was that I was to suffer in silence.

Conclusion of *Woman's Day* Findings

The *Woman's Day* findings lead us to several conclusions. One is that the clergy probably has contact with a much larger number of battered wives than was previously thought. The second conclusion is that the clergy is, as a whole, perceived to be relatively ineffective in its efforts on behalf of the battered women. There is certainly much room for improvement in the performance of the clergy. In-service education programs for the clergy are in order, as are educational modules dealing with marital violence in seminary programs.

Members of the clergy must not only improve their own performance in aiding the wives who come to them, but also learn more about the availability and relative effectiveness of other community resources that can be used by battered wives. This is a matter of networking, or realizing that secular and religious institutions need not act as if the others do not exist. They can be mutually enhancing if they work toward common goals in appropriate areas.

Conclusion

Religious leaders must face up to ideas related to traditionalism and paternalism in their religions, ideas that often undermine the rights of women who are under the spiritual care of the clergy. At the same time, it would not be fair to expect the average member of the clergy to become a skilled family counselor or feminist therapist. A comprehensive referral network will leave the clergy free to concentrate on what it does best.

For some members of the clergy, this will mean helping battered wives solve moral dilemmas associated with ending the violence in their lives and helping batterers to see the inconsistencies between their abusive behavior and religious teachings. However, individual counseling and referrals do not end the responsibilities of the clergy with respect to wife beating and other forms of family violence. Sensitive, progressive clerics will also want to develop initiatives to increase congregational awareness about these problems through directed sermons and extraliturgical education programs.

Much of the networking between religious and secular institutions could eventually be accomplished by congregational members rather than the clergy. Such activities by congregational volunteers would be the strongest possible evidence of the increased effectiveness of the clergy in dealing with family violence in a comprehensive way.

Notes

1. See, for example, J. J. Gayford, January 1977, "Wife Battering: A Preliminary Survey of 100 Cases," *British Medical Journal,* 25:194–197; J. P. Flynn, January 1977, "Recent Findings Related to Wife Abuse," *Social Casework,* 58:13–20; S. Prescott and C. Letko, 1977, "Battered Women: A Social Psychological Perspective," in M. Roy, ed., *Battered Women: A Psychosocial Study of Domestic Violence* (New York: Van Nostrand), 72–96; B. E. Carlson, November 1977, "Battered Women and Their Assailants," *Social Work,* 22:455–460; M. S. Ashley, 1978, "Shelters: Short-Term Needs," in United States Commission on Civil Rights, *Battered Women: Issues of Public Policy,* Washington, D.C., 371–400; and R. E. Dobash and R. Dobash, 1979, *Violence Against Wives* (New York: Free Press).

2. L. H. Bowker, 1982, "Battered Women and the Clergy: An Evaluation," *The Journal of Pastoral Care,* 36:226–234.

3. B. H. Gottlieb, April 1978, "The Development and Application of a Classification Scheme of Informal Helping Behaviors," *Canadian Journal of Behavioral Science,* 10:103–115.

4. A. Lake, March 9, 1982, "New Hope for Battered Wives," *Woman's Day,* 65:120–123.

5. Where percentages do not total 100, it is due to statistical rounding procedures. Note: Some of the data presented in this chapter were collected under NIMH grant number 1 RO1 MH33649.

26

Women Who Ended Abuse: What Religious Leaders and Religion Did for These Victims

Anne L. Horton
Melany M. Wilkins
Wendy Wright

This year thousands of battered women will approach clergymen, community agencies, and various mental health professionals for advice about their violent situations. Though methodologically challenging, the 1986 study presented here gathered these victims' reports and their perceptions of what worked for them and what did not. How did their faith and religious leaders contribute to their success in stopping wife battering in their lives?

This chapter focuses on the important relationship between women and abuse and identifies what part these victims themselves see religion and religious leaders playing in their abuse, their strategies for ending the violence, and their satisfaction with their choice of remedy. What did they do when praying was not enough?

Background

Although empirical data directly related to religiosity are very limited or, at best, generalized from the unidimensional measurement of church attendance or affiliation, feminist theorists believe that violence against wives is historically structured into marriage under the patriarchal order. Cameron in 1979 declared in the *The Feminist Connection:*

> The religious battered woman must come to see reality—that religion has been part of her problem and that true mental and emotional health can come about only when she can reject her religious dependency sufficiently to recognize a fact: that the degradation of women is a cornerstone of most religions.

Clearly, this position and other past research views religion as placing these abuse victims at risk.

Though religiosity is a critical dimension in the lives of many clients, it is also clinically important to note that religion is totally meaningless to others. Therefore, since the religious faith of certain clients will greatly affect treatment decisions, according to Maloney (1985) it "is probably just as important to assess as ego strength, interpersonal relations, self-concept and emotional control." Yet how does one measure religiosity? And what effect does it have on the treatment and recovery of victims? Is it working for them or against them?

For one group of caregivers (Advocates for Battered Women, National Coalition Against Domestic Violence [NCADV], shelters), physical safety may be the sole concern of the service provider. For religious leaders there is a long-term, more complex aspect to their counsel. It has been primarily a concern for this spiritual and eternal dimension that has divided those who advocate separation and immediate safety from those who emphasize relationship preservation and long-term well-being. However, the actual practices of religious leaders and the level of victim satisfaction have not been reported in depth.

Most researchers have chosen to define religiosity in terms of church affiliation or church attendance. These measures, however, do not seem to be sufficiently comprehensive measures of a victim's religiosity or commitment to her religion as it affects her physical abuse by her spouse.

Although women may report themselves as being affiliated with one particular religion, they often do not consider themselves to be religious, nor do they consider such a religious affiliation to be important in their lives. Others, though not involved with a specific group or weekly services, see their relationship to a higher being as life-saving. To account for these differences, self-definition of religiosity was chosen as the focus for this study. Different behavioral and ideological measurements were used to validate the women's self-definitions and personal perceptions of their use of, or need for, religion in their lives. These measures are reported here. While these definitions are broad and highly personal, they do reveal the victim's orientation and perceived use of her belief system. Religion was generally viewed by those sampled as being "very important" (a 9 or 10 rating) or "not at all important" (a 1 or 2 rating). For most, it was not a middle-of-the-road issue.

Methodology

For this study, public service announcements requesting physically abused spouse victims (postabuse for one year or more) were published in local newspapers throughout the United States. Areas of publication were selected from the *Statistical Abstract of the United States,* 1985 edition, as being geographically representative. This method, though scientifically limited, was chosen to report the diverse cultural and social orientation of as wide a range of victims as possible. A 272 item questionnaire was sent to victims who expressed a willingness to participate. Of the 462 victims who responded to the ad, 187 qualified as being abuse-free for one year or more and returned the completed form. This in-depth survey approach was used to describe and analyze the 187 victims' background, relationship history, use of professional help, religiosity, and satisfaction with the various counselors and solutions they sought.

The Straus Conflict Tactic Scale was modified to reflect the levels of abuse and specific acts suffered by the victim. Some critics see this as a limited instrument, but it was used in this study only to distinguish three broad levels of violence (mild, moderate, and severe), not to extrapolate further (Straus, 1981). This chapter gives basic profiles of the religious and nonreligious victims and describes in detail how these victims used religion as a strength and coping mechanism, as well as their criticisms of its limitations.

The Findings of the Study

Background and Marital Description

Although Straus (1981) presents 11.6 percent of women as being the only abusive partner in relationships, tradition and socialization apparently still discourage men from reporting abuse. Of the 187 victims participating in this study, 182 were female. Also, the victims were generally older than those in the shelter studies, with an average age of 38.8 (see Table 26–1). This information was particularly valuable because it indicated how long it takes most victims to actually end abuse in their lives.

The areas of education and job skills are stressed in the literature as resources that lead to early disengagement (Pfouts, 1978; Field and Field, 1973), and these findings support that premise. The average level of formal education was 13.6 years, and the average level of income was $1,546.00 per month. Only 11 percent received Aid to Families With Dependent Children benefits. Sixty-four percent of the victims worked outside the home. The average number of children per respondent was 2.5. Ninety-one percent of the sample were Caucasian and 9 percent nonwhite. The groups of victims from various geographic regions was approximately equal for the West, Midwest, East, and South.

Thirty-two percent of the sample were married at the time of the survey. Of these, 36 percent of the religious women were married, compared with 27 percent of the nonreligious. However, only 22 percent reported that they

Table 26–1
Victim's Social and Marital Profiles: A Comparison of "Religious" and "Nonreligious" Victims

Variable	Total Sample (187)	Religious (116)	Nonreligious (71)
Age (x̄ average)	38.8	39.5	37.6
Years Education (x̄)	13.6	14.0	13.0
Employed (%)	64.0	63.0	64.0
Income (x̄)	$1,546.0	$1,549.0	$1,542.0
AFDC Recipient (%)	11.0	9.0	12.0
Ethnicity (%)			
White	91.0	89.0	94.0
Nonwhite	9.0	11.0	6.0
Currently Married (%)	32.0	36.0	27.0
To new partner (%)	10.0	13.0	7.0
To abusive partner (%)	22.0	23.0	20.0
Living with abusive partner (%)	15.0	15.0	14.0
"Satisfied" (%)	9.0	12.0	4.0
Length of Abusive Marriage (average)	10.3	11.4	8.6
Number of Children (average)	2.5	2.8	2.1

were still married to their formerly abusive partner, and only 15 percent were still living with their formerly abusive spouse.

Of that 15 percent who were able to end the abuse and continue to cohabit with their formerly abusive spouse, 60 percent (or 9 percent of the total sample) reported being "satisfied" with their present relationship. Those who reported being religious and "satisfied" made up 7 percent of the total population, and those who were "not religious" and "satisfied" made up 1.7 percent of the total population.

Abuse History

For the purposes of most research, domestic abuse victims are generally self-identified, and the reported characteristics are always limited as a result of this self-selection. Nonetheless, these victims defined themselves both psychologically and behaviorally as "battered," and generously described their own abuse history, often in great detail, which added much to the richness of the data.

Forty-six percent of the respondents indicated they were abused as children, and 64 percent reported their partners had been also. Over a quarter

Table 26–2
Abuse Profiles: A Comparison of "Religious" and "Nonreligious" Victims

Variable	Total Sample (187)	Religious (116)	Nonreligious (71)
Abused as Child (%)	45.0	45.0	45.0
Witnessed Abuse (%)	27.0	26.0	28.0
Partner Abused As Child (%)	64.0	59.0	70.0
Partner Witnessed Abuse (%)	64.0	64.0	64.0
Abuse Prior to Marriage by Partner	25.0	25.0	25.0
Level of Abuse			
Low (%)	100.0	100.0	100.0
Moderate (%)	100.0	100.0	100.0
Severe (%)	96.0	96.0	96.0
Length of Abuse Period (x)	8.7	9.5	7.4
Abuse by Others as Adult	28.0	27.0	28.7
Childhood Witnessed Abuse (years)	80.0	85.0	72.0
Children Abused	44.0	49.0	36.0
Use of Resources			
Attempted suicide (%)	34.0	35.0	32.0
Shelter (%)	38.0	39.0	37.0
Counselor (%)	64.0	74.0	49.0
Religious leader (%)	48.0	54.0	38.0
Told no one	25.0	23.0	28.0
Separation (%)	82.0	80.0	84.0
Filed for divorce (%)	80.0	79.0	83.0
Alcohol Involved (%)	36.0	36.0	36.0
Husband Sought RX/ Change Behavior (%)	70.0	78.0	56.0

of the victims in the study acknowledged being abused before marriage, had observed spouse abuse between their parents, and/or experienced abuse in another relationship. Over half the victims stated that their spouse had been abusive in other relationships, and over half believed their spouses had witnessed abuse between their own parents (see Table 26–2).

The average length of time in a conjugal-type relationship was ten years, with an average of 8.7 of those years spent in an abusive relationship. The mean number of abuse incidents over the period of the relationship was 43, with a mode of 4 and a median of 6. Fully 100 percent of the respondents had been the object of some type of physical abuse according to the modified Conflict Tactics Scale (Straus, 1981), with 96 percent experiencing severe abuse at least once during the relationship. Thirty-four percent of the victims had attempted suicide.

Previous research has reported that religious women appear to attribute a higher value to marriage as an institution by their definition of its importance, by the percentage remarrying or remaining, and by the total years in the marriage. This research is supported by the longer marriages and extended abuse periods reported in this study. Severity level did not appear to vary.

While religious women do appear to have more children and longer marriages, they are not less educated, less frequently employed, poorer, less satisfied, less resourceful, or more dependent than their nonreligious counterparts. Perhaps the most interesting victims are those who remained in the relationship, stopped the abuse, and were satisfied. Higher levels of religiosity appeared to increase chances for an abuse-free, happy future. Also, those religious women who had religious partners showed a greater likelihood of remaining together. Not only does the religious victim appear to stay married longer, but she also goes to greater lengths to save her relationship.

Use of Religious Resources

About half the victims stated that they currently felt as though they were actively part of a religious group (see Table 26–3). When asked for a denominational preference, 58 percent defined themselves as Protestant, 20 percent as Catholic, 1 percent as Jewish, 10 percent as "other," and only 11 percent responded "none." Therefore, had religiosity in this sample been done according to denomination—the most common measure used—about 90 percent of the victim would have been seen as religious.

Forty-four percent were weekly attenders of church; thus, a number of victims who see themselves as "highly spiritual" or "extremely religious" would not have been counted as such. Interestingly enough, the percentage of frequent attenders includes 14 percent who do not see religion as a high value for them. Just over half the victims made financial religious contributions, and only 3 percent of the victims stated that they "never" prayed.

Religious victims, by definition, gave a much higher importance to religion and the value it had in their lives. It is also not surprising to find that many religious victims felt religion helped them and said they grew stronger during the abuse period. Those areas in which religion helped and hurt are discussed in depth later in the chapter.

The use of resources is of particular importance to those caregivers who are concerned with religion as a factor in the service area. Though reputedly more isolated, the religious victims were as likely to tell someone about their abuse as the nonreligious victims. It appears that religious victims were just as likely as those less religious, if not more so, to report their abuse to a family member, friend, lawyer, counselor, shelter, crisis line, police, medical

Table 26–3

Religiosity Profile: A Comparison of "Religious" and "Nonreligious" Victims' Use of Religious Resources

Variable	Total Sample (187)	Religious (116)	Nonreligious (71)
Have Current Religious Affiliation (%)	56.0	74.0	23.0
Stated Denomination			
Protestant (%)	58.0	63.0	50.0
Catholic (%)	20.0	21.0	16.0
Jewish (%)	1.0	1.0	2.0
Other (%)	10.0	12.0	8.0
None (%)	11.0	4.0	24.0
Church Attendance (%)			
Weekly	44.0	62.0	14.0
1–3 times a month	5.0	7.0	0.0
Occasionally	18.0	15.0	23.0
Seldom	16.0	9.0	29.0
Never	17.0	7.0	34.0
Prayer (%)			
Daily or more	74.0	90.0	32.0
Occasionally	23.0	10.0	59.0
Never	3.0	0.0	10.0
Stated level of religiosity (%)			
Very strong	28.0	45.0	0.0
Strong	34.0	55.0	0.0
Not strong	13.0	0.0	56.0
Inactive	25.0	0.0	44.0
Financial Contributions (%)	53.0	76.0	33.0
Religion "Most Important" In Life (%)	38.0	58.0	12.0
Value of Religion (%)			
Helped	47.0	52.0	34.0
Hurt	27.0	21.0	41.0
Both	26.0	27.0	24.0

doctor, support group, other professional, Alcoholics Anonymous, drug rehabilitation program, or county attorney. They also used separation as frequently but did not file for divorce as often. Interestingly enough, only 54 percent of the religious victims sought out religious leaders for guidance, while 38 percent of the nonreligious victims also saw clergy about their abuse.

Comparing resources by preference, the study found that family and friends were seen as the most helpful resource by 29 percent of the victims. Counseling, shelters, and crisis lines were helpful to 40 percent of the victims. Religious leaders were viewed as most helpful to 14 percent of the religious victims, but to only 3 percent of the nonreligious victims. Lawyers, police, and physicians, though widely used by most victims at some point in the abuse process, were not highly regarded as helpful, and the police were considered by many victims to be the least beneficial group they appealed to for assistance.

Unfortunately, of the religious victims who consulted religious leaders, one-third regarded these leaders as the "least helpful" care providers, whereas only 13 percent of the nonreligious victims rated them in that category. It would appear religious victims have much higher expectations from these advisors and are thus more disappointed. The next section will address those expectations and criticisms. Other professionals were also seen as nonbeneficial by some and extremely beneficial to others.

Satisfaction with Religious Leaders

In-depth content analysis of the victims reporting contact with religious leaders indicated that seventy-eight victims saw a pastor, minister, or bishop; twenty-two saw priests; and one saw a rabbi. Thirty of these victims reported their contact as "very satisfactory" or "satisfactory." Twenty-nine reported a "dissatisfactory" contact, and forty-two reported a "very unsatisfactory" relationship.

Those victims who enjoyed positive experiences with their religious leaders reported that they received "validation" and "approval." The most positive responses were to religious advisors who agreed that safety, even divorce or separation, was imperative or at least acceptable for the battered victim. While some clerics rated in this category did not advocate leaving, they expressed concern, showed a willingness to listen, believed the victim, and were willing to support her decision. A few members of the clergy recommended and even helped pay for outside counseling or education for the victim, and that was seen as helpful. Two Catholic priests were willing to work with victims toward getting annulments.

On the other hand, twice as many of the "very dissatisfied" respondents reported some of the following advice:

"Stay and work things out. God expects that."

"Christians don't get divorced unless adultery is involved."

"Hope for the best. God will change him. Pray."

"He is hopeless and cruel but you are married to him."

"Forgive and forget."

"Try harder not to provoke him."

Twenty-five victims reported at length that their pastor focused on their behavior and that they should change. Such suggestions as "wear him out with sex," "cook more appetizing meals," and "don't talk" were not well received by victims. Sixteen victims were told specifically not to get a divorce and to learn to live with the abuse. Sixteen counselors advised the victims that there was just nothing they could do or else that they did not know how to react. Religious cures such as prayer, reading the Scriptures, and coming to services and singing hymns to raise one's spirits were suggested to numerous victims, sometimes but not always in combination with other more helpful suggestions. Victims complained most about clerics who denied the problem existed, who said they were exaggerating or lying, and who were unwilling to listen because they considered the victim as the cause of the problem.

Religion as a Strength

Forty-five victims reported that their religious beliefs gave them "courage," "strength," and "hope." Seventeen reported that their beliefs gave them "support" and increased their "self-esteem." Eighteen reported prayer had been rewarding to them and had helped. Fifteen felt "peaceful," "trusting," and "protected by God's love." Twelve said the abuse increased their faith, and ten felt it was somehow part of a greater plan. Five felt their beliefs "eased their loneliness"; six reported their religion helped them get out of the abuse. However, most helpful of all, perhaps, was the faith of the eleven victims who felt their religiosity prevented them from taking their own lives or killing someone else.

In responding to the ways religion helped the victims cope, most responded that knowledge of God's love for them, the power of prayer, inner peace, trust, and calm were their best helps. Thirteen victims emphasized that religion reinforced their feelings of self-worth. These messages of self-worth and personal value are particularly critical to abuse victims who have been repeatedly berated and criticized. The power to forgive and to understand were also seen as real strengths. Nine victims, however, interpreted the history and righteousness of suffering as helpful and of spiritual benefit. This use of religiosity would undoubtedly be very open to criticism by most care-providers who do not agree that needless suffering is beneficial and recognize it as life-threatening.

Religion as a Detriment

Thirty-nine victims reported that they were told they could not leave the relationship, or that it would be sinful to do so, and that divorce was strongly discouraged. They reported they felt trapped by their religion. Thirteen stated that they felt that there had been a misuse of the scriptures or of male authority. Ten felt that religion promoted tolerance and rationalization of their pain instead of safety or hope. Nine felt their prayers were unanswered, and four believed they got what they deserved.

Discussion

In many ways, the women in this study do not fit the stereotype of the battered wife found so often in the popular literature. Granted, a large number of respondents were victims of abuse as children, but the women tend to be well educated, with the majority of them working outside the home. Additionally, only a minority of the respondents receive government assistance. Minority ethnic groups, unfortunately, composed a small percentage of the sample which was not seen as representative. But perhaps the most notable finding was that only 15 percent of the women somehow ended abuse while retaining a conjugal relationship with their partner. These are not very promising odds when predicting probable outcomes with clients—particularly when it is noted that of those few, only 60 percent are satisfied.

Contrary to some authorities' declarations, though highly religious women were found in this study to stay in their marriages longer and did remain in abusive situations longer than women of lower religiosity, they did not appear to be more severely abused. Quite surprising, though, was the finding that the more religious victims had used more resources and were generally more willing to reach out for assistance and guidance in an effort to resolve their situation. Divorce was not seen as the easiest course to follow and was not pursued without many attempts to retain the relationship.

Instead of withdrawing, a large majority made use of friends and family. Legal intervention of one type or another was used by well over 50 percent of the women. Professional counselors, community agencies, doctors or hospitals, and women's shelters provided care to a greater number than the other agencies.

Friends, professional counselors, and shelters were judged to be the most effective. Religious leaders, family members, lawyers, crisis lines, and police were mentioned as being beneficial as well as detrimental. Most telling, though, is the fact that a quarter of the women did not list any resource as being useful, and most did not approach any external sources. Overall, religiosity proved extremely helpful to many victims and was even seen as life-preserving to some.

The victims' criticisms of religious leaders and religion focused mainly on (1) feeling trapped within a dangerous relationship, (2) facing lack of understanding, validation, and minimization of the abuse, (3) having no alternatives or practical suggestions offered, (4) being blamed or made to feel responsible for the abuse, and (5) feeling helpless to change or escape.

The respondents, by and large, offered three major recommendations for dealing with abusive relationships. First, the women advocated being aware of the problem and realizing that it is not one's lot in life to be abused. Second, respondents emphasized the need for the victim to take the initiative in building self-esteem and escaping the relationship if necessary. Finally, and overwhelmingly, the women advise others who are being abused to get professional counseling quickly. Praying appears to bring comfort, but not to guarantee safety.

Conclusion

Religious women can no longer be considered as barefoot and pregnant, weak and unable to change. They have shown a very different character and a positive approach to violence in their lives and for their families. They are not disadvantaged, nor should they be "treated" for religiosity instead of abuse. This study also indicates several areas where services to abused women generally can be improved.

Doctors, police, lawyers, and clergy—the most commonly used and criticized community resources—are all trained to treat only a portion of the person's environment: the doctor to heal the body, the police to keep the neighborhood and home quiet, the lawyer to advocate for a person's legal rights, and the cleric to look after morality. The relatively low number of women who viewed these individuals as being extremely useful in dealing with abuse indicates a need to increase the skill of such professionals in delivering appropriate counseling, treatment, and referrals.

Interdisciplinary respect and communication is the logical road to increase expertise in these areas. Lacking cooperation from these professions, secular counselors must ensure that abused clients, religious or nonreligious, caught up in medical, legal, and ethical processes receive support and guidance to compensate for any possible lack of insight on the part of these other care providers.

The overwhelming number of women in the sample who turn to family and friends indicates a need to increase community education about the causes, symptoms, and treatment of spouse abuse. Certainly, the fact that few women use community resources other than doctors, hospitals, and shelters indicates a lack of awareness of possible resources. Not only do abused women need to be informed of the wide range of possible roads out of an abusive relationship, but the population in general needs to be educated about spouse abuse and ways treatment and family unity can be established.

The perceived effectiveness of counselors, both secular and religious, may be seen as a challenge to these professionals. The good counselor must retain well-honed therapeutic skills as well as empathy for the abused woman. Certainly religion should also be reevaluated for its positive therapeutic influences. Whether it is working for the client is important; whether it fits with the therapist's views is not. Care providers must note that 25 percent of the women did not find *any* outside help (including counselors) to be truly effective in helping stop the abuse.

This and other studies emphasize that the most competent expert is often someone who has personally experienced abuse, met its effects head-on, and successfully ended it in her life. The expertise of such women, particularly those of a similar religious persuasion, should be available to currently abused women so that they may pinpoint the formal and informal coping styles that will help others end their abuse.

Meanwhile, those who remain in these relationships may be educated about the wide range of options available to them and the likelihood of reaching their various goals. Secular counselors need to acknowledge that religion is the foundation that holds many women together so that they can help build upon that strength. The religious leader, meanwhile, needs to increase his or her substantive knowledge, investigate a larger repertoire of available resources, and focus on safety. A victim seeking help must be validated and encouraged to recognize that her own actions and abilities must be used effectively when praying is not enough.

References

Cameron, A. 1980. The Battered Woman: Why Does She Stay? *The Feminist Connection* 10:12.

Field, M. H., and H. F. Field. 1973. Marital violence and the criminal process: Neither justice nor peace. *Social Service Review* 47(22):221–240.

Maloney, H. 1985. Assessing religious maturity. In *Psychotherapy and the religiously committed patient,* ed. E. M. Stern. New York: Hawthorn.

Pfouts, J. H. 1978. Violent families: Coping responses of abused wives. *Child Welfare* 57(2):101–111.

Straus, M. A. 1981. Ordinary violence versus child abuse and wife beating: What do they have in common? Paper presented at the annual meeting of the National Conference on Family Violence Research, University of New Hampshire.

U.S. Department of Commerce: Bureau of the Census. *Statistical abstract of the United States, 1985.* Washington: Government Printing Office.

27

How Men Who Batter Rationalize Their Behavior

James Ptacek

Throughout the past decade of feminist work on violence against women, the testimony of battered women has been indispensable in making public the oppressiveness that had long been hidden from view. With the growth in social services for men who batter, researchers and activists have recently had the opportunity to talk with batterers about how they perceive their violence.

What can we learn about wife beating from men who batter? Surely we cannot accept their words at face value; their testimony must be examined critically. But if batterers' accounts are treated carefully, they reveal much about both the reasons and the rationalizations for the violence.

The Sample

For this study, I interviewed eighteen men who had been to Emerge, a Boston-area counseling service for men who physically abuse their wives or partners. The length of involvement in counseling had ranged from a single intake session to twenty-four weeks in the group counseling program. Most had been out of contact with Emerge for over a year. In all but two cases, the violence had reportedly stopped.

While this is clearly not a representative sample of batterers in any scientific sense, particularly since they were self-referred clients at Emerge, this group of men is nonetheless quite diverse as far as demographic data and levels of violence are concerned. The age range is broad, from twenty-two to fifty-three years, although most of the men are in their thirties. All but two of the men are white. Only half of the men were married during the period of the violence; three men had not even been sharing a common residence with their partner during the time of the abusiveness. The data on education, occupation, and income indicate that the proportion of working-class and middle-class men is about equal.

In half the relationships, the men became violent less than a year after the relationship began. Based on their own testimony, the violence involved shoving, slapping, dragging by the hair, throwing objects such as a plate or an ashtray, punching, kicking, bodily throwing, choking, "beating up," threatening with a knife, and rape. One-third of the men reported that their partners sustained broken bones or other substantial physical injuries as a result of the violence. It is my opinion that this is at best a conservative estimate of the violence these men inflicted; underreporting by batterers is frequently noted in the clinical literature.

Batterers' Excuses and Justifications

Initially, these eighteen men had all come to the Emerge counseling program for help. Whether they defined the problem as their violence, or as is more likely, saving their relationship, the very existence of a program for men who batter established the sense that their violence was wrong. And once they arrived, this sense of wrongness was made explicit by the counselors.

On an average of 1.8 years later, these men returned to talk with a man, identified as both an Emerge counselor and a researcher, about their violence. The sense that the violence is wrong is institutionalized in the very setting of the interviews. In this context and to this interviewer, how do these men talk about their abusiveness?

When an individual whose behavior is regarded as socially unacceptable is questioned about such behavior, the individual's response may be called an account, according to Scott and Lyman (1968). Such accounts represent a complex of anticipated judgment, face-saving, and status negotiation. Scott and Lyman distinguish two types of accounts that serve to neutralize socially disapproved behavior: excuses and justifications.

Excuses are those accounts in which the abuser *denies full responsibility* for his actions. *Justifications* are those accounts in which the batterer may accept some responsibility, but *denies or trivializes the wrongness* of his violence. These descriptive categories offer a way of exploring the issues of wrongness and responsibility. The meaning of excuses and justifications will become clearer when they are applied to the batterers' testimony.

Scott and Lyman emphasize that in making excuses and justifications, the deviant individual employs "socially approved vocabularies" which are "routinized within cultures" (pp. 45, 52). In this analysis, the batterer is thus seen as appealing to standard rationalizations in an attempt to make sense of or normalize his behavior.

Excuses: Denial of Responsibility

Perhaps the most common way that batterers attempt to excuse or deny responsibility for their violent behavior is by an *appeal to loss of control*. Such appeals take several forms. Loss of control is usually spoken of as either the result of alcohol or drug use, or as the result of a build-up of frustrations. In either case, the loss may be expressed as partial or complete. The sense here is that physiological or psychological factors lead to a state in which their awareness or will is impaired, thus diminishing their responsibility. Of the eighteen men interviewed, 94 percent ($n = 17$) employed an account that falls into one or more of the following subcategories: appeal to alcohol or drugs, frustration, and complete loss of control. Of the sample of eighteen batterers, 33 percent ($n = 6$) maintain that their self-control was diminished by alcohol or drugs:

> It's taken the edge off my self-control. That's what I call it, being intoxicated. It's taken my limits off me and let me do things and become disruptive in a way I would not become.

> I can get angry with people, really violent, stone sober. But the more I was drinking on a day-to-day basis, the more easy that was to come across.

> I've been involved with A.A., and that's why I'm much better. And a lot of my problems—not all of them—but most of my problems at the time were due to that. And it's just amazing to know that there was a reason for the way I acted.

Asked whether they thought they would be violent with a woman again, it was common for these men to say no, so long as they were able to remain free of alcohol or drug dependency (most of them said they had successfully quit).

To what extent does alcohol cause loss of control over one's behavior? In a study of family violence, Gelles (1974) cites anthropological data that establish drunken behavior as learned, rather than purely chemically induced, behavior. Drunken comportment varies widely from culture to culture, according to Gelles. Because it is *believed* to lead to loss of control, people behave as though it has that property, and they use this "loss of control" to disavow or neutralize deviant behavior, such as wife beating, Gelles argues. As shall be shown, the contradictions in the batterers' own testimony support this argument.

A frustration-aggression description of violence is present in the accounts of 67 percent ($n = 12$) of the men. This duplicates a finding in Bograd's study of men who batter and battered women (Bograd, 1983). As in that study, these accounts present temporary loss of control as resulting from an accumulation of internal pressure. This pressure is often described as building with a hydraulic type of inevitability:

> I think I reach a point where I can't tolerate anything anymore, and it's at that time whatever it is that shouldn't be tolerated in the first place now is a major issue in my life. I do better now. It used to come out at one thing.

It didn't matter what it was. It just, you know—I couldn't hold it back any-more. It just came out in a tirade.

We used to argue about picayune-ass things anyway. And a lot of this was building and building. And I was keeping it all inside. All of the frustration and anger.

You're supposed to sit there and take this stuff from your wife. And, like I say, I'd take it for a while, but then I'd lose my head.

But as Bandura argues regarding the frustration-aggression hypotheses, aggression is only one of a number of responses to frustration. Other possible responses include dependency, achievement, withdrawal and resignation, psychosomatic illness, drug or alcohol use, and constructive problem solving (Bandura, 1973, p. 54). Most of the men in this sample must have responded to frustration in ways other than violence, for they indicate that their violence is very selective. For 39 percent ($n = 7$) of these men, their frustration led to violence *only* in the presence of their wives or lovers; for another 33 per-cent ($n = 6$), their frustration led to violence *only* when they were in the presence of their partners, children, and mothers. In only 28 percent ($n = 5$) of these cases were the men violent both within and outside the family.

In the accounts of 56 percent ($n = 10$) of the batterers, descriptions of the violence are presented in terms of being *completely* out of control:

When I got violent, it was not because I really wanted to get violent, it was just because it was like an outburst of rage.

I was a real jerk for almost a year. And anything would set me off. Anything. I was like uncontrollably violent. I would slap her, knock her down, choke her, and call her a slut and a whore.

I struck her once before, and I guess it made me see something of myself that I didn't like to see, the way I had no control over myself. And I knew that the anger that I had inside me was very hard to control.

It was all booze. I didn't think. I didn't think at all. I was just like a madman. It was temporary insanity. I really, all's I really wanted to do was crush her. There was nothing there but—I wanted to cause pain and mess her looks up.

Of the ten men claiming such total loss of control, only three of them blamed this on alcohol. Blackouts or partial memory losses were reported by two of the men who claimed they had been intoxicated; but such memory losses were also reported by two men who allegedly had not been drinking.

The second main category of excuses is *victim-blaming*. As in the case of the loss of control excuses, the wrongness of the violence is more or less accepted; but here, the men deny responsibility by claiming they were provoked. In a few isolated incidents, the batterers presented their violence as a response to the woman's physical aggressiveness:

> She slapped me across the face hard. It hurt . . . and that did it. Then I slapped her, and punched her, and kicked her, and knocked her down. I mean, I just let her have it.

More commonly, the batterers asserted that their violence was a response to the woman's verbal aggressiveness. Some 44 percent ($n = 8$) of the sample blamed the victim in this fashion:

> She was trying to tell me, you know, I'm no fucking good and this and that. . . . And she just kept at me, you know. And I couldn't believe it. And finally, I just got real pissed and I said wow, you know. I used to think, you're going to treat me like this? You're going to show me that I'm the scumbag? Whack. Take that. And that was my psychology.

> Women can verbally abuse you. They can rip your clothes off, without even touching you, the way women know how to talk, converse. But men don't. Well, they weren't brought up to talk as much as women do, converse as well as women do. So it was a resort to violence, if I couldn't get through to her by words.

> On some occasions she was the provoker. It didn't call for physical abuse. I was wrong in that. But it did call for something. . . . You know, you're married for that long, if somebody gets antagonistic, you want to defend yourself.

These men seem to regard verbal aggressiveness as equivalent to physical aggressiveness. In these examples, they speak as though a woman's verbal behavior somehow excuses them of responsibility for their violence. There are serious deficiencies in this argument. As Dobash and Dobash (1979, pp. 133–137) point out, even if one takes the extreme position that verbal aggressiveness warrants a physical response, the question can then become who provoked the verbal aggressiveness? Furthermore, the provocation argument presupposes that there is a standard delineating the proper ways in which a wife can address her husband, a standard which the husband is empowered to maintain. The accounts above reveal just such a male arrogance, along with the sense that while his retaliatory behavior is acceptable, her verbal excesses are not. Thus, the provocation excuse is based on and solidifies male dominance. The batterer's responsibility is excused, for he is only responding to his wife's improprieties.

Appeals to loss of control and victim-blaming have been shown to be common ways that these men excuse their violence. While excuses represent denial of responsibility, justifications are denials of wrongdoing on the part of the offender.

Justification: Denial of Wrongness

The first of two categories of justifications is *denial of injury*. According to some clinicians who have worked with men who batter, many batterers neutralize the unacceptability of their behavior by denying or minimizing the injuries battered women suffer. With this sample, it was not possible to obtain reports from the abused women in order to determine the full extent of minimization. Nonetheless, trivialization of the woman's injuries is apparent in the accounts of 44 percent ($n = 8$) of the men. With some men, this takes the form of a denial that the behavior was violent. With others, the abusers maintain that the woman's fears were exaggerated. And a number of men minimize the nature of the injuries.

A euphemistic redefinition of violent behavior is presented in the accounts of two men:

> I never beat my wife. I responded physically to her.

> Yes, I do believe my physical punishment as a child can contribute to me having tendency to react violently and think nothing of it. When I say violent, "physically," I think, would be a much more appropriate term.

Looking at the behavior these men report, the first admitted he pushed, grabbed, and slapped his wife, and that she received bruises and injured her knee as a result. The second man admitted to slapping, punching, and grabbing a woman by the hair and dragging her across the floor. One of the many women this second individual was "physical" with received a black eye. He was arrested five or six times for assault and battery on men.

Other men claimed that women exaggerated the severity of the violence. This respondent's account is representative:

> These people told her that she had to get all of these orders of protection and stuff like that because I was going to kill her, you know. Well, I wasn't going to kill her. I mean, I'd yell at her, and scream, and stuff like that, and maybe I'd whack her once or twice, you know, but I wasn't going to kill her. That's for sure.

This individual did admit to slapping and punching his wife, giving her a black eye, and throwing and breaking furniture. During one episode, he stated that his wife fled the house screaming. Yet when asked whether she was frightened of him, he said "no."

A number of men minimized the extent of the women's injuries by attributing black and blue marks to the ease with which women bruise. This is how three men responded to the question of whether the woman was injured:

> Not really. Pinching does leave bruises. And, I guess, slapping. I guess women bruise easily, too. They bump into a door and they'll bruise.

> Not injured. She bruises easily.

> Yeah, she bruised. Yeah, she bruises easily anyway. If I just squeeze like that, you know, next day she'll get a mark . . .

The statement that "women bruise easily" goes beyond an observation of comparative anatomy. By admitting that they have bruised a woman, and yet denying that this is very significant, the less apparent injuries are also denied: the instilling of fear, the humiliation, the degradation, and the assault on her identity as a woman.

These other kinds of injuries become more visible in this last category of justification. One batterer reported that he threatened his partner with these words: "I should just smack you for the lousy wife you've been." This rationale underlies the following justifications. Among the reasons for the violence given by men who batter, there is a pattern of finding fault with the woman for not being good at cooking; for not being sexually responsive; for not being deferential enough to her husband; for not knowing when she is supposed to be silent; and for not being faithful. In short, for not being a "good wife." Bograd (1983) titles this category of justifications *failure to fulfill obligations of a good wife.* Of the 18 men interviewed, 78 percent ($n = 14$) gave accounts falling into this category. These accounts come from both married and unmarried men. On cooking:

> Until we were married ten years or so there was no violence or anything. But then after a while, it just became, it just became too much. . . . I don't know if I demanded respect as a person or a husband or anything like that, but I certainly, you know, didn't think I was wrong in asking not to be filled up with fatty foods.

On availability for sex:

> A couple more incidents happened over the next year . . . where I did strike her, and for basically the same reason. I just tried making love, and making love, and she couldn't do it.

It was over sex, and it happened I guess because I was trying to motivate her. And she didn't seem too motivated.

On not being deferential enough:

I think a lot of it had to do with my frustration of not being able to handle children. You know, they'd tell me to shut up. "You're not going to tell me to shut up." And then [my wife] would tell me, you know, "let me handle this." I said, "I'm the man of the house." Then we'd start arguing. That's basically how they used to happen.

The intent is to have her see it my way. You know, "there's no need for you to think the way you're thinking. And you should see it my way. And if you don't see it my way, there's something wrong with you. You're being abusive to me by not seeing it my way."

On not knowing when she is supposed to be silent:

I don't think I used to like to be confronted about being high (on heroin), even though I was high. And it would bother me. It bothered me to a point where I would strike out.

I was working, but I wasn't making any money . . . "The baby needs this, and the baby needs that," Jesus Christ what do you want me to do, you know? We were at the table . . . I just picked my plate up and threw it at her.

On not being faithful:

I walked right over and slapped her right across the face . . . I think it was probably around the time when she was telling me she wanted to see other guys, you know. She was too young to get involved with me, or one guy. And I didn't want to hear that.

I was eighteen. And I was going to be true to somebody, for once, to see what it's like. And it turned out two years later, two and a half years later, she was going out on me. And it totalled me. Because I had made that commitment. It was like a big deal, the first time I was acting like a man and I got it. I got betrayed. And I almost killed her.

These accounts illustrate more than just the way that individual men seek to control individual women. As in the example of provocation, a theme of self-righteousness about the violence pervades these accounts: "I didn't think that I was wrong"; "she couldn't do it"; "she didn't seem too motivated";

"she had gone too far"; "I got betrayed." But here the sense is not that "she provoked me"; rather it is a sense that the privileges of male entitlement have been unjustly denied. This is evident in the gendered terms used to express this self-righteousness: "I should just smack you for the *lousy wife* you've been"; "I don't know if I demanded respect as a person or a *husband* or anything like that, but . . . "; "I'm the *man of the house*"; "the first time I was *acting like a man* and I got it." There is a sentiment here about the way that women should behave when they are sexually involved with a man, whether married or unmarried.

Adrienne Rich speaks to this sense of male entitlement, or, to use her term, husband-right. She sees husband-right as

> . . . one specific form of the rights men are presumed to enjoy simply be-
> cause of their gender: the "right" to the priority of male over female needs,
> to sexual and emotional services from women, to women's undivided atten-
> tion in any or all situations . . . (Rich, 1979, pp. 219–220).

With this assumption of male entitlement, the wrongness of the violence is denied; the batterer sees himself as punishing the woman for her failure to be a good wife. Other investigations have found a similar pattern in the batterer's violence (Gelles, 1974; Elbow, 1977; Dobash and Dobash, 1979; Coleman, 1980). But this assumption of male privilege is not limited to the expectations of men who batter; feminists have been pointing out for years the way that this vocabulary of male entitlement has been routinized within the culture at large.

Patterns and Contradictions in the Batterers' Testimony

The definitions of excuses and justifications turn on the denial (or accept-ance) of responsibility and wrongness. Most of the men made statements falling into both categories. Often, the violence was first excused as being out of control, then described as deliberate and justifiable, and then as somehow beyond rational control again. Within the context of individual interviews, this pattern presented a great deal of inconsistency.

But there is more here than inconsistency: there is contradiction. The batterers' excuses of loss of control and provocation are undercut by the cal-lousness they display about their partners' injuries, and by the goal orienta-tion that appears in their own words. The transcripts reveal that these men were motivated by a desire to silence their partners, to punish them for their failure as "good wives," and to achieve and maintain dominance over these women. And their objectives were accomplished: according to the men, the women fell silent; they were taught a lesson; and they were shown who was in control of the relationship, and to what length the batterer would go in maintaining control. The violence, then, had clear *benefits* for these men, however brief or enduring these benefits were.

The batterers' denial of responsibility is further contradicted by other evidence they provided about their behavior. In none of these relationships was the violence completely anomalous to the batterer's other actions toward his wife or lover. In every case, the men's testimony offered other examples of behavior directed at achieving or maintaining dominance. This behavior does not include merely subtle controlling behaviors, but such things as writing threatening letters to the woman, driving her back to her mother's house to learn how to cook, forcing sex, threatening the woman if she talks about leaving, tearing the phone off the wall to prevent her from calling the police, and spying on the woman's house and lying in wait to assault her new boyfriend.

Thus a pattern of intentional, goal-oriented violence is established by the batterers' testimony, despite the contradictory denials of responsibility. Loss of control and provocation cannot explain the violence; they merely serve as excuses, as rationalizations, as ways of obscuring the benefits, however temporary or enduring, that the violence provides.

Conclusion

Scott and Lyman insist that excuses and justifications are "standardized within cultures," that they are "socially approved vocabularies" for avoiding blame (1968, p. 46). In this connection, it is important to recognize the cultural patterns in the batterers' excuses and justifications: these rationalizations represent culturally sanctioned strategies for minimizing and denying violence against women. For example, many clinicians writing about batterers appear to accept notions of "loss of control" and "provocation." Victim-blaming, minimization of injuries, and other justifications for wife beating are also commonly encountered in the criminal justice system. The batterers' rationalizations detailed above are therefore *affirmed* by such vocabularies within mental health and criminal justice institutions.

Jurgen Habermas speaks to this relationship between individual rationalizations and collective interests:

> From everyday experience we know that ideas serve often enough to furnish our actions with justifying motives in place of the real ones. What is called rationalization at this level is called ideology at the level of collective action (Habermas, 1971, p. 311).

The excuses and justifications I have detailed must therefore be seen as ideological constructs; at the individual level they obscure the batterer's self-interest in acting violently, while at the societal level they mask the male domination that underlies violence against women. To the extent that mental health practitioners, the criminal justice system, or any other institutions accept these rationalizations, they fail to hold batterers accountable for their violent actions.

Batterers have a lot to tell us about their violence. Their own words reveal the intentionality, the cruelty, the goal-oriented nature of their actions. While they would like to claim that their violence is beyond rational control, they simultaneously assert that the violence is deliberate and warranted.

Batterers' testimony, then, cannot be taken at face value. What these men have to say can be fully understood only in the context of the terror, injury, and degradation their violence creates. Yet these are the consequences that batterers are so quick to minimize and deny. It is therefore essential that battered women's experiences form the basis of any intervention with men who batter.

References

Bandura, A. 1973. *Aggression: A social learning analysis*. Englewood Cliffs, NJ: Prentice-Hall.

Bograd, M. 1983. Domestic violence: Perceptions of battered women, abusive men, and non-violent men and women. Unpublished doctoral dissertation. University of Chicago.

Coleman, K. H. 1980. Conjugal violence: What 33 men report. *Journal of Marital and Family Therapy* (6):207–213.

Dobash, R. E., and R. Dobash. 1979. *Violence Against Wives: A case against the patriarchy*. New York: Free Press.

Elbow, M. 1977. Theoretical considerations of violent marriages. Social casework 237–232.

Gelles, R. J. 1974. *The violent home: A study of physical aggression between husbands and wives*. Beverly Hills: Sage.

Habermas, J. 1971. *Knowledge and human interests*. Boston: Beacon Press.

Rich, A. 1979. *On lies, secrets, and silence: Selected prose 1966–1978*. New York: W.W. Norton.

Scott, M. B., and S. M. Lyman. 1968. Accounts. *American Sociological Review* 33(1):46–62.

28

What Incest Perpetrators Need
(But Are *Not* Getting)
from the Clergy
and Treatment Community

Anne L. Horton
Doran Williams

Incest has been one of the best-kept family secrets for a long time. However, recently it has made an impact on the research and treatment community, demanding long-overdue remedial and preventive care that so far has little empirical foundation. According to Russell (1982), incest involves 16 percent of the female population as victims. While clinicians and lawmakers now agree that society does have a problem, great disparity of opinion still exists within the treatment area itself. Incest perpetrators are simply the family member no one wants to treat. Is incest "a sin and a caution"? Is it a criminal or a mental health issue?

Incest perpetrators need help too! They have few resources or social support systems, and no incentive for seeking early help (Roberts, 1982). Most offenders believe confession and counseling will certainly lead to censure and probably to arrest. While current public outcry is understandable, it also encourages greater family fear and secrecy. This chapter reports the findings of a national study of incest perpetrators and answers, in part, these questions: What do the perpetrators themselves want from their clergy and the treatment community, and what are they currently receiving?

A Brief Background

The major thrust of the legal system has been to involve incestuous families with the courts rather than the treatment community. By criminalizing family problems, immediate safety is achieved. However, the family continues to suffer long-term hardships and stigmata. At a time when our treatment goals should be to strengthen families by offering comprehensive help to them (Newberger, Newberger and Hampton, 1983), the current practice is usually one of punishment and added pain.

If reporting is to lead to prevention and treatment, it is absolutely essential to train all helping professionals to recognize and treat the whole family unit and support a total intervention effort. And this total treatment effort will involve many disciplines and much cooperation. Thus far, good case management in the area is sadly lacking. Many of these families elect to remain together, and treatment resources need to be engaged to help all members. Such intervention necessitates a pooling of efforts on the part of the religious and helping communities in conjunction with the criminal justice system.

Many families want to stay together and are burdened with loss of income, social stigma, and criminal consequences in addition to the incest. Thus far, treatment has focused primarily on support for victims and blame toward the perpetrators, two approaches that, from a religious and mental health standpoint, are unlikely to produce change. Yet change is the primary goal. Thus the perpetrator, the family member who initially must make the greatest change, has historically had the least available and most hostile treatment providers.

Many helping professionals do not wish to work with perpetrators and most are not trained to do so (Edelson, 1984). The victim and other family members can seek counselors, but at present incest perpetrators are very limited in their choice of professional help. Social science literature offers little information on treatment or empirical data on perpetrators. Their needs are relatively ignored by the clinical and religious treatment communities; little resource and referral information exists, and therapists are not being trained to work with them. Most early intervention is done with victims while the perpetrator—the one generally regarded as "sick" or degenerate—goes without treatment.

Today, incestuous families represent a large population in the treatment community—families in which members desire to change their patterns or in which court-ordered changes are demanded. Since family treatment is so urgently needed for these perpetrators, a research project was designed to explore the needs of these key actors. While incest perpetrators historically hold no credibility in the research area, their responses to what they want and feel they need reflects a perspective that is certainly critical to making any realistic attempts at program development and personal assessment. This study focused directly on these questions, this population, and their observations.

Methodology

In March 1987, questionnaires were sent to all 155 Parents United chapters and affiliated treatment centers throughout the United States listed in the March 1986 *Chapter Contact List: Child Sex Abuse Treatment Program.* A total of 274 perpetrators involved in 27 of these programs volunteered to take part and completed an extensive questionnaire. Many questions required a short answer or a yes/no response. Several open-ended questions allowed participants to rank their preferences and explain in more precise terms the subjective feelings and emotions related both to their offense and to those religious leaders and counseling services they contacted.

The Perpetrators' Responses

Background Characteristics

The sample consisted of 98 percent men and 2 percent women who ranged from seventeen to seventy-four years of age with a median age of thirty-nine. The largest number of perpetrators lived in the western part of the country (43 percent)—which also had the greatest number of Parents United affiliates—followed by the Midwest (25 percent), South (19 percent), and the Northeast (13 percent). Eighty-four percent of the respondents were Caucasian, and 81 percent expressed a religious preference: Protestant (43 percent), Catholic (21 percent), Jewish (1 percent) and other (16 percent). The educational mean was 12.5 years, and 79 percent were currently employed full-time while only 6 percent were employed part-time and 15 percent were unemployed. Sixty-one percent of the perpetrators were currently married; of those who were married, 75 percent were still married to the same partner they were married to at the time the incest occurred. This statistic alone emphasizes the great need to work with the entire families toward joint treatment.

The Use of Resources

Few perpetrators sought help or confided in anyone before arrest. Upon arrest, however, perpetrators reported turning to the following individuals or agencies.

	Percent (%)
therapist/counselor	21
Parents United	16
clergy/God	16
spouse	14
family	12
CPS worker/police	8
friend	4
lawyer	4
M.D./hospital	3
A.A.	2
	100%

Many perpetrators (18 percent) initially said they did not discuss their problem with anyone. However, since arrest or subsequent public exposure, 84 percent reported receiving some individual or group counseling, and 65 percent reported contact with some religious group or member of the clergy.

When asked which resources were *most helpful,* 45 percent listed Parents United first; 34 percent individual counseling; 7 percent prison/jail/police; 6 percent listed the clergy; 5 percent selected A.A.; and the remainder found their wife or a family member most helpful. Those resources considered *least helpful* were police/jail (40 percent), Child Protective Services/D.F.S. (18 percent), hot lines (11 percent), clergy (9 percent), therapist (7 percent), Parents United (7 percent), and family/friends and others made up the remainder.

Discussion

Parents United was extremely well supported by the participants. Although the sampling method used in this study can be faulted for this bias to some extent, it must be noted that these are currently the only existing outpatient programs, and the observations of the members are certainly well worth noting and should be considered in making referrals.

Advantages of Parents United

1. This organization, unlike Child Protective Services, the police, and many other community agencies, views the perpetrator as its client. Therefore, specific focus is given to this individual from a treatment standpoint, whereas many of those agencies less popular with the offenders clearly defined someone else or the community as their client.

2. Parents United is usually far more knowledgeable and has more resources for the perpetrator than other agencies. Upon arrest, offenders need to have practical, procedural, and legal information in addition to psychological and emotional guidance. Other counselors usually cannot fill this repertoire of needs.

3. Incest is the entire focus of this agency, and the agency has the ability to act as a clearing house and centralized treatment unit. Agencies that divide their services in many directions or toward another population do not have this ability.

4. Parents United provides a variety of services that includes treatment within a group setting, which allows perpetrators to have contact with other offenders going through the same process. They become aware of dynamics involved and the steps needed for treatment, and they have an experiential peer group to work with them. These offenders and their leaders do not

allow for the rationalization, excuses, and denial that some private therapists might.

5. Sexual and incest problems are well understood and openly discussed, and full disclosure is demanded. Several perpetrators commented specifically that it was not possible to "snow" or "bullshit" at Parents United as they could with other therapists or marriage counselors.

A number of perpetrators also found individual counselors very useful, particularly in conjunction with group work, because they could work on their own personal and historical development. Marital counseling also received wide support, as did family involvement. Of particular interest was the recognized need for long-term treatment and the emphasis on encouraging other perpetrators to stay with both group and individual work for at least two years—much longer for most.

Those who felt the police and jail were helpful expressed an awareness that drastic steps were needed to bring them into treatment. However, those expressing dissatisfaction with law enforcement pinpointed primarily attitudinal problems on the part of the police, and said they experienced a lack of information, personal disrespect and disgust, or an unwillingness to cooperate.

Interaction with the Clergy

Initial Response and Level of Cooperation

The perpetrators in this study were far more satisfied with the support and response they experienced from the clergy and their church community than might have been expected. Of those reporting contact, 49 percent reported they were "very satisfied" and 34 percent said they were "satisfied." Only 11 percent reported any dissatisfaction, and 6 percent stated they were "very dissatisfied." When compared with the victims' level of satisfaction with the clergy (see Chapter 26), there is a considerable difference.

Positive Responses to the Clergy

Since perpetrators were generally pleased with their contact with the clergy, it is apparent that their expectations overall were not particularly high, nor were the perpetrators anticipating support in the way victims expected it. When asked how religious leaders responded, the replies ranged from "at first he said he wanted to punch my lights out," "you make me want to throw up," and "shocked" to "nonjudgmental," "tolerant," "compassionate," "understanding," "warm," and "you certainly aren't the first person to come to me with this problem." While offenders preferred the more supportive approaches, they did not appear to anticipate warm responses. Because the nature of the problem is so morally sensitive and censorship was expected, perpetrators still gave high ratings to pastors using more harsh approaches. The advice from religious leaders that was seen as most helpful fell into four basic categories:

1. *"Get help and get it now!"* These perpetrators reported that recommending counseling was the most frequent advice given by the clergy. Some suggested groups; some suggested individual treatment. Few attempted to provide it themselves. Three insisted the offender arrange to see someone about it during the meeting with the leader. Concrete suggestions of whom to see, where to go, and how to pay for it were highly valued. It appears that the more specific and practical the advice, the more highly it was valued.

2. *"Turn yourself in."* Many religious leaders encouraged the perpetrators to self-report, to leave the home, and to get help for the rest of their family. "Let the authorities know about the incest and take what's coming to you," "call the social service department and tell them you need help," or "be honest about what you've done and get the treatment you need" are some of the common variations.

3. *"Change your ways, pray for forgiveness, and look to the Lord."* Most religious leaders recommended prayer, repentance, church attendance, faith and hope, scripture reading, and assistance for the victim as a means of resolution. Perpetrators felt comforted to be offered the possibility and reassurance of some form of spiritual recovery. However, these suggestions were also accompanied by the pastor's emphasizing change and usually treatment. Perpetrators, at least those in treatment, knew that without additional help, prayer alone was not enough.

4. *"I'll be there with you."* The response that seemed by far the most helpful and appreciated was from the religious leader who not only encouraged the offender to resolve the problem, but also let him know that he (the minister) was always available and would go with the perpetrator to the authorities, to court or church officials, or to whatever lengths were necessary.

> My pastor not only listened to me, but he loved me and my family enough to go down to the police station with me. He had faith in me and assured me I could make it through when I didn't think I could.

> He must have spent more hours with me and my wife than he did his own.

> I didn't think he'd ever look me in the face again, but he's supported me for over two years now.

Negative Responses to the Clergy

The major complaints—and complaints were few—about the clergy were that (1) they did not know what to suggest, (2) they did not understand the problem or the perpetrator, and (3) they minimized or ignored the incest. Perpetrators, like all clients, want informed counselors and need guidance and direction. Such suggestions as "just stay with God," "I really don't know what to say," and "don't bring up the past; you've repented, so let bygones be bygones," were defined as "unsatisfactory" advice.

Of those perpetrators who did not elect to go to a religious leader, most gave one of the following explanations for his decision: "not a churchgoer" or "didn't belong"; felt "ashamed" or "embarrassed"; "it was too personal to talk about" or "he wouldn't understand how I could do such a terrible thing"; or "how would he know what to do about it?" (uninformed).

Some General Suggestions to Improve Clergy Response

Perpetrators made the following suggestions on how religious leaders and other counselors might improve services.

1. Be more knowledgeable about incest generally. Attend training sessions. Read about it. Talk to perpetrators.

2. Refer members to counselors and agencies that are specifically trained to work with these offenders. (Clergy are encouraged *not* to counsel about the incest because they are not specifically trained in that area or confrontive enough. Clergy can help offenders spiritually but need to refer them to others to treat the sexual abuse itself.)

3. Talk about incest in public, openly and honestly, so that members will be informed and will be willing to come forward to get help for themselves or others. Arrange for speakers and lectures on the subject. Do not pretend it does not exist in your membership!

4. Work with the whole family. Give support to all family members. Advocate for family treatment and preserving the unit, but recognize that doing so takes time. Do not rush these families or this treatment and do not push for easy repentance or quick, unrealistic forgiveness.

5. Know referral sources and investigate community agencies so that sensitive and appropriate referrals can be made.

6. Maintain confidentiality within the religious community if the family desires this. Keep incest within the counseling or treatment area.

7. Be supportive, even if the family separates or divorces. They will need help more than ever.

8. Be available. Perpetrators need twenty-four-hour-a-day service. Perhaps clergy could work to get appropriate "hot line" or emergency services for offenders. Many complaints about current crisis lines involve the listener's lack of understanding of this problem.

9. Follow up on incest. Do not just see the offender once and assume everything is taken care of.

10. Help arrange for listeners and some sort of network system within your church to help these families and provide support for them.

11. Ask direct questions and help identify incest in families. Do not avoid or minimize what offenders are doing. They know it is wrong and they know you know it is wrong.

12. Develop some financial resources for (1) perpetrators who need therapy but cannot afford it, (2) housing for offenders when they cannot live at home, and (3) legal services.

Conclusions

Overall, incest perpetrators seem satisfied with most of the services they have encountered with the clergy. Their general concern seems to be for more practical, direct service. Though they may come seeking reassurance and peace, offenders urge the clergy to work with them over time and not assume cures come quickly. The perpetrators stated that "Hail Mary's" and "kneel therapy" are not enough. Most offenders want clergy to be informed, sensitive, and understanding, but agree that sexual abuse treatment is best left to the experts. They emphasize the need to coordinate and cooperate. Many services are required for the incestuous family. Law enforcement, treatment, and spiritual recovery need to be combined as a joint effort to ensure total care for all family members.

References

Edelson, J. 1984. Working with men who batter. *Social Work* 29:237–242.

Newberger, C. M., E. H. Newberger, and R. L. Hampton. 1983. Child abuse: The current theory base and future research needs. *Journal of American Child Psychiatry* 22:262–268.

Roberts, A. R. 1982. A national survey of services for batterers. In *The Abusive Partner,* ed. M. Roy. New York: Van Nostrand Reinhold, pp. 230–243.

Russell, D. E. H. 1982. The incidence and prevalence of intrafamilial and extrafamilial sexual abuse of female children. *Child Abuse and Neglect* 7(2):133–146.

29
What a Shelter Is Really Like:
A Victim's Perspective

Judy Williamson

The clergy may often play an important role in the counseling of the battered woman. However, no other time may be more critical or opportune for counseling intervention than the time just prior to, during, and following a woman's stay at a shelter facility. During this time the battered woman is making decisions about herself, her children, and her husband that may have consequences not only for time but also for eternity. The battered woman is in as much crisis during this period as she was during the actual abusive incident. Therefore, it is crucial for the religious leader to understand just what leaving home and being at a shelter may mean to the battered woman.

Leaving home to stay at a shelter involves a variety of feelings and experiences, some of which may be as terrifying to the battered woman as staying at home. Going to a shelter is more than going to a safe place; it is living with rules the woman does not understand and with people she does not know or trust. It is worrying that she made the right decision and about what will happen to her when you leave. It means admitting to others that her marriage is less than ideal. It is receiving counseling that makes her face a problem she may have been trying to hide for years.

There are numerous shelters and safe houses across the United States. Each has its own criteria for admissions, policies, procedures, and house rules. However, the purpose of this chapter is not to examine shelters in the terms of buildings, rules, criteria, policies, or procedures, but to examine shelters in terms of the intensity and similarity of experiences and feelings associated with them.

A cross section of women was interviewed who had used different services offered by shelters throughout three states. Some had stayed at the shelter, while others had only received counseling, either individually or as part of a support group. Several conversations were also held with the children of these women in an effort to obtain a perspective on how a stay at a shelter affects the children of battered women.

The Four Stages

The women interviewed identified four stages involved during their shelter experience. These stages represent different needs, feelings, emotions, and decisions that the woman may have experienced during various contacts with the shelter. It is critical to recognize these needs in order to facilitate more appropriate treatment. The stages as identified by the women were making the decision to leave, the shelter stay itself, leaving the shelter, and the aftermath.

Phase I: Making the Decision

> I had been abused for eight years. I had never told anyone at all. After all that, the trust and the belief that things were going to change just were not there anymore. It was like a light bulb going off in my head. Things were not worse than before; I had just lost the hope of things getting better. I began to look at him differently. I began to compare him to his friends that I had always hated. I had previously thought that he was different from them and now I realize that he wasn't. If he knew I was leaving he would try and stop me. He would never let me take the kids, and then things would be worse. I found the number of the shelter in the phone book and called. After the first call I made my decision. Over the next several days I gathered what I needed and just waited . . . for the chance to leave.

Not all women, however, are able to plan their departures; others needed to leave immediately:

> We had a fight the night before. He had broken my nose and ribs. I decided that it was time I called them (shelter). I was really scared but I knew the abuse was getting worse and I was afraid that if I stayed he would kill me.

> I didn't even take a change of clothes. There had been a horrible fight that night and the police were called by my neighbor. I don't even remember much about what was said, I was so upset. I remember the police taking me there, but little else. I figured whatever happened or wherever I was going couldn't be any worse than what had just happened.

> He had just left the house and I knew he would be back soon and when he came back I knew I would be in for it. I just left. . . . I was afraid they weren't going to let me come and then I wouldn't know what to do. I was terrified he would find and kill me. I didn't believe there was anywhere that could be safe enough but I knew I had to try.

Phase II: The Shelter Stay

The level of satisfaction with the actual stay at the shelter varies. This is based not only on the services provided, which are similar throughout all shelters, but on the woman's personal issues. Her level of satisfaction will be based on her own expectations, fears, agendas, feelings, personal history, and the intensity with which she is experiencing these issues at the time she enters the shelter.

Many battered women come from multiproblem families, and the spouse abuse incident may not be the only issue the woman is dealing with when she leaves home. It often initiates a floodgate of old issues and feelings from previous relationships, including parental, sibling, stranger, or other spousal relationships. A stay at a shelter will also be colored by the daily stressors (financial, medical, and so on) that are affecting the family unit.

The woman may also be experiencing a sense of loss. This loss will be not just of the relationship, but of her role within that relationship. A woman may not feel confident that she can manage or even exist outside of that particular role. For instance, her spouse may have controlled events so tightly that she has never made decisions about daily events. Her role may reflect only her husband's expectations, desires, and decisions. Now she must redefine her own identity upon leaving her spouse.

She may subconsciously decide to seek this same role again in order to give herself a sense of security, or she may try to redefine herself within her new environment or, more appropriately, within herself. Whichever direction she chooses, her stay at the shelter and the services she receives there will play a critical role in the decisions she makes.

Another issue commonly dealt with in a shelter was the question of theology. Many of these women's religions did not support separation within the family unit. For the religious woman the stay at the shelter may have represented not only a break with her husband but—if she did not receive support from church leaders—a break from her theological beliefs. The feeling of guilt associated with just leaving home may have been immense; it may never end unless she can justify in her own mind her separation within the framework of her theology.

The next step, after the decision to leave is made and special issues and considerations are evaluated, is the shelter stay itself. Several women's comments about their shelter experience follow.

> For the first time in a long time I was O.K. I was safe. I slept through the night without waking up to see if he was up to something. I kept pinching

myself to see if it was real. I got on welfare until I could get a job. Being there was the best thing I ever did.

I didn't think that it would be like this but, then again, I really didn't know what to expect. I mean I planned it and everything. It wasn't like I had to leave in the middle of the night or anything. But when I got there it was such an odd feeling. I was half relieved and half terrified. I knew my husband probably would not have guessed where I was, and even if he did he couldn't find me, at least for the moment. But the fear of what was to come was the thing that kept coming back at me. He used to say that if I ever left him he would hunt me down like a dog and kill me and the kids. Sometimes I used to think that that would probably be best.

I can't hide from him forever and I can't stand worrying about if that's his car or who's at the door or on the phone. He'd said at other times that if I didn't do what he wanted me to that he would take the kids away and I'd never see them again. He would have too. Before I left home I hadn't really thought about anything other than getting away from him.

But when I got here all this other stuff sort of hit me in the face. I didn't even know if I should put the kids in school because he could go and take them out at any time, and I would never see them. I didn't have money to go anywhere or I would have just disappeared. I realized I was afraid he would find me no matter what I did. I felt things weren't really going to be any different except for the fact that we were living apart.

My mind began to go wild with all the things that could happen. I began to have nightmares about the abuse. I began to wonder if I had done the right thing by moving out. The moment I arrived I began to think of all this stuff.

Being in the shelter for me was as terrifying as being at home, but in a different way. I didn't fear for my safety. No, for the first time I felt safe. No, here I feared something different. For the first time in my life I had to make decisions I had never had to make before.

My husband was so possessive he wouldn't let me go anywhere by myself. He would have to go with me wherever I went. He wouldn't let others come to the house. I forgot what it was like to talk to friends. He ran everything. I did and said only what he wanted me to, even when he wasn't there.

At the shelter this was all gone. I could come and go for the first time in my life. I had freedom. It seemed so basic. Everybody else has it, but I didn't know what to do. For the first time in my life, I had to make my own decisions. These decisions were going to affect the rest of my life. I had to decide if I was going to leave him, when, and where I was going to go.

Would I stay here (in town) and risk further harassment or would I move away? How could I support myself and my kids? I was afraid I wouldn't do the right thing. I didn't have any practice making even little decisions. Everything had always been done his way. So in the end I just tried to put things off, hoping something would just happen to solve everything.

I hated it. I felt trapped and confined. I felt the very same as if I were at home. The rules were extremely confining. I know all of that is there for security but it made me feel as if I were in prison. Every time the alarm on the door went off a streak of panic would shoot through me. I expected to see my or someone else's husband walk through that door every time the alarm went off.

It was the hardest on the kids, though. They couldn't understand why they could not live the way they did at home. There they could play, eat, or sleep when they wanted. They were the reason I left . . . I wanted things to be easier for them.

I couldn't even make a call without them [staff] listening to it. My husband wouldn't let me make calls without him listening either. I had to talk to a counselor every day I was there and I really wasn't ready to talk. I had just left. I felt I just needed some time to myself. I even had to go to bed and get up at certain times. I hadn't had a curfew even as a kid. My biggest goal once I was there was getting out. I wanted to get out badly, but I had no money and no family or friends that could or would help.

I decided to leave and go back home. At least the kids would be happier and I now know what to expect. I made a mistake to leave him now. If I ever do leave again, next time I will be more prepared so that maybe we can move right into an apartment. I don't ever want to go back to the shelter. The people were nice and the place was great but it just wasn't for me.

Other Stressors: Child Abuse and Psychological Problems

For some women, being at the shelter not only included the anger, fears, and emotions attributed to the spousal abuse but may have been an even more threatening experience if the woman had some inconsistencies in her own life. Some women may be experiencing psychological problems, or may be abusing their own children.

I knew I was doing and saying things I never had before. I kept hoping things would get better if I were just away from him. I was afraid they would take me away and then I would lose my kids. So I was even more resistant in not telling them what was really going on. They suggested I go to a private hospital. For a while I thought my husband had gotten to them and they had believed all the things he was saying about me. I just left. I just grabbed my things and told them I would be back, but I never did go back.

For me it was as threatening, I'm sure, as it was for my husband. I was as guilty of abuse as he was. He was abusing me, but I was abusing the kids. Being at the shelter put a lot of pressure on me. I was afraid I would be found out. Several years ago I had even broken my baby's arm. I still could not get that out of my mind. I wanted help but I was terrified. There were counselors that spent time with the kids. Sometimes I wanted to threaten them [kids] not to tell anyone. Other times I wanted them to tell so I would get some help. I felt the counselors suspected and that it was just a matter of time before they reported me.

I knew I was depressed. I had even talked about killing my husband, my kids, and myself. I was talking about it more and more. The people at the shelter tried to make me get help. I called my minister. He told me to get out of there, the Lord would take care of me. I did. I wish he would have understood how much I needed help. I came so close to killing those kids.

Children at the Shelter

Children also experience the trauma of spouse abuse even if they are not the direct target of the abuse itself. Most shelters do not have children's programs, and those that do more often than not are child-care rather than treatment oriented. Frequently, even if the mothers had attempted to explain what was happening, younger children often did not understand. However, many women failed to take the opportunity to explain why they were at a shelter at all, assuming the child would just know or was capable of dealing with it. Other women were too involved with their own concerns to be aware of their children's problems. More often than not the children were confused and unhappy and wished to return home; they frequently did not see the necessity for being at the shelter.

My mommy never told me why we were here. She just told me to get in the car. I could tell she was scared but I didn't know why.

I was away from my friends, school, toys, and my dog. I just wanted to go home.

She tried to tell me why we were here but I didn't really want to know. I sort of did but I didn't know why things couldn't be worked out. I didn't know why we were here. This particular place.

I really missed my daddy. Every time I said that my mom got mad. My daddy was always nice to me.

My mom leaving home and leaving my dad was the best thing she ever did. All he did was cause trouble. I never want to see him again.

Phase III: Leaving

Leaving the shelter is one of the more difficult times for the battered woman. It is the time she probably will meet with her spouse again and have to make decisions she is probably not ready to make. In other cases, even if she does not return home, she may become a victim of abusive behavior in the form of harassment. No matter what situation she encounters or returns to in the community, things will never be quite the same for the battered woman, for she knows she has options. Even if the woman returns home, she will know she does not have to accept the abuse. She knows she can leave. She can implement what she has learned and hope that it is enough to sustain her through all the abusive situations that may follow. The following are excerpts from the women's interviews.

I knew my husband would bother me. I just wanted the strength to say no to him. I knew I didn't have it yet. I knew no one could really protect me from him either.

I was afraid to leave the shelter. It had been the first time I had experienced peace in a long time. I knew that whatever was about to happen I wouldn't feel this safe again. It was like leaving the only person who understood what was happening to me.

I was scared but I was excited to start over. I could have the freedom I wanted and I would not let myself get into that kind of situation again.

Phase IV: The Aftermath

It is important to remember that the victim has identifiable characteristics and will have reacted to the various stages of the cycle of violence (see Chapter 2) with her own cycle of behavior. She will need help to break it. One of the comments many of the interviewed women made was that once the woman had left the relationship and was set up with new quarters, the support from informal support systems was frequently withdrawn or reduced. This was equally true if the woman chose to return home. By returning home, she was frequently perceived as accepting or even desirous of the abuse. Either way, emotional support to sustain the woman's decision was eliminated or drastically reduced as indicated by the following comments.

In the beginning it seemed as if everyone was there helping me. My bishop especially. He had been the one to counsel me to leave my husband, and then when I left he had volunteers from the church help me move. The church even gave me food and paid my first month's rent. But then that was the end. Sixteen years of abuse and it seemed moving was supposed to be the answer. I had so many questions I needed answered. I needed to talk about some of the things I was still feeling. My bishop didn't see the need to counsel with me anymore; after all my husband wasn't around anymore. I didn't have the money to go to anyone else. In the beginning it was just as bad as being at home. There was still no one to talk to. I was just as isolated and I was not ready to pretend that nothing had happened and just forget about it.

When I was at the shelter it seemed as if everyone wanted to help . . . the people at work, church, my family and friends. But when I went back home, they all left. They didn't understand why I had to try again. They thought I was stupid and that whatever happens to me now is my fault. I only had support as long as I was doing what they wanted.

Several weeks, months, or even years may not be sufficient to remove problems the abuse has left behind.

Three years after the divorce I met another man. The more we dated, the more fearful I became. He had never been abusive or showed any signs of it but I was just so afraid of it happening again, I did things on purpose to sabotage the relationship. I'd flip flop back and forth. I got so angry at my ex-husband. It was as if all the things he had done were going to ruin my chances for happiness for the rest of my life. I had gone to counseling and all. I just panicked every time I got close to a man and I didn't know how to stop it. No one seemed to understand. They all seemed to think that everything should be all right just because *he's* not here anymore.

I came to the shelter as a volunteer. I had previously been abused. When I entered the shelter for the first time (since the abuse had ended seven years ago), I felt my stomach drop. It triggered all the old memories. I felt scared, not of the shelter, but of the abuse. I felt as if I didn't belong there and that I should go back home. I have been divorced a long time, but those feelings never seem to leave no matter what or how well you do.

I have been divorced eleven years and my husband continues to harass me. He's tampered with my car, cut my phone lines, broken into my house, and follows me much of the time. The police can't stop him. I feel like I'm living in some kind of purgatory and being punished for something. I don't understand. My kids, family, and friends are afraid and they stay away now. I just don't understand why I'm being punished this way.

The memories of the shelter experience never fade, and women who have been abused will need continued support long after the abuse may have ended. The clergy may play a vital role in the counseling of the battered woman and her children.

Conclusion

Shelters, safe houses, or domestic violence programs usually offer counseling for the battered woman. Some offer counseling for the abusive partner, and still others offer programs for children. These programs offer a safe place to go—a time out from the abuse.

These women will have a number of concerns upon leaving the shelter. Some will worry about finances, others about day care. Some will worry about their children, and still others will continue to be abused. Others will worry about their roles and their churches' stands on the abuse and their separation. Some may have an occasion to worry about all of these and other concerns too numerous to mention. Many of these women will feel that the full scope of their problem was overlooked or minimized by clerics who have treated their abuse as simple marital discord.

No one description of a shelter or safe house and its services will adequately describe what happens there—the feelings, the experiences, the decisions, and so on. After all, a shelter is only a physical structure made of wood and brick. What a shelter is really like is based on what it represents to the women who come there, and it will change with the women who are there at any one time.

30

A Model Treatment Program That Would Work toward Family Unity and Still Provide Safety

Constance Doran

M ost traditional counseling programs hold family unity as a primary goal. When confronted by a family experiencing conflict, they work hard to keep that family together, even if the costs of doing so are high. However, in the last fifteen years, a number of programs have been developed that specialize in working with victims of family violence so severe that the cost of keeping the family together might be the death of the victim. For many of these programs, family unity has come to be regarded as a dangerous fantasy, not a primary goal of treatment.

Nevertheless, it is true that many victims of family violence have a strong desire to remain with their abusers, even at the risk of their lives. Most studies of battered women who leave shelters show that slightly more than half return to their partners within six months (Giles-Sims, 1983; Snyder and Fruchtman, 1981; Walker, 1979). For these women, as for the much greater number of victims who suffer in silence and never make an attempt to leave, the pressure to remain united in the family comes from many sources, including economic dependency, hope for reform, and religious values that condemn divorce or separation. For these individuals, family unity is indeed a primary goal, and their desires must be taken seriously by anyone who wishes to help them.

The Duty to Warn

Mental health professionals have a legal duty to warn and protect victims of violence (Hedlund, 1983; Jablonski, 1983; Tarasoff, 1976). Since one of the best predictors of future violence is past violent behavior (McNeil and Binder, 1987; Monahan, 1981), people who have been victims of family violence are likely to continue to be abused as long as they remain in that family situation. The legal and ethical standards of helping professions therefore require that victims be warned to get out and stay out until their safety can be reasonably assured.

Many religious leaders encourage the abuser to apologize, pray for forgiveness, and promise to reform. But is that enough assurance? Not in my experience. In fact, this cycle of alternating violence and penitence is part of the classic battering syndrome identified years ago by Walker (1979) and others. What about counseling for the abuser, or better yet, the whole family? Is that a guarantee of safety? Unfortunately, no known treatment program offers 100 percent success rates.

Counseling takes time and effort. Not even the best counseling programs produce immediate change, or, in fact, any change at all *if* the client is unmotivated and uncooperative. So while entering counseling is hopeful in the long run, in the short run the risk of continued violence remains high. It may even be higher than before counseling was started.

Counseling itself is stressful. Previously hidden painful memories are brought out into the open, and suppressed feelings of anger are expressed openly by the victims. Embarrassing incidents of abusive behavior are now dissected by a professional person who possesses some authority. All these elements frequently make counseling painful—especially for the abuser. Since abusers are people who have learned to deal with stress by aggressive outbursts, the risk of violence may be increased during the early stages of counseling. Until they have learned new ways of dealing with stress and of handling their angry feelings, the probability of abuse remains high.

The S.A.F.E. Program

How can we protect the potential victims in the family while this process of new learning is going on? At the S.A.F.E. (Stop Abusive Family Environments) Program at Fuller Theological Seminary, a model of treatment was developed that attempts to take into consideration the legal and ethical requirements of protecting victim safety, while still offering treatment to all members of the violent family (Doran, 1984). Though this model is not unique, it does focus on family unity and has been developed with consideration of the work being done in many other settings (Margolin, 1979; Neidig and Friedman, 1984; Nelke-Dunn, 1982; Novaco, 1975; Purdy and Nickle, 1981; Sonkin, Martin, and Walker, 1979).

The model is described here in some detail simply as one example of how this problem is currently being addressed professionally. While this model has been used successfully in cases of child abuse, abuse of parents by adolescent and adult children, violence between adults of the same sex, and in a few cases abuse of a male by a female partner, it has been used primarily with battered women and their male abusers. For that reason, the following description will focus on that situation.

Stage One: Initial Separation

During the first phase of treatment the parties are advised to separate. The purpose of this is primarily to ensure safety to the potential victims of violence, but also secondarily to foster assessment of the clinical issues involved. It is important to recognize that in-depth assessment cannot be done—and should not be attempted—with the abuser and the principal victim in the same room. In such a situation, the victim is highly unlikely to tell the whole story, and in fact risks subsequent violence if she tries.

There are other reasons besides victim safety for insisting on initial separation. Violent relationships involve symbiotic attachments, in which the partners become overly dependent on one another to meet all their needs. Separation breaks that excessive attachment and forces family members to develop new, healthier ways to meet their needs.

Furthermore, violence can become an addictive pattern in that it offers an immediate way to release tension, which is a powerful payoff for someone who knows no other way to find relief. In addition, there are external payoffs through victim compliance and intimidation. These reinforcements are some of the reasons that violent behavior is so hard to give up—it works. Like drugs and alcohol, violence offers an effective short-term escape from stress and tension. Like drug and alcohol addiction, violence addiction is very difficult to overturn unless the abusers are withdrawn from their "fix"—no longer permitted to have ready access to the target of abuse. In domestic violence situations, this means being denied access to the former victim. When the addictive behavior is no longer possible, the abuser experiences increased pressure to develop alternative ways of coping with stress. Like withdrawal from any "fix," this will be a painful experience and will evoke intensified feelings of frustration and rage.

In counseling the abuser during this process, both support and confrontation are necessary, and both individual and group therapy are recommended. The principal issue for the abuser is to learn to manage his anger nonabusively, which involves four steps:

1. Breaking through his minimization and denial that he has a problem.
2. Accepting responsibility for his own behavior.
3. Learning to recognize his stress levels and identify his emotions.
4. Developing assertive, rather than aggressive, ways of meeting his needs.

Exploring unrealistic expectations of himself and others, especially sex role stereotypes, are important parts of this process.

Meanwhile, the battered woman has somewhat different issues to address. First, she needs to be safe. In order to ensure her safety during this period, the use of shelters and restraining orders should be carefully considered. A detailed safety plan must be worked out with the woman; the plan will fully inform her about the legal and social resources available and will include a plan of action should emergencies arise.

If the past level of violence has not been life threatening or of long duration, and if the abuser is a highly motivated and active participant in treatment, then informal separation may be sufficient, in which the abuser or battered woman moves out to stay with friends or relatives. A local church has offered this option to violent families by allowing battered women or batterers who are in counseling to stay with trained volunteer families in the church until the family is ready to reunite.

Once the battered woman's safety is ensured, she can begin to recover from the effects of the trauma she has suffered. Her reactions initially may involve numbness and loss of sense of control over her world. She may also initially minimize the trauma she has experienced. However, as she feels safer, her memories of past abuse will surface, and along with them, feelings of fear and pain that may be terrifying in their intensity and frequency. A safe and supportive environment is essential for her at this point. She also needs to learn to recognize her stress levels, identify her emotions, and develop assertive, rather than passive, ways of meeting her needs. For her, too, both individual and group therapy are recommended.

During this phase of counseling for both men and women, the focus is primarily on the individual rather than on the relationship. If any family issues are considered here, they are likely to be related to the individual's family of origin, because it is in *that* family that the individual's present pattern of coping with problems was probably learned.

At S.A.F.E., the battered woman is typically seen weekly by an individual therapist, preferably female. Participation in various support groups is also encouraged, including a battered women's group at the local shelter, Al-Anon, AA, Parents Anonymous, Parents United, self-defense classes, and so on. Meanwhile, the abuser is being seen by another therapist in S.A.F.E., again preferably of the same sex, or is referred to a nearby agency that specializes in working with abusers.

In addition to individual therapy, the batterer is also encouraged to participate in a batterer's group, as well as other relevant community support and self-help organizations. Any children requiring treatment are seen by counselors who specialize in child therapy, either at S.A.F.E. or at child development clinics in the community. When necessary, S.A.F.E. offers a place for court-ordered, monitored visitation of children by the noncustodial parent.

All therapists involved with the family obtain releases of information from their own clients. Doing so allows them to remain in communication with the other therapists throughout the course of treatment and also to make periodic "reality" checks with the other family members. At least monthly, the various therapists are contacted to update one another on the progress of treatment.

During this phase of treatment, the family's religious community can be helpful in counteracting the loneliness and fear of abandonment that are often experienced during this period of separation. Participation in small groups and social activities in the church can help overcome the social isolation many violent families experience and can help the family members develop new relationships outside the family. The length of this period of separation varies, but it is rarely less than three months. The end is signaled by notification from the abuser's therapist that reliable anger-management skills have been acquired, and that the abuser is ready and willing to have more contact with the family. If the battered woman is also willing for this to occur, we then proceed to Stage Two.

However, it must be pointed out that during this period, a significant percentage of batterers simply drop out of treatment before achieving any significant improvement in anger control. In these cases, in my judgment, the legal and ethical constraints noted above require that we recommend continued separation from abusers, despite their often intensely intimidating attempts to move back into the family. At this point, arrest, restraining order enforcement, or escape to shelters may be necessary for the family's safety. At S.A.F.E., we have at times become the target of hostility by the abusers, who may see us as responsible for denying them access to the family.

We have consistently encouraged such batterers to remain in dialogue with us and have offered to relay messages they wish to convey to the family. With rare exceptions, this has markedly reduced the abuser's anger and has in some cases led to his eventual resumption of counseling. However, despite S.A.F.E.'s good fortune (to date) in avoiding any staff injury, the risks to those who intervene in this situation are great and must be addressed through staff training, environmental security, and the presence of multiple back-up staff when in contact with the abuser.

Stage Two: Limited Contact

Once the batterer's therapist and the battered woman have given permission, the next phase of treatment may be started, in which the family is gradually encouraged to increase contact. This contact will occur at first only in the therapist's office, and then outside as well. In my experience, this works best if the abuser's therapist and the battered woman's therapist are both present. This, then, is a conjoining, male-female "co-therapy" period of treatment, and the focus changes from the individuals to their relationship. Improved communication, problem-solving, and conflict-resolution skills are the initial goals, with the parties eventually attempting to resolve major underlying issues of conflict that are identified during the therapy. Once again, sex role stereotypes and patriarchal expectations typically emerge as major issues in most violent families.

After a few conjoint sessions, the worker may alternate conjoint with individual sessions so the clients can still experience a safe and confidential forum in which to ventilate feelings and develop agendas for the conjoint sessions. Both clients are encouraged to continue their participation in their respective support groups during this time.

If good anger-management skills are demonstrated in the office, *and* the battered woman is willing, *then and only then* should the parties be encouraged to see each other outside the therapy situation. If restraining orders are in effect, they should be amended to specify precisely the level of permissible contact at this time. I recommend that the first outside contact be brief, time limited, and always in the presence of neutral third parties (but not the couple's children, siblings, or parents). Here the participation of friends from church can be invaluable. The experience of the clients during these outside contacts becomes the basis for much of the work in therapy. If there is a return of violence, the contacts should be terminated and a return to Stage One conditions obtained. However, if the outside contacts go well, they may be gradually increased and may include overnight stays. If children are involved, or other family members are critical in these contacts, these persons may also be included in the therapy sessions—always, of course, with the permission of the primary clients.

When these limited contacts, or dates, are going well, and there has been no actual or threatened violence for a period of time (my personal recommendation here is at least 90 days), cohabitation may be recommended, but only if *all* parties genuinely consent. Many battered women reluctantly consent, under pressure from their husbands, children, and therapists (who are so proud of their handiwork), only to have violence erupt again. Trust the woman's instincts. She knows this person better than you do, and if she is uneasy about it, it is probably not safe.

Stage Three: Family Reunification

During this period the family resumes living together, and conjoint family therapy is recommended—preferably with the same male-female cotherapy team which has been working with the couple. Individual sessions as well as participation in their respective support groups should also be continued periodically for the abuser and the battered woman. If restraining orders have been in effect, they should now be terminated or amended to reflect the current living situation.

The focus of healing now is building healthy, peaceful patterns of interaction in the family. Contact with other families in the religious community who have become successful at doing this is important for providing healthy models, which neither the man nor the woman may have had in their own families of origin.

The process of reunification is typically very stressful for the family members, but they often want it so desperately to work out that they may not wish to face the problems that emerge. They may start denying that anything is wrong and drop out of therapy prematurely, before things are really stable.

At this point, the support and involvement of others, especially friends, clergy, and members of the religious community, may become critical in continuing to help this family back to health. At this point, S.A.F.E. staff have served as consultants to concerned clergy and friends who want to know how to be helpful in these specific situations. Of course, the confidentiality of any information given to us by clients must be preserved, but general information based on current literature and research can certainly be presented to interested community caregivers.

Even when families remain in therapy during Stage Three, they may experience a return to old patterns of interaction, including physical violence. Because they want things to work out, they may all join in denying that this is occuring. If violence is made known to the therapists, a return to Stage One is, of course, immediately advised, and is a condition of further treatment.

Another problem is that physical abuse may be replaced by psychological or verbal abuse, which is often not admitted as occurring at all by the abuser, or is rationalized as not being harmful. However, psychological abuse can be even more destructive to the victim than physical battering.

It is important that everyone in the family be aware of these possibilities, that they be discussed openly *before* and after the family reunites, and that the family understands the hardest period of work is now before them.

Conclusion

Returning to our analogy of drug and alcohol abuse: During the period of family reunification the abuser is like a recovering alcoholic who is now returning to work as a bartender. It takes a constant struggle in the familiar setting of past abusive behavior not to return to the habitual abusive patterns. Abusive individuals will need a lifetime of personal vigilance and effort to overcome these patterns, which often have been with them since childhood.

Recovering from this kind of ingrained pattern requires development of even stronger patterns of nonabusive family life. That, in turn, requires clear-cut norms that label family violence as wrong, clear-cut models that demonstrate loving, nonviolent, and nonsexist patterns of family interaction, and compassionate support for families "in transition."

These are not tasks for therapists alone. These are tasks for each community of faith as well. These are spiritual as well as psychological issues, involving questions of not only sickness and health, but also good and evil, the worth of human beings, and the nature of love. Each tradition may verbalize these concepts in different ways, but we can, I believe, all unite in working to stop domestic violence and no longer allow this virulent form of abuse to masquerade as love.

References

Doran, C. M. 1984. Wife abuse and the training of psychologists: The S.A.F.E. program. Paper presented at the 92nd Annual Convention of the American Psychological Association, Toronto, Canada.

Giles-Sims, J. 1983. *Wife-battering: A systems theory approach*. New York: Guilford.

Hedlund v. Superior Court of Orange County, 34 Cal 3d 695. 1983.

Jablonski by Pahls v. United States of America, 712 F. 2d 391.19. 1983.

Margolin, G. 1979. Conjoint marital therapy to enhance anger management and reduce spouse abuse. *American Journal of Family Therapy* 7(2):13, 23.

McNeil, D. E., and Binder, R. L. 1987. Predictive validity of judgments of dangerousness in emergency civil commitment.

Monahan, J. 1981. *Predicting violent behavior: An assessment of clinical techniques*. Beverly Hills, CA: Sage.

Neidig, P. H., and Friedman, D. H. 1984. *Spouse abuse: A treatment program for couples*. Champaign, IL: Research Press.

Nelke-Dunn, J. 1982. Appropriate couples counseling. Paper presented at the Second National Conference of the National Coalition Against Domestic Violence, Milwaukee, WI.

Novaco, R. 1975. *Anger control: The development and evaluation of an experimental treatment*. Lexington, MA: Lexington Books.

Purdy, F. and Nickle, N. 1981. Practice principles for working with groups of men who batter. *Social Work with Groups* 4:111–122.

Snyder, D. K., and Fruchtman, L. A. 1981. Differential patterns of wife abuse: A data based topology. *Journal of Consulting and Clinical Psychology* 49:878–885.

Sonkin, D. J., Martin, D., and Walker, L. E. A. 1985. *The male batterer: A treatment approach*. New York: Springer.

Tarasoff v. The Regents of the University of California, 17 Cal. 3d 425. 1976.

Walker, L. E. 1979. *The battered woman*. New York: Harper & Row.

Resource Directory

Organizations

Center for the Prevention of Sexual and Domestic Violence, N. 34th St., Suite 105, Seattle, Washington 98103

Center for Women Policy Studies, 2000 P St., NW, Suite 508, Washington, D.C. 20036 (202) 872-1770

Ending Men's Violence National Referral Directory, To RAVEN, P.O. Box 24159, St. Louis, Missouri 63130 (314) 725-6137
Copy of directory $10.00., includes postage and handling.

Marital Rape Information, University of Illinois at Urbana-Champaign, 415 Library, 1408 West Gregory Drive, Urbana, Illinois 61801 (217) 244-1024

National Center on Child Abuse and Neglect, 8201 Greensboro Drive, Suite 600, McLean, Virginia 22102 (703) 821-2086

National Clearinghouse on Marital and Date Rate, Women's History Research Center, 2325 Oak Street, Berkeley, California 94708 (415) 548-1770

National Coalition Against Domestic Violence, 2401 Virginia Avenue, NW, Suite 305, Washington, D.C. 20037 (202) 293-8860

National Coalition Against Sexual Assault, Volunteers of America, 8787 State Street, Suite 202, East St. Louis, Illinois 62203 (618) 398-7764

National Committee For Prevention of Child Abuse, 332 S. Michigan Avenue, Suite 950, Chicago, Illinois 60604 (312) 663-3520

National Criminal Justice Reference Service/NCJRS, Victims Specialist (800) 851-3420

National Organization for Victim Assistance, 717 D Street, NW, 2nd Floor, Washington, D.C. 20004 (202)-393-6682

Publication and Media Resources

Battered Women: Behind Closed Doors, produced and available from Motocoln Tele-program Center. Also available from Minnesota Coalition on Battered Women, 435 Aldine Street, St. Paul, Minnesota 55104

Bussert, Joy M. K. 1986. *Battered Women: From a Theology of Suffering to an Ethic of Empowerment.* Division for Mission in North America, Lutheran Church in America. Contact DMNA Interpretation, 231 Madison Avenue, New York, New York 10016

Fortune, Marie, 1983. *Sexual Violence: The Unmentionable Sin.* New York: The Pilgrim Press

Walker, Lenore. 1979. *The Battered Woman.* New York: Harper and Row

Index

About the Contributors

Craig M. Allen, Ph. D. Associate Professor, Department of Family Environment, Iowa State University, Ames, Iowa

James M. Alsdurf, Ph.D. Clinical Psychologist, Psychological Services, Hennepin County Bureau of Community Corrections, Minneapolis, Minnesota

Phyllis E. Alsdurf, M.A. Freelance writer and editor, Minnetonka, Minnesota

Rosie P. Bingham, Ph.D. Director of Student Development, Memphis State University, Memphis, Tennessee

Tillie Black Bear. Director, White Buffalo Calf Women's Shelter. Rosebud Indian Reservation, South Dakota.

Lee H. Bowker, Ph.D. Dean, College of Behavioral and Social Sciences, Humboldt State University, Arcata, California

Judith L. Brutz, Ph.D. (Candidate) Department of Family Environment, Iowa State University. Director, Friends Family Service, Ames, Iowa

Rev. David W. Delaplane. Director. The Spiritual Dimension, Sacramento, California

Constance Doran, Ph.D. Clinical Psychologist, Fuller Theological Seminary, Pasadena, California

Rev. Mitzi N. Eilts. Minister, United Church of Christ. Executive Director, Battered Women's Shelter, Dane County Advocates for Battered Women, Madison, Wisconsin

Rev. Marie M. Fortune. Minister, United Church of Christ. Executive Director, Center for the Prevention of Sexual and Domestic Violence, Seattle, Washington

Virginia M. Friedemann. Director, Migima Designs, Inc., Eugene, Oregon

Rev. James Friedrich, M.S.W. Area Coordinator, Lutheran Social Services of Northern California, San Jose, California

Edward Gondolf, Ph.D. Research Fellow, University of Pittsburgh, Western Psychiatric Institute and Clinic, Pittsburgh, Pennsylvania

Carol C. Haase. Program Specialist III, C. Henry Kempe National Center for the Prevention and Treatment of Child Abuse and Neglect, University of Colorado Health Sciences Center, Denver, Colorado

Geraldine G. Hanni, M.S.W. Clinical Director, Intermountain Sexual Abuse Treatment Center, Salt Lake City, Utah

Barbara Harris. Director, Transition Center, Gustave Hartman YM/YWHA, Far Rockaway, New York

Cassandra Hoffman-Mason, M.S.W., L.I.S.W. Outpatient Therapist, Private Practitioner, Southeast Community Mental Health Center, Columbus, Ohio

Pam Johnson, B.S. University of California, Riverside, California

Robert J. Kelly, Ph.D. Assistant Research Psychologist, University of California, Los Angeles Department of Psychology, Los Angeles, California

Judith A. Kowalski, Ph.D. Associate Director for Studies, The American Lutheran Church Office of Church in Society, Minneapolis, Minnesota

Donna LeClerc, Wheaton College, Norton, Massachusetts

Marcia K. Morgan, M.S. Director, Migima Designs, Inc., Eugene, Oregon

Ginny NiCarthy, M.S.W. Co-Director, Women's Counseling Group, Seattle, Washington

Mildred Daley Pagelow, Ph.D. Adjunct Research Professor of Sociology, California State University, Fullerton, California. Director, Educational Consulting Services (private practice, clinical sociology)

Ellen Pence. Minnesota Program Development Incorporated, Duluth, Minnesota

James Ptacek, Graduate Student in Sociology, Brandeis University, Waltham, Massachusetts. Counselor and trainer, EMERGE, Men's Counseling Service on Domestic Violence, Cambridge, Massachusetts

Albert R. Roberts, Ph.D. Associate Professor of Social Work, Indiana University School of Social Work, Indianapolis, Indiana

Gail Ryan. Director of Information, Resources and Referrals, National Child

Abuse and Neglect Resource Center, Kempe National Center, Denver, Colorado

Constance Hoenk Shapiro, Ph.D. Associate Professor, Department of Human Service Studies, New York State College of Human Ecology, Cornell University, Ithaca, New York

Barbara W. Snow, D.S.W. Licensed Clinical Social Worker, Private Practice, Salt Lake City, Utah

Penny Tokarski, M.D. Medical Director, Child Protection Team, Orlando Regional Medical Center, Orlando, Florida

Susan Turner, B.S.W. Program Director, Robinson Development Center, Robinson, Texas

Lenore E. Auerbach Walker, Ed.D., A.B.P.P. Clinical and Forensic Psychologist, Walker and Associates, Denver, Colorado

Melany M. Wilkins, M.S.W. American Fork Hospital, Social Services, American Fork, Utah

Doran Williams, M.S.W. (Candidate) Research Assistant, Brigham Young University, Provo, Utah

Wendy J. Wright, M.S.W. Outpatient Therapist, Timpanogos Mental Health Center, Provo, Utah

Kersti Yllo, Ph.D. Associate Professor of Sociology, Coordinator of Gender-Balanced Curriculum Project, Wheaton College, Norton, Massachusetts

About the Editors

Anne Horton received her Ph.D. in Social Welfare from the University of Wisconsin-Madison (1983) and is currently an assistant professor in the School of Social Work at Brigham Young University. She is a Licensed Clinical Social Worker and does all her research and private practice in the area of domestic abuse. She has over fourteen years of clinical practice and has spent eight years as a crisis intervention specialist and program director. She is the 1987–88 president of the Board of Trustees for the Center for Women and Children in Crisis, and is also on the Board of Directors for Parents United, Crisis Line, Family Living Council, and the Utah County Council on Domestic Abuse. She is a member of the Council on Social Work Education, National Association of Social Work, National Council on Family Relations, International Pediatric Social Service Workers, Utah Association of Marriage and Family Counselors, and the Association of Mormon Counselors and Psychotherapists. She is the author of numerous professional articles and textbooks, and does a great many workshops and presentations on domestic violence.

Judy Williamson has a B.S.W. degree from Brigham Young University and is employed as a counselor in the Child Welfare unit for the Division of Family Services, Provo, Utah. In addition, Judy is the coordinator for the Children's Program at the Center for Women and Children in Crisis, where she does part-time intake, crisis intervention, grant writing, and program development.

Abuse and Religion

When Praying Isn't Enough

Anne L. Horton
Judith A. Williamson

Domestic and sexual abuse does not occur in religious homes. . .or does it?

This year, thousands of abuse victims, mostly women, will seek help from the clergy—and many will find their urgent needs unmet and their problems dangerously unresolved. Few clericals are trained to work with abusive families, and their advice is often limited to theological issues and values. Yet, when religious people turn to secular counselors, they often find that these professionals are not sensitive to their deeply felt religious values and beliefs. This dilemma typically leaves the abuse victim confused, uninformed, and unprotected, despite the best efforts of helping professionals in their community.

In this unique new handbook, experts on family violence, religious leaders, and members of abusive families offer practical, "how-to" insights on every significant aspect of the needs of this large and generally unacknowledged population. The contributors provide practical, basic guidelines for identification and diagnosis, strategies for change, intervention and treatment choices, and suitable referrals for both religious and secular counselors. This unique book provides a fresh, long-needed contribution towards resolving the special interests of victims of abuse. Through improved education and training, by forging new alliances between religious and other

facilitating the
h community's
fessionals can
domestic
ently prevalent

clergy of all
vill find that this
ifying approach
domestic
nvironment
or the greater
egrations, and

professor in the
igham Young
president of the
enter for Women
has been
ily crisis for

counselor in
amily Services,
es the Children's
Women and